# AN INTRODUCTION TO CONTEMPORARY ITALIAN THOUGHT

# AN INTRODUCTION TO CONTEMPORARY ITALIAN THOUGHT

## From Posthumanism to Cyberfascism

**Tim Christiaens, Joost de Bloois, and Stijn De Cauwer**

BLOOMSBURY ACADEMIC

LONDON · NEW YORK · OXFORD · NEW DELHI · SYDNEY

BLOOMSBURY ACADEMIC
Bloomsbury Publishing Plc, 50 Bedford Square, London, WC1B 3DP, UK
Bloomsbury Publishing Inc, 1359 Broadway, New York, NY 10018, USA
Bloomsbury Publishing Ireland, 29 Earlsfort Terrace, Dublin 2, D02 AY28, Ireland

BLOOMSBURY, BLOOMSBURY ACADEMIC and the Diana logo are
trademarks of Bloomsbury Publishing Plc

First published in Great Britain 2026



Cover design: Ben Anslow
Cover images: November 1947: Milan workers demonstrate in the Cathedral
Square against the decision made by the Confederation of Industries to dismiss
many workers. (Photo by Keystone/Getty Images); Street art murals in Rome,
Pasolini's eye.
(© Antonio Sena | Dreamstime.com)



A catalogue record for this book is available from the British Library.

A catalog record for this book is available from the Library of Congress.

ISBN:   HB:     978-1-3504-0760-2
        PB:     978-1-3504-0761-9
        ePDF:   978-1-3504-0762-6
        eBook:  978-1-3504-0763-3

Typeset by Integra Software Services Pvt. Ltd.
Printed and bound in Great Britain

For product safety related questions contact productsafety@bloomsbury.com.

To find out more about our authors and books visit www.bloomsbury.com and
sign up for our newsletters.

# CONTENTS

# INTRODUCTION: "WHAT IS ITALIAN THOUGHT?"

## Chapter Summary

Since the turn of the century, "Italian thought" has emerged as a prolific tradition in European and American academia. The writings of Giorgio Agamben, Antonio Negri or Roberto Esposito proved to resonate so deeply with the concerns of the time that they quickly became international academic superstars. The deceptively simple question "What is Italian Thought?" has played a key role in giving shape to Italian thought as a style of thinking, with its own central concepts and concerns, such as biopolitics, power, and issues of class and labor. In this introduction we are skeptical vis-à-vis attempts to construct a unilinear genealogy for Italian thought, even when such a genealogy would emphasize the trans-historical porosity of Italian thought. Moreover, we situate Italian thought in a global academic context where "Italian thought" is now produced and discussed well beyond Italy. Italian thought constitutes an assemblage of ideas of which Italian academia is but one element. The meaning of "Italian thought" is hence subject to change in a world undergoing massive technological, environmental and geopolitical changes. We consider Italian thought to constitute an interventionist practice that turns both poststructuralist and Marxist ideas into instruments for intervening in contemporary debates concerning political power, work or migration. The post-1970s Italian political and intellectual idiosyncrasies act as a catalyst for the renewal of continental philosophy.

It seems only appropriate to begin a book on Italian Thought with the question "What is Italian Thought?" This question, however, is deceptively simple. As we hope to explain in this introduction, this very question may have been instrumental in the invention of "Italian Thought" itself. We may even exaggerate and claim that much of the work on (and perhaps, at a certain point, even *in*) contemporary Italian philosophy consists of variations on this question. This is not to say that the latter, and subsequently Italian Thought itself, is mere smoke and mirrors, or postmodern *mise en abîme*. Even if Italian Thought appears self-referential to a degree, the repeated question "What is Italian Thought?" has proven to be highly productive and affirmative of the very thing it allegedly contemplates. The *effetto Italian Thought*,[1] foremost, has been the creation and promotion of a new, discernible style of thinking. Often, the question "What is Italian Thought?" is asked *from within* the Italian philosophical community to grasp what is at stake in contemporary Italian philosophy and critical theory at large. Many of the contributors to volumes, special issues, monographs, and roundtables on Italian Thought since the early 2000s are, in fact, themselves key figures in contemporary Italian philosophy: Roberto Esposito, Toni Negri, Mario Tronti, Pier Aldo Rovatti, and others. Even those theorists who are skeptical of the validity of such a thing as "Italian Thought," like Rovatti and Negri, often return to the question.

However, as several contributors to the debate claim, one of the defining characteristics of Italian Thought is the latter's sustained engagement with its *outside*.[2] Despite its continued self-reflection, Italian Thought is anything but self-obsessed, a simple matter of philosophical navel-gazing of little relevance outside of Italian academia. Emphatically, contemporary Italian Thought orients itself toward the outside world, as it grapples with our contemporary political and social contexts. Italian Thought looks beyond the confines of philosophy as an academic discipline and engages with a range of fields, such as political theory, theology, contemporary technology, history, science studies, and biology. Contemporary Italian thought—regardless of whether it is packaged or not as Italian-Thought-with-a-capital-T—has made extremely relevant interventions in discussions regarding contemporary capitalism, new forms of labor, new types of (political) governance and surveillance, precarity, new modes of resistance, and new forms of subjectivity. Therefore, in this book, we primarily define "Italian Thought" as *interventionist thought*; that is to say, as simultaneously a sequence of interventions into various contemporary political controversies, *and* in philosophical debates, primarily on the foundations of politics and society. In this sense, the *effetto* of *Italian Thought* can be understood as its *impact* on our conception of a range of social and political issues, from new labor issues to the very idea of "life" in a posthuman or post-pandemic context.

As underlined by some of its representatives, Italian Thought is a *practice*. Its ideas, concepts, and analyses emerge not from behind the scholar's desk—although the university, both in Italy and abroad, remains crucial for the production of Italian thought—but *in response to* socio-political events and developments. Perhaps more so than any other contemporary strand of thought, Italian thought is firmly embedded in its historical moment and socio-political context, even if its assessment of both is often far from optimistic. However, Italian thought does not necessarily tackle contemporary political issues head-on. It does not conform to the standards of opinion pieces or columns that tackle the news of the day with little to no staying power. Rather, it takes detours through archaeologies of the history of thought, be it philosophy, theology, or literature, to explore the potential of past ideas and contexts for our contemporary world. The contemporary is not just a steady flow of news stories but a complex assemblage of power-relations, conceptual apparatuses, and communal tensions that carry the weight of past ideas and developments. Within the contemporary, thoughts from the past find their moment of legibility. The task of philosophical archaeology is, then, to reveal this persistent presence of the past within the present in order to open up potential action for the future. Moreover, although Italian thinkers often address questions that have been fundamental to postwar European philosophy and critical theory in general,[3] their interventions always display unique perspectives emerging from, on the one hand, the Italian socio-political context of the past decades, and, on the other hand, the idiosyncrasies of Italian debates, academic vocabularies, and local genealogies in philosophy and the social sciences. Even if Italian theorists only metaphorically walk the streets of Paris and Frankfurt, their steps resonate with those taken in Rome, Turin, or Naples.

In this book, we express some doubts about the homogeneity of Italian thought (we prefer the small "t" to the capital "T"), but we do claim that contemporary Italian thought is defined by its interventionist, strategic, and practical disposition, insofar as these interventions are inspired by the Italian historical context and Italian intellectual genealogies. As we will see, these interventions often concern specific debates: politics and governance (particularly biopolitics), labor, political subjectivity and identity, but also epistemological debates putting *affirmation* before critique and negation. In this book, we would like to honor the activist character of Italian thought and gauge its significance for today's debates regarding questions of labor in a digital world, (re-)emerging forms of fascism, post-pandemic politics, populism and identity issues, migration and decolonization, and the decentering of the human. What is the enduring significance of Italian thought in our current "outside?" What is the continued urgency of Italian thought beyond its identification with biopolitics? What remains of Italian thought when we are no longer haunted by the question "What is Italian Thought?" Before we examine the characteristics of contemporary Italian thought in detail—as we will see, "characteristics" here should be understood as "resonances" between various theorists perhaps more than as "shared DNA"—we will need to briefly explain the three components of this notion: "Italian," "contemporary," and "thought."

## What is "Italian" Thought?

Of the three components of "contemporary Italian thought," the geographical denomination "Italian" seems the least complicated. The opposite may be true … Much of the work that goes under the heading of Italian Thought is written *outside* of Italy, even in exile (from Braidotti to Negri). Moreover, "Italian Thought" as a canonical term emerges from a sustained engagement with other continental and Anglo-American schools of thought and individual thinkers. Even if explicitly Italian genealogies and idiosyncrasies can be distinguished within Italian thought, and can be said to be fundamental to it, their trajectory is often erratic, consisting of many detours through other traditions and intellectual contexts. When the representatives of Italian thought write their own genealogies, they often include non-Italian authors, like Michel Foucault, Walter Benjamin, Baruch Spinoza, Martin Heidegger, and Friedrich Nietzsche, in the family tree. Therefore, it is important to distinguish between philosophy and critical theory as it is practiced *in* Italy and Italian thought as a constellation of ideas, topics, and political engagements, which emerges partly outside of Italy and resonates internationally.

In contrast to other countries, philosophy is fairing relatively well in Italy. Despite increasing pressure by successive populist governments, and the quasi-monopolization of news and cultural media by a handful of consortia, certain theorists (such as the philosophers Maurizio Ferraris and Donatella Di Cesare, or the psychoanalyst Massimo Recalcati) contribute often and polemically to debates concerning ethics, new media, the rise of neo-fascism, the wars in Ukraine and Gaza and other conflicts—as were, before them, figures such as Pier Paolo Pasolini or Gianni Vattimo. Philosophy has a significant presence in the Italian public sphere. Admittedly, the role of the public intellectual has been on the decline in Italy and beyond after the 1970s. But the specter of Antonio Gramsci's organic intellectual continues to haunt Italy's highly politicized and fragmented public debate. In addition, as a discipline, philosophy continues to occupy a central place in the humanities, although Italian academe is increasingly receptive to interdisciplinary types of study, such as media studies, environmental Humanities, queer- and gender studies, and post- and decolonial studies. To some of these, Italian thought has been a crucial source of inspiration, often boomeranging back to Italy *via* Anglo-American academia. However, the practice and relative popularity of philosophy and critical theory *in* Italy does not necessarily constitute a coherent "Italian Thought." What has emerged over the past decades as "Italian Thought" is a nebula of themes, concepts, and ways of thinking—a "style of thought" as Esposito and others claim—that neither overlaps with popular, mediatized philosophy nor with academic philosophy per se.[4]

Italian thought does not coincide with critical theory produced and taught in Italy, even though some of the key figures in Italian thought, like Vattimo or Esposito, have built their entire academic careers in Italy. Many contemporary Italian theorists work abroad or have gained significant professional experience internationally, in particular in French (Emanuele Coccia, Toni Negri, Maurizio Lazzarato) and anglophone contexts (Silvia Federici, Rosi Braidotti, Federico Luisetti, Alberto Toscano). Consequently, Italian Thought is not even exclusively expressed *in Italian*. In the past decades, Italian academic and intellectual life has suffered from a veritable brain-drain, as many younger theorists have left for more welcoming institutions elsewhere in the Euro-Atlantic world, and now publish primarily in English for an international public more receptive to Italian thought as a "style of thought" than the Italian public itself, which remains often divided along political and institutional bloodlines. As the editors of the journal *Lo sguardo* write in their special issue on *La "differenza italiana." Filosofi(e) nell'Italia di oggi*: "'Italian philosophy' can no longer mean (exclusively) philosophy written in the

Italian language, a language that is encountering increasing marginality in the international community and, it is not difficult to predict, will suffer a similar fate in the national community of scholars."[5]

Moreover, Italian thought is partly the result of *exile*. In the aftermath of the political repression of left-wing movements in the late 1970s, many activist-thinkers associated with *operaismo* ["workerism"] and *autonomia* (Negri, Bifo, Lazzarato, Virno, Scalzone) were forced into exile, in particular in Paris,[6] where their earlier Marxist ideas amalgamated with French poststructuralism (specifically with the work of Michel Foucault, Gilles Deleuze and Félix Guattari). On the other hand, a major figure such as Giorgio Agamben spent much of his life outside of Italian institutions, in London or Paris. For reasons that are often at the same time political, socio-economic, or biographical, Italian thought refuses to be restricted to the geo-political as well as intellectual and linguistic boundaries of modern-day Italy. Additionally, the discussions in Italy concerning the consistency and genealogy of a "properly Italian" thought are often initiated in response to mostly Anglo-American attempts to internationally present "Italian Thought" as a single body.[7] Tellingly, a first milestone in the fashioning of Italian Thought is Michael Hardt and Paolo Virno's *Radical Thought in Italy*, first published in the United States in 1996. The production, reception, and manufacture of "Italian Thought" is decidedly international and multilingual. Perhaps Italian thought is best imagined as a network of entanglements of intellectual and political concerns, the intersection of which is highly idiosyncratic, and of which Italy is not so much the epicenter, or its "proper place," but rather a launchpad, sending off into the world a specific set of concepts, engagements, and methods.

## Genealogies and Actualities

Crucial to the debates concerning the meaning of Italian Thought, within and beyond Italy, is the question of its supposed *genealogy*, or better still, *genealogies*. It is by establishing a genealogy for contemporary Italian thought that theorists like Esposito or Toscano attempt to distill a coherent set of ideas and themes that would constitute "Italian Thought."[8] These genealogies, however, vary widely, both in terms of content and timescales. For example, in *Living Thought: The Origins and Actuality of Italian Philosophy*, Esposito traces the alleged characteristics of Italian thought—i.e., the emphasis on the here-and-now, a preference for difference rather than sameness or unity, a certain openness or porosity, a penchant for action rather than contemplation—all the way back to the Renaissance, particularly to Machiavelli. Esposito paints a family tree of Italian thinkers that includes Machiavelli, Giordano Bruno, Leonardo da Vinci, Giambattista Vico, and closer to our age Benedetto Croce, Antonio Gramsci, Pier Paolo Pasolini and workerist Marxism. Toscano and Chiesa's *The Italian Difference: Between Nihilism and Politics*, much like Hardt and Virno's *Radical Thought in Italy*, situates the inception of Italian thought with the emergence of workerist Marxism in the social struggles of the 1960s and 1970s, a much shorter family tree. In recent work by Dario Gentili, Elettra Stimilli, and others,[9] Italian thought is presented as the surprising yet highly productive assemblage of Italian Marxism (Gramsci, workerism) and poststructuralist ideas (most notably those of Foucault), which puts the moment of Italian thought's inception even closer to the present. These different genealogies primarily fulfil a strategic function of recombining elements from a radically fragmented Italian intellectual tradition into more or less coherent strands of thought. The yearning for genealogy in much of contemporary Italian thought may in reality be a symptom of a fundamentally fragmented philosophical landscape: the lack of an undisputed family tree. This may, as a matter of fact, be very Italian. Just like Italy itself failed to constitute its own uniform nation until deep in the nineteenth century, the unity of Italian thought might also be belated. Modern Italian history constitutes a tension between an aspiration to unity and the many resistances to national political, geographical, socio-cultural, and intellectual unification. It ostensibly prefers the Spinozist variegated multitude over the Hobbesian–Hegelian universal State. As Gentili argues, "Italian critical thought is in fact a field of tension whose territory is mapped and delineated exactly by differences and conflicts."[10] In this sense, for Gentili, the very term "Italian Theory" risks neutralizing the radical difference between various thinkers and, we may add, the centrality of "difference" itself in Italian thought.

## What is Italian "Thought"?

In this book, we agree with Gentili, Esposito and others that "Italian Theory" may not be the most suitable denomination. At the very least, we should use the plural. Moreover, as we will see, the notion of "Italian Theory" derives from that of "French Theory," a household name in global academia for decades, which does not do justice to the originality of Italian thought or to its complicated relationship with postwar French philosophy. Italian thought should not be presented as yet another ready-made "Theory" made palatable for global, neoliberal, and anglophone academia. However, we recognize that the attempts, conscious or not, to do so by Esposito, Gentili, and others, may simply result from a lack of choice. The prerequisite for any visibility on the international academic scene today is to turn one's intellectual tradition into a brand. On the other hand, neither does the traditional designation of "Philosophy" do full justice to Italian *thought*. Although the thinkers discussed in this book are mostly philosophers, if not by profession at least by training, their thought is characterized by a certain open-mindedness toward questions that lie beyond the jurisdiction of academic philosophy (i.e., biology, politics, technology, art), and by a porousness vis-à-vis other disciplines and other forms of writing, and even by a certain marginality with respect to academic philosophy, in particular the history of philosophy.

The term "thought"—taken here as a nod to Vattimo's *pensiero debole* ["weak thought"] (see Chapter 5), but also to Esposito's *living thought*, as well as to Heidegger's *Denken* conceived as alternative to a "philosophy" deemed anachronistic—captures Italian thought as an open-ended and dynamic refusal of institutional rigidity. To recognize the strategic function of the many genealogies that have been established for Italian thought is not to diminish their importance. In fact, they are highly revealing of the stakes of the philosophical and political debates in Italy over the past decades. In this book, instead of siding with a particular genealogy, we consider "the genealogical question" a central part of this complex assemblage of debates, often conflicting ideas and schools of thought; political position-taking; and geographical, historical, and cultural eccentricities that constitute "Italian Thought." In this light, the absences and silences within these genealogies—the sawn-off branches of the family tree, as it were—are as interesting as the names and schools included. For example, the complicated position or downright exclusion of Vattimo's *pensiero debole* and postmodernists like Mario Perniola, from attempted genealogies of "Italian Thought" is revealing. They constitute potentially repressed origins of contemporary Italian thought on which, perhaps painfully or embarrassingly, postmodern or weak thought itself would have loved to linger.

Moreover, genealogy as a method of philosophical inquiry plays a significant role in the work of thinkers such as Giorgio Agamben, Massimo Cacciari, and Roberto Esposito; it is by no means a matter of mere archiving but a means to critically and carefully analyze received ideas. We do not assume Italian thought to possess a unique genealogy, and we would like to resist the temptation to elevate Italian thought into a monolithic "Italian Thought." But we would also like to avoid dismissing Italian thought as mere fabrication packaged and made digestible for impatient international academics in search of new buzzwords for their publish-or-perish careers. This book is not an encyclopedia of Italian Theory, let alone of the immensely rich tradition of Italian philosophy.[11] The relevance of Italian thought, for us, resides in its porosity and malleability, in its engaged and interventionist character that defies any essentialist take on it. In this book, we would like to show the continued relevance of Italian thought, as it has developed over the past decades, including some of its canonical thinkers and concepts, in new and resolutely contemporary contexts. Even if the genealogies of Esposito or Negri differ wildly, they do share the assertion that Italian thought is a practical, *worldly* thought, even if it frequently juggles metaphysical concepts and belabors long-forgotten historical texts. It *does* something, it seeks to understand and *intervene* in its historical and political context, and often sides with those who find themselves at the margins of that context. Gentili points out that the concept of biopolitics, which acted for two decades as shorthand for "Italian Theory," may be disappearing as the reference paradigm of Italian thought.[12] Given the open-endedness of Italian styles of thinking, we argue this is not a loss but the prologue to a new chapter in Italian thought.

## What is the "Contemporary"? Beyond the "Italian laboratory"

Although we are reluctant to provide Italian thought with a date-stamp that would certify its origin, we do stress the role of political context in its formation. The political emphasis in Italian thought recurs in many of the introductions and debates. Hardt and Virno's *Radical Thought in Italy* sets the tone. Not only does their book provide Italian thought with a discernible genealogy, firmly rooting Italian thought in workerist Marxism and its role in the social and political upheavals of the 1960s and 1970s, it also introduces a series of key notions that have continued to dominate discussions of the origins and characteristics of Italian thought ever since. Hardt and Virno directly embed Italian thought in the ideological and conceptual constellation of Italian workerist Marxism. Italian thought constitutes for them a politics of experimentation, practice, subjective agency, struggle and resistance, autonomy. Moreover, Hardt and Virno explicitly speak of "the Italian laboratory": Italian political, intellectual, and social experimentation are seen as a prefiguration for radical progressive politics across the Euro-Atlantic world. Hardt writes: "I take Italian revolutionary politics as a model … because it has constituted a kind of laboratory for experimentation in new forms of political thinking that helps us conceive a revolutionary practice in our times."[13] The image of the "Italian laboratory" has, to an extent, become an origin story that has persisted in the academic imagination.[14] In his preface to the re-issue of the Semiotext(e) *Autonomia* issue (originally published in 1980), Sylvère Lotringer notes that the Italians may be "the only political philosophers capable of *re-inventing politics affirmatively*, 'post-politically'."[15] For Hardt and Lotringer, Italian thought remains relevant because it is entangled with political *practice*, or at least primarily concerned with the question of *praxis*.

In their book, Hardt and Virno present Italian thought not just as a tool to reconsider and inspire contemporary revolutionary politics, but also describe the "difference," the defining characteristics of Italian theory in terms of its "real political immediacy." For Hardt and Virno, theory follows practice, as the former "can effectively address only questions that are raised in the course of practical struggles, and in turn, this theorizing can be articulated only through its creative implementation on the practical field."[16] Akin to Italian society in the 1960s and 1970s, the relationship between theory and practice becomes a laboratory of sorts "for testing the effects of new ideas, strategies and organizations."[17] Hardt and Virno join earlier analyses by, among others, Guy Debord and Félix Guattari of the Italian 1970s, as opening a window for radical experiments at the very moment the revolutionary spirit of 1968 seems to fade away in Paris, Berlin, or Berkeley. For Hardt and Virno, "revolution can be nothing other than this continually open process of experimentation."[18] In establishing this nexus between theory and practice, between philosophy and social struggles, Hardt and Virno clearly situate Italian thought under the aegis of workerist Marxism.[19]

For workerists like Tronti and Negri, "*self-valorisation* was thought of as the building block for constructing a new form of sociality, a new society."[20] The recognition and subsequent reclaiming of the autonomy of the working class vis-à-vis capital unleashes the "power to generate and sustain social forms and structures of value independent of capitalist relations of production."[21] According to Hardt and Virno—and Lotringer some twenty years later—Italian thought originates in this Marxist frenzy of political, social, and cultural experimentation in Italy in the 1960s and 1970s, culminating in the *Autonomia* movement, also known as the *Movimento 77*. The latter experimented with new forms of radically horizontal social organization, new political subjectivities (women, homosexuals, psychiatric patients, the emerging precariat, the "Metropolitan Indians"), underground culture and drugs, and new media (free radio and TV stations, such as Radio Alice).[22] About the twenty years that separate the end of the autonomist movement in Italy and the post-historical, globalized world of the late 1990s, Hardt writes, "the convergence of social conditions, reducing the gap of Italian exceptionalism, has brought Italy close to us."[23] Again, Italy serves as laboratory for the Euro-Atlantic world: the rise of "new forms of diffuse and flexible production"[24] known as post-Fordism, the monopolization of cultural production by media-moguls like Silvio Berlusconi, the emergence of populist and technocratic politics as embodied by the same Berlusconi, that is to say the "postmodernization"[25] of the economy, of society and politics. All of these developments have fundamentally reshaped Italian life, and therefore, once more, turned Italy into a privileged laboratory for new forms of social relations that are rapidly spreading across the globe. "This is why the experiments conducted in laboratory Italy are experiments of our own future," Hardt claims.[26]

Admittedly, Hardt's narrative is tempting, especially since today's Italy seems yet another socio-political experiment. Governed by populist far-right politicians like Giorgia Meloni and Matteo Salvini, contemporary Italy looks like a petri dish of neofascist experimentation. And to Hardt and Virno's credit, they were partly proven right about the global importance of the Italian left of the 1970s. The so-called anti-globalization movement of the 1990s and 2000s, which culminated in the protests in Genoa in the summer of 2001, as well as the subsequent global social movement—including Occupy Wall Street and the anti-austerity and anti-precarity movements of the 2000s and 2010s—were in part inspired by Italian autonomist and workerist thought. Theorists such as Negri, Franco "Bifo" Berardi, Maurizio Lazzarato, and Virno and Hardt themselves did occupy the global intellectual scene for years, and many of their core ideas on post-Fordism, precarity, or cognitive capitalism are now part and parcel of the academic as well as activist idiom. However, Hardt and Virno's model genealogy of the "Italian laboratory" is not unproblematic from a historical as well as intellectual perspective.

First, the implicit vanguardism in the metaphor of the "laboratory Italy" may not do justice to historical reality. In their preface to *The Italian Difference*, Lorenzo Chiesa and Alberto Toscano express their skepticism as to "the Italian *difference*": Rather than being a laboratory for radical politics and thought, Italy may simply have been late to the progressivist party that culminated in May 1968 in Paris.[27] In Italy, the social and political upheavals of the 1960s took place a decade later, and were accompanied by widespread political violence (left- and right-wing terrorism) and state repression during the so-called *anni di piombo* ["years of lead"].[28] In this light, radical experimentation may also be a sign of the absence of a popular or mainstream emancipatory movement that would effectively realize large-scale social and cultural changes. As Chiesa and Toscano argue, this periodization is relevant insofar as it points to an Italian *difference* rather than to an *exception*. In the period following the *anni di piombo,* the spectacular neoliberalization of Italian society and the commercialization and profanation of culture, as exemplified in the crass figure of Berlusconi, create perhaps not another "laboratory"—this time around for neoliberal governance, post-Fordist production, and populist politics—but a local, particularly condensed and symptomatic incarnation of a global state of affairs.[29] For Chiesa and Toscano, Italian thought thus offers a kind of parallax view on global questions and processes, a "peculiar admixture of the extremely parochial ... and the intensely universal."[30] Second, to situate the origins of Italian thought in the social movements of the 1960s and 1970s can also be understood to conflate Italian thought and workerist Marxism, to present the key concepts of Italian thought as derivatives of workerist-autonomist ideas. Before tracing Italian thought back to its Machiavellian beginnings, even Roberto Esposito argues that "the germinal nucleus of Italian Thought is the 1960's Italian Operaism in its various souls."[31] If, for Esposito, "Italian thought constituted itself in its own making," it did so as it emerged from the student movements and social struggles of the

1960s, clearly connecting its fate with politics, or as Esposito puts it, with politics as its "outside."[32]

Workerist notions and thinkers have undeniably been crucial to the gestation of Italian thought and a key factor in its success, as notions such as "immaterial labor," "cognitive capitalism," and "precariat" are vital to understanding many of our current predicaments. But we are hesitant to *reduce* Italian thought to the workerist tradition. The monopolization of Italian thought as an offshoot of workerism not only excludes important voices from outside the Marxist tradition (Vattimo, Rovatti, Braidotti, Adriana Cavavero), it also distorts the history of workerism itself. In his essay "Post-Operaism? No, Operaism," Negri boldly claims that such a thing as post-workerism "simply does not exist,"[33] as workerism has never really ceased to be. Fitting in Italian thought as a late offshoot of workerism or as a *post*-workerism might postulate discontinuities absent in historical reality. According to Negri, there is a direct continuity between workerist theory and politics from the 1960s to today. "Italian thought," in Negri's narrative, merely signifies "*operaismo* in its progressive updates."[34] For Negri, today's questions remain those that were at the heart of the workerist project:

> How can we position ourselves within/against capitalist command as we recognize that we have no alternative, and as we fight it by blocking its power to exploit the individual and its power of collective "extraction" of value? How can we forcefully take away its knowledge and power instruments? I believe these questions constitute the heart of workerism.[35]

Notwithstanding the urgency of the questions raised by Negri, his reappraisal of workerist theory does gloss over the caesura in workerist as well as broader Italian history, a caesura we believe to be essential to the constitution of Italian thought today. As Sylvère Lotringer reminds us, the autonomist movements of the sixties and seventies were tragically defeated, resulting in the exile and imprisonment of many of its key thinkers (Negri, Bifo, Lazzarato, Virno).[36] It is from this caesura that Italian thought, *including post-workerist/post-autonomist theories*, emerged. Italian thought, as a constellation of ideas rather than a homogenous school of thought (from Negri to Vattimo, from Agamben to Braidotti), constitutes a *response* to the dissolution of social and political movements, such as *operaismo* and *Autonomia*, and the radical socio-political and cultural changes in Italy since the mid-1970s. Despite Negri's hostility towards the prefix "post-," we consider Italian thought to be a thinking posterior to the caesura of the mid-1970s, which was famously diagnosed by Pasolini as a profound anthropological mutation shortly before his own violent death in 1975, a death that perhaps can be considered to be the most prominent marker of the caesura. After the 1970s, humanity was never quite the same anymore.

In this sense, Italian thought is not the resurrection of workerism, yet neither does it have a centuries-long more-or-less consistent history as claimed by Esposito. It is the reflection on and the working-through of, albeit in different philosophical idioms, the historical transformations that took place in Italy with the collapse of the social movements and the institutions of the postwar society of the *miracolo economico*, i.e., Italy's economic miracle of the three decades following the Second World War. To put it slightly more pessimistically, Italian thought constitutes the requiem of Italian—and by extension European—post-1945 social democracy and its promises of social, economic, and political emancipation. Pier Aldo Rovatti adequately summarizes what is at stake in contemporary Italian thought: "Our society is the society crafted after the anthropological mutation that Pasolini denounced. We have to reinvent new battles and strategies of thought *starting from here*."[37] For Rovatti, if there is such a thing as Italian thought, it surfaces as a strategic—and eminently *practical*—response to the caesura of the 1970s, which we take to be equally constitutive of both Negri's post-workerism and Rovatti's own "weak thought."

As Elettra Stimilli suggests, there may be an "Italian laboratory" after all, but in a different sense from Hardt and Virno's: a laboratory for the analysis of the changing nature of the State, of surveillance and repression, of de-industrialization;[38] a laboratory that churns out concepts and modes of thought to comprehend, challenge, and intervene in (perhaps more so than to revolutionize) our contemporary. For Esposito, it is the final Pasolini, in his cinematic testament *Salò* and the articles collected in *Scritti corsari*,[39] who captures "the unbearable" within our contemporary (or better still, our contemporary *as* unbearable).[40] The descent of young Italians into the circles of hell in *Salò* represents how true hell consists of the absence of hope. In the waning of the revolutionary hope of the twentieth century, there remains only the eternal present of capitalism and concomitant consumerism. Pasolini painfully demonstrates how neither the future nor the past can act any longer as refuge (if only in thought), everything being violated by unfettered commodification—from the bodies of the young to the patrimony, traditions, and communities of Italy. What reigns in the infernal villa of *Salò* is absolute illegality, the anarchy of a new and absolute power that no longer has any opponents, no outside, and that manifests itself in its unfiltered obscenity. We argue that Pasolini's final works capture the context of political disenchantment, of the rapid neoliberalization of Italian society, of the postmodernization of Italian culture, in which contemporary Italian thought has gestated. Pasolini painstakingly expresses the festive, perversely joyful character of contemporary power that no longer represses libidinal energy but unleashes it, turns it into an integral part of the exercise of power, and uses it to seduce us into its claws.

In the final scene of *Salò*, we see how one of the libertines, played by Aldo Valetti, watches a series of unbearable torture scenes through his binoculars. Perhaps the unbearable truth of post-1970s Italy is that what ultimately has stared back at us through these binoculars is an invitingly smiling Silvio Berlusconi. The truly "unbearable" of contemporary Italy is not only that we are the hapless victims of sadistic powers but that we are also happily invited to come join the *bunga bunga* party, always already complicit in the obscene libidinal excesses of power. Rather than playing Negri's blame-game of shaming the alleged saboteurs of revolutionary Italian philosophy, we prefer to identify Italian thought as a bundle of different attempts—including that of post-workerists, such as Negri himself—to forge ways out of this unbearable predicament, if only intellectually or apophatically in cases like Agamben or Vattimo's *pensiero debole*.

As Gentili observes, in the late 1970s, "there was a shift from thinking of crisis in an antagonistic sense, as an occasion for rupture, tension and radical ideas, to the idea of a *government* of the crisis, i.e., the field of tension that the crisis brings into play can be governed."[41] If we can speak of Italian thought as a constellation of recurrent and at times overlapping ideas, it is because Italian thinkers have tried, from different philosophical, ideological, and institutional angles, to come to terms with the societal and political mutations since the 1970s. These attempts have created a sequence of concepts ("biopolitics," "*homo sacer*," "immunity," "precarity," "immaterial labor," "multitude"), as well as novel methods of inquiry (from *pensiero debole* to archaeological inquiry), that allow them to gauge the political conjunctures of our unbearable times. In this book, rather than promoting a particular lineage for Italian thought, we believe that the conception of Italian thought outlined above allows for an open-ended and more inclusive sense of Italian thought, which also comprises those voices that were pivotal for the formation of Italian thought but are routinely glossed over or excluded in many of the introductions in Italian thought issued over the past two decades.[42]

## The Political Outside

In *Living Thought,* Esposito stresses that Italian philosophy is a thought of the *outside.* Italian thought, he argues, "came into the world turned upside down and inside out, as it were, into the world of historical and political life."[43] Esposito distinguishes a kind of repeated primal scene of Italian thought. From Machiavelli to *operaismo* and biopolitical theory, Italian thought is enmeshed in politics, in historically specific social struggles over power. There may not exist a direct line from Machiavelli to Agamben, but both their philosophies are reflections on and interventions in the political life of their times. Italian thought, according to Esposito, has always ventured outside of the confines of philosophy as an academic discipline, and it is *politics* that represents the nexus between history and life.[44] Rovatti expresses caution concerning a notion of politics that may be overgeneralizing: "I fear that the main focus of Italian Theory could be limited to Politics with a capital 'P.'"[45] Such a "Grand Politics," ultimately, forces us to take sides. As Rovatti says, the implicit question here is always "are you a leftist or not?" It shoehorns the idea of politics into that of macroscopic struggle, with its implications of violence and grand gestures, but it ignores politics in its "microphysical, everyday sense."[46] Rather than assuming politics to constitute the epicenter of Italian thought, Rovatti proposes the ethical–political task of "weakening the truth [by] fighting against the inner theoretical violence of the hegemonic policy of truth,"[47] including and especially in our daily experiences and habits. Micropolitics can constitute another nexus between history and life. This prominence granted to politics or the nexus life-history allows Esposito to situate Italian thought explicitly outside of the horizon of much of contemporary thought. He sees the latter as determined by a linguistic turn and a concern for the instability of language that is notably more secondary to the Italian focus on politics and micropolitics.

As we will see, the horizon of contemporary thought in Esposito coincides with French poststructuralist and postmodern thought, which themselves are seen as culmination point of German-written European philosophy from Nietzsche to Heidegger, via Theodor Adorno and Ludwig Wittgenstein. Italian thought, then, proposes an affirmative thinking, outside of the limitations of deconstruction and negative dialectics, but without resorting to a naive and outlived realism or empiricism. As such, Italian thought may offer the humanities "some leverage to resume functioning in an affirmative mode."[48] The affirmative tone of much of Italian thought can also be interpreted as an attempted affirmation of Italian theory's autonomy in relation to French poststructuralism. As we will also see, Italian thought, whether it is Negri, Esposito, or Agamben, entertains a highly ambiguous relation with poststructuralist or postmodern thought. It crucially engages with poststructuralist thinkers like Foucault, Derrida, or Deleuze and situates itself vis-à-vis poststructuralist ideas, often developing or reworking poststructuralist concepts in a contemporary context geographically, politically, historically distinct from 1960s Paris. This ambiguity results in a series of disjunctive syntheses characteristic of Italian thought, combinations of seemingly incompatible ideas from poststructural thought, from Esposito's affirmative deconstructive biopolitics to post-autonomist admixtures of Deleuze and Marx, to Agamben's cross-eyed reading of Heidegger with Walter Benjamin, Guy Debord with Pasolini. The pivotal role played by French poststructuralism for Italian thought is both acknowledged *and* repressed as an "outside" that continues to haunt Italian thought on the inside. The porosity of Italian thought, however, is not always fully conceded by Italian theorists themselves. This explains the precarious place occupied by Vattimo, Emanuele Severino, and Rovatti's *pensiero debole* in current genealogies of Italian thought. On the one hand, "weak thought," in its persistent refusal of permanent affirmation and its withdrawal from power, including the power and exclusionary violence of "strong thoughts" and master concepts such as biopolitics or class, undermines the affirmative aspirations of Italian thought as envisioned by Negri or Esposito. As a result, weak thought finds itself casted out of genealogies of Italian thought. Symptomatic of this exclusion is Negri's violent dismissal of Vattimo, who calls *pensiero debole* "a plan to repudiate the history of the insurgencies and resistances that had accompanied the first construction from below of a public space in Italy, the first democratic construction after fascism."[49] With undeniable machismo, Negri dismisses weak thought as *pensiero molle* [limp or impotent thought],[50] a "renewed ontology of fascism," but this time around dressed up as Berlusconi's showgirls. On the other hand, weak thought is perhaps the most extensive engagement in recent Italian philosophy, with the epistemological concerns of poststructuralism at the pivotal, transformative caesura of the late 1970s and early 1980s, and it remains a touchstone (albeit often in negative terms) for the thinkers who emerge in its slipstream, from Agamben to Esposito and beyond. Hence the importance of incorporating weak thought in genealogies of contemporary Italian thought.

## Original Differences: From French Detours to Italian Geophilosophy

This brings us to a constant in Italian thought: the detour through so-called French Theory. As is recognized by some of the principal contributors to the discussion and many roundtables on the alleged nature of "Italian Theory," the very idea that there may be a more-or-less consistent body of thought that can be labeled as "Italian Theory" is clearly modeled on the global phenomenon and success of "French Theory," itself a shorthand for poststructuralism. French Theory has established itself in anglophone academia as a ready-made repertoire of conceptual moves and theoretical talking points to inform teaching and research in European philosophy and literary theory. Italian Theory is, in that context, sometimes suggested as the "next big thing" for aspiring academics. Despite the suspect motivations for establishing Italian Theory as a uniform school of thought, there are clear historical connections between French and Italian thinkers. As suggested by Stimilli in her introduction to *Decostruzione o biopolitica?*, any attempted genealogy of Italian thought should start from its foundational and continued engagement with French poststructuralism and its key thinkers: Foucault, Derrida, Deleuze.[51] Even more outspoken is Rovatti in his categorical assertion that:

in my opinion there is no such thing as a national peculiarity of Italian thought, although it may be true that in Italy there is, and always has been, a unique and independent reaction to some significant French authors, simplistically labeled as 'poststructuralists' ... recasting their conceptual tools in an original fashion.[52]

What makes Italian thought relevant for global philosophical audiences is the fact that the Italians have underlined and re-energized the radical dimension of theorists such as Foucault, whose politics are often toned down in anglophone academia.[53] The question "What is Italian Thought?" makes sense only in the wake of the victory march of French Theory in the global humanities. It provides a valuable corrective to the homeopathic versions of critical thought that sometimes inform academic discourse.

As some of the protagonists (Rovatti, Esposito) and chroniclers (Gentili, Stimilli) of Italian thought are well aware, the concoction that is Italian Theory can easily be misread as an attempt to replicate the successes of French Theory, to brand the disparate landscape of Italian philosophy as marketable unit for global anglophone academia. It reveals a kind of double detour: a first loop through French poststructuralism, followed by a second loop through a US-centered global critical theory industry largely modeled after, and highly receptive to, French Theory. But as Sandro Chignola suggests, the very idea of an Italian thought only makes sense in a contemporary that, philosophically speaking, is posterior to poststructuralism and that is still coming to terms with poststructuralism. In this sense, any attempt to create a genealogy for Italian thought anterior to poststructuralism is an anachronistic gesture, an attempt to antedate.[54] In a sense, Italian thought constitutes a powerful resumption and revival, *in and beyond the caesura of the late 1970s*, of poststructuralism and some of its key conceptual innovations and concerns: biopolitics, power, assemblage, becoming, deconstruction, and genealogy as method. After the violent decline of the ideals of the 1960s and 1970s that saw the birth and heyday of poststructuralist thought, Italian thought picks up where the French left off, but in the idiom of Italian intellectual contexts.

Whether it is the post-workerist amalgam of Marx, Foucault, and Deleuze, or Agamben and Esposito's continuation of Foucauldian analyses of biopolitics, or Braidotti's vitalist-Deleuzian feminism, or Bifo's Baudrillardian-Guattarian takedowns of contemporary "semiocapitalism," the principal interlocutors for Italian thinkers remain French poststructuralist philosophers. In many cases, these are direct interlocutors, i.e., Vattimo's extensive collaboration with Derrida, Agamben's dialogues with Jean-Luc Nancy and others, Negri's work with Guattari. If the worldly "outside" of Italian thought, first and foremost, is politics, then the philosophical outside is French poststructuralism. In fact, as Stimilli affirms, it is because French theory "took philosophy outside of itself" [*la filosofia fuori di sé*] that it became such an attractive and relevant model for Italian thought.[55] As Esposito claims, Italian thought attempts to overcome some of the antinomies and perhaps antipathies of French poststructuralism. It does not read Foucault-against-Derrida (or Deleuze, or Lyotard) but rather Foucault-*with*-Derrida, Derrida-*via*-Foucault.[56] If French poststructuralism can be said to have a double genealogy, post-Heideggerian (Derrida) versus post-Nietzschean (Foucault, Deleuze), Italian thought reconsiders these legacies as they intersect, at the confluence between being *and* becoming. Esposito stresses that poststructuralism (most notably Derridean deconstruction) and Italian analyses of biopolitics were first articulated in two different conjunctures [*congiunture*] of contemporary philosophical history and history *tout court*. We have shifted from the paradigm that inspired the so-called linguistic turn that gave birth to poststructuralism toward a biopolitical paradigm in which the tenets of poststructuralism take on a different meaning.[57] As Esposito argues, deconstruction radically changes its meaning (or rather, our perspective on the poststructuralist project shifts dramatically) "in a world that is already broken" [*un mondo che da sé cade in pezzi*].[58] In such a world, we need to "push Derrida beyond Derrida" [*spingere Derrida oltre Derrida*] by means of Foucault.[59]

Esposito adequately captures a basic maneuver in Italian thought: re-reading and recombining French poststructuralist thinkers, soldering seemingly contradictory thinkers in order to grasp our contemporary. Chignola speaks of Italian thought as an assembly of "thought machines," of often surprising hybrids of thinkers, foremost French contemporaries. Such thought-machines combine different philosophical perspectives to push the latter beyond themselves.[60] Foucauldian power with Deleuzian becoming or Derridian deconstruction with Deleuzian vitalism bring forth key insights into the political and the nature of reality more generally.[61] Chignola adds that because of its hybrid, porous character, "it is possible to talk about an Italian Theory only in a very weak way."[62] In this book, we embrace the notion of a "weak genealogy." Rather than seeking to establish paternities, continuous bloodlines, we consider Italian thought to be a sequence of potential couplings, of attempts to take poststructuralist figures of thought beyond their context of inception into the contemporary, to gauge their tactical potential as instruments for intervening in present political and socio-cultural debates, often altering them fundamentally in the process.

But then, once again, where does this leave the adjective "Italian" in "Italian thought"? Could it not be argued that a sizable chunk of the humanities today, not in the least in Anglo-American academe, consists of various recalibrations of French poststructuralism? Esposito proposes the term "Italian geophilosophy" to avoid regressing into either an essentialism of a-historical Italianness or a generic Theory-with-a-capital-T that would be indistinguishable from a now globalized critical theory and its many "-studies". Borrowed from Deleuze, Guattari, and Massimo Cacciari, "geophilosophy" disrupts the phantasy of a unified European philosophy that would consist of a straight line from its Greek origins to today.[63] On the contrary, "geography is what tears history away from the claim of simple progression but also from the regressive cult of origins, to trace out lines of flight, undiscovered passages, and sudden diversions that tamper with the order of time by overturning the usual relationship."[64] Geophilosophy infuses the history of philosophy with the particular, the exceptional, the idiosyncratic, and the unpredictable; it does not so much enclose national philosophies into a claustrophobic narrative of alleged national characteristics, but it deterritorializes, fractures, and multiplies what "philosophy" means; it opens up philosophy to an outside, as it reveals "philosophy" as a patchwork of traditions and vocabularies, each bordering on others, and thus opening toward the outside. It encourages us to conjoin Italian thought with German idealism, French critique, American pragmatism, etc.[65] For Esposito, Italian thought is perhaps best understood as geophilosophy, as it is paradoxically characterized by a constant deterritorialization, a relentless back-and-forth between its historical, political, cultural, and institutional contexts, and adjacent European philosophical traditions with their universalizing aspirations. In this sense, Italian geophilosophy refers to a peculiar tradition of thought that distinguishes itself not so much by transmitting a quintessential "Italian" philosophical canon but by the constant engagement with a historically shared social and political outside.

According to Esposito, in contrast to the German desire for reterritorialization and closure (a return to Greek origins) as well as the French suspension and perpetual deferral of the origin (of *différance* and *différend*), Italian thought encapsulates an incessant, creative exodus, a productive and affirmative recasting of other critical traditions via distinct Italian concerns.[66] To an extent, Esposito argues, Italian thought has always been a marginal thought: "positioning itself instead at its external margins"[67] as Italy has never been a strong, monolithic nation-state; moreover, for Esposito, Italy has remained marginal vis-à-vis "the historical-conceptual horizon in which it is situated," known as *modernity*.[68] Esposito presents Italy as a kind of *alter-modernity*: neither anti-modern—avoiding Romantic mythologies of ancient origins—nor falling for the modernist myth of a radical rupture with whatever precedes it. Whether we agree or not with the exact phrasing of Esposito's view, contemporary Italian thought is not so much a philosophy of new beginnings but of potentials.

From Agamben's archaeology of the theological sources of our political economy to post-workerist reappraisals of labor and class, to the Spinozist revival of Braidotti and Negri, to Vattimo's oxymoronic "return" to Christianity and communism alike, to the continual exchange with poststructuralism, Italian thought taps into "the *actuality of the originary*."[69] Italian thought taps into the archives of the philosophical canon and past historical struggles as sources of energy, and it recovers hitherto concealed meaning and critical use-values that can be reactivated in critical interventions into contemporary debates. It is this "inoriginarity"[70] of Italian thought, its historical, intellectual, and institutional off-center position, that imbues it with its originality and agility. Italian thought does not shy away from conflict. Its often radical reconsiderations of fundamental concepts (life, politics, community, class, being) originate in unruly, historically specific contexts. In this sense, it is both immanent *and* transhistorical. Italian thought chooses "the perspective of innovation not preservation."[71] It delivers conceptual tools to carry out careful reconsideration of fundamental categories of contemporary politics and society: labor, life, identity, security, violence, populism, fascism, immunity, etc. If not exactly a laboratory for experimentation, Italian thought does deliver an affirmative deconstruction of sorts that seeks out potential in the present, on the threshold of actualization.

Finally, with Sandro Mezzadra, we would like to highlight another aspect of Italian thought understood as geophilosophy, which is only slowly emerging in current genealogies of Italian thought: its "outside" is rapidly expanding. First, Mezzadra reminds us of the tragic fact that "thousands of young Italians are forced to leave the country to have a future as researchers." To cling to an image of Italian thought that is either "auto-referential" or even Eurocentric makes little sense in this new diasporic reality.[72] Italian thinkers are no longer exclusively engaged in a dialogue with European schools of thought like French poststructuralism or German critical theory, but more and more intensively with post- and decolonial thought, feminism, black studies—to which we can add environmental thought, queer studies, posthumanism, science studies, and so on.[73] The habitat for Italian thought is no longer reduced to the archaic universities of metropolitan Italy but resembles what Braidotti imagines as the "global multiversity."[74] Mezzadra (but also Braidotti and Luisetti) takes a step beyond Gentili, who affirms that Italian thought continues to move "within the framework of Europe," even if, as a space for thought, "Europe" is conflictual and complex.[75] Mezzadra opposes what he calls a "centrifugal reading" of Italian thought, as such a reading would "run the risk of being reduced to a merely academic exercise. And Italian Theory would remain a theory of the world of yesterday."[76] If Italian thought is to remain relevant for the now global humanities, it must engage with other vantage points for thought, be it non-human others, migrants, new technologies, new identities, and new bodies.

For Mezzadra, this different vantage point consists of the question of migration, which has become prominent since the 1990s and has now reached its crescendo in the refugee crisis, among other places on the island of Lampedusa. It offers a radically different point of departure for critical thinking, which did not originate in questions of class struggle or emancipation, not in the notion of autonomy, not in biopolitics in its historical shapes and forms, but in an urgent, contemporary kind of biopolitics.[77] Mezzadra's subsequent work (see Chapter 5) shows that there are multiple ways into Italian theory—but always setting off from an outside—and the importance of questioning the Eurocentrism underpinning much of it (including the supposed universality of "Theory" and "Philosophy") in response to, and a means of thinking through the geopolitical transformations of the past decades.[78] The key to the continued relevance of Italian thought lies in admitting this shifting of perspective and turning it into a productive displacement, a continuous critique of the "homogenizing vectors" of Western theory, including concepts such as biopolitics, class, and labor.

The principal aim of this book is not to provide Italian thought with yet another genealogy or to prove current genealogies wrong. It would be more than pedantic for three obscure Northern-European academics to tell world-renowned Italian thinkers what they should or should not write about themselves and their own traditions of thought. The point here is to stress strategic and productive moves made in these various genealogies, in particular insofar as these are often self-undermining as they emphasize the openness and, in a sense, the "inauthenticity" of Italian thought, its fundamental Machiavellian suppleness. Genealogy, in Italian thought, is deployed as an effective means of identifying and energizing recurrent or overlapping concepts and concerns, even if these originate in a wide variety of often conflicting and even mutually exclusive intellectual traditions. The sole constant in these genealogies is the fact that Italian thought can best be thought of as a practical, interventionist thought, which delivers heuristic tools for intervening in historically situated debates (from social and labor relations to biopolitical regimes, from migration to medical ethics, from postmodernism to national identity to the new fascisms). Italian thought often ventures further into pathways opened by other traditions, transforming and recontextualizing ideas in the present; it does so in continued dialogue with the vast corpus of Italian philosophy, political theory, literature and art, and in light of Italian politics, geography, as well as cultural and historical fractures.

In the first chapter, we assess the contemporary relevance of one of the key concepts of Italian thought: biopolitics. During the Covid-19 pandemic, the term "biopolitics" played a surprisingly insignificant role in the academic and public debates surrounding the pandemic. Apart from discussion in specialist circles, the impact of biopolitical theory on general politics was minimal. Nonetheless, securing the health of the population became the number one concern of nation-states across the globe, placing biopolitics at the core of national politics on an unprecedented scale. It seemed that in spite of a biopolitical crisis affecting the planet, the term "biopolitics" had lost its conceptual value. Esposito has described various problems surrounding the use of the term: conceptual unclarity, a lack of historical precision, and a lack of attention to the mediating factors between life and politics.[79] Four general issues surrounding the term will be addressed. First, in a reaction to the claims that everybody was equally affected by the virus, Daniele Lorenzini has emphasized that biopolitics always entails a division within the population.[80] Biopolitics installs an unequal distribution of vulnerabilities within society. This places inequality at the heart of biopolitics. When Foucault or the Italian workerists turned to the notion of "biopolitics," it was because this notion allowed them to analyze the dynamics of a particular historical conjuncture. Therefore, the present use of the term should not merely repeat analyses from the past but serve to understand the present conjuncture, including the various inequalities that are systematically reproduced. Second, for Esposito, the term "biopolitics" as such does not clarify how "life" and "politics" relate to each other, suggesting an unmediated relation between them. To overcome this ambiguity, Esposito proposed that the dialectic between "immunity" and "community" is a better framework to understand the dynamics of biopolitics, such as the tendency of biopolitics to become a form of thanatopolitics.[81] In his recent books, Esposito has focused on the mediating role of institutions between politics and living beings. He pleads for an "instituent praxis," demanding institutions to change to meet the demands and needs of the people.[82] One of these mediating institutions is the media. Maurizio Lazzarato and Tiziana Terranova have argued that new media technologies have fragmented the population into various smaller publics. Managing these publics is what they have called "noopolitics," which acts as a supplement to the process of biopolitics aimed at the population.[83] Third, while for some authors, biopolitics is mainly a negative dynamic, Esposito also explores the possibility of developing what he calls an "affirmative biopolitics." In such an affirmative biopolitics, the notion of the "commons," a focus on relationality and the importance of care play a central role. This resonates strongly with the focus on care and the commons that has always been at the heart of Italian feminist theory, such as the work of Adriana Cavarero and Silvia Federici. One final issue that will be addressed is the fact that theories of biopolitics have always been implicitly human-centered. Now that we are increasingly faced with a climate catastrophe, should "*bios*" not be rethought to include non-human life as well? Or, to rephrase this, is *bios* not the close intertwined relation of human with non-human life? However, while several authors in the Environmental Humanities have sought to distribute agency across all forms of life and to develop more expanded ontologies involving non-human life, Esposito's emphasis on instituent *praxis* reminds us that the human/non-human relations, no matter how closely interwoven they may seem, are also institutionally mediated and the subject of institutional politics.

In Chapter 2, we will heed Esposito's call for an affirmative biopolitics and a biopolitics beyond the human. As we have noted extensively, the concept of "life" takes center stage in Italian thought, in particular in the painstaking analyses of "biopolitics" (in Agamben, Esposito and others). The distinction between *bios* [human cultivated life] and *zōē* [naked life] is foundational to much of Italian thought. In this chapter, we discuss contemporary Italian theorists like Braidotti, Coccia, and Luisetti, who question and venture beyond this distinction, as their thinking is rooted in a materialist and Spinozist-Deleuzian paradigm that is radically different from the Foucauldian genealogies of Agamben or Esposito's archeologies of biopolitics. On the one hand, we will explore how this "other" trajectory for Italian thought allows us to move *beyond biopolitics*; for example by privileging *zōè*, as raw living matter, over *bios* (Braidotti), by considering "earth beings" as part and parcel of a new political ecology (Luisetti), and by radically expanding our view of politics toward an "atmospheric" or true *cosmopolitics* (Coccia). On the other hand, by reading these recent theories in dialogue rather than against biopolitical philosophies, we will highlight the potential for a different reading of biopolitics in Agamben and Esposito. We will also see how these new readings of and beyond biopolitics allow Italian thought to resonate with ecological and environmental, posthuman, and decolonial theories.

In Chapter 3, we focus on the world of work and the workerist legacy in philosophies of technology. New digital technologies are invading the workplace at a mind-blowing pace with little time for reflection on their impact. Artificial Intelligence is replacing human mental labor, digital platforms are "Uberizing" a workforce of outsourced precarious micro-entrepreneurs, and new forms of digital surveillance are creeping into office buildings and remote workers' homes. While techno-optimistic narratives originating in Silicon Valley praise these new technologies as harbingers of increased efficiency and labor productivity or as inevitable signs of progress to which workers must only submit, common people themselves are often less enthusiastic about being subjected to constant datafication and digital surveillance. Workers often resist the introduction of new workplace technologies that erode their bargaining power and reduce their autonomy. In this chapter, we study the conceptual history of Marx' notion of "general intellect" in Italian workerism to articulate a critique of contemporary workplace technologies. Marx took the term from British political economist William Thompson to investigate the role of technology in workplace power relations between capital and labor. Marx noted that capital invests in new technologies to absorb human collective intelligence in privately owned machines, which capitalists could subsequently introduce into the labor process to deskill workers. While pre-industrial, artisanal workers could still autonomously coordinate their own labor, because they possessed know-how and skills to which their managers did not have access, industrialization enacted a separation of the moments of coordination and execution. The general intellect, embodied in industrial machines, possesses the knowledge and know-how required to coordinate the labor process, while workers are reduced to the role of mere living appendages to the industrial automaton. They can do nothing more but execute the orders they receive from machines. Over time, their skills and craft atrophy until they become wholly dependent on the machinery to valorize their labor. New digital technologies push this subsumption of labor under capital even further: even thought processes and the mind itself can be captured by the general intellect. Digital technologies absorb human communication directly into their databases and automate this thinking through algorithmic operations. In Chapter 3, we study what this entails for the prospects of worker autonomy under digital capitalism.

Chapter 4, on the other hand, focuses on the interplay between social media and politics. Upsurges in the popularity of far-right extremism seem oddly related to the successful use of the affordances of new communication technologies. It looks like the communicative infrastructure of social media platforms like Facebook, X, and YouTube are specifically suited to the formation of a fascist public sphere. While there are clear resonances between the public rallies and speeches of, for example, Donald Trump and Benito Mussolini, late fascism today would never have been so successful without the online war machine of the alt-right. The online far-right is composed of white supremacists, a resentful manosphere of incels and gaming geeks, New Atheists, and even trolls without ideological commitment who are there only "for the lulz." Maurizio Lazzarato has called this patchwork, loosely kept together through the viral dynamics of social media, "cyberfascism." Using the notion of plebiscitarian public sphere as developed in the writings of Giorgio Agamben, Alberto Toscano, and Alessandro Baricco, we argue that there is an elective affinity between fascism and social media that becomes visible in the tactics of the cyberfascism. While social media do not cause fascist upsurges, their design is also not neutral to political struggle. They constitute a unique terrain in which some political tactics operate better than others. Social media establish an attention market that thrives on engagement and cults of personality that fit extraordinarily well with the fascist understanding of the public sphere as the domain of acclamation for a political leader. Cyberfascism constitutes the right's response to the structural transformation of the public sphere in the age of social media.

In the final chapter, we consider the question of national and cultural identity as touched upon in Chapter 4 from a different angle. We will look at how the alleged disappearance or imminent decline of Italian and European popular identity plays a key but ambiguous role in much of contemporary Italian thought. In this chapter, we will first analyze Pasolini's somber diagnosis of the disappearance of the fireflies in Italy's post-1960s hedonist capitalism, that is to say, the rapid decline of an ecosystem which, for Pasolini, is both natural *and* cultural. The disappearance of the natural life world also entails the disappearance of popular, historically and locally rooted forms of (collective) life. The double-bind that characterizes Pasolini's analyses—"emancipation" now means tapping into the potential of rapidly disappearing traditional forms of life—continues to haunt contemporary Italian thought, in particular the recent work of Giorgio Agamben. Agamben's radical anarchist pleas for a fundamentally porous coming community, or his conceptualization of the refugee as the new paradigm for political subjectivity, are, paradoxically, shot through with cultural nostalgia. Political binaries, like the lifeless technocratic State versus the living potential of the people, sometimes uncomfortably echo culturally conservative or populist tropes. In contrast, we will set forth the renewed significance of Gianni Vattimo's weak thought for a radical critique of such residual Pasolinian nostalgia in our context of resurgent nativist ontologies. Moreover, we will closely look at the work of Sandro Mezzadra as an antidote to the latent Eurocentrism in many of the leading theorists in Italian thought. We will see how Mezzadra reformulates key notions in Italian thought in a resolutely post-colonial perspective, resituating Italian thought beyond its geographical and historical borders. Moreover, taking our cues from Mezzadra's call to provincialize Italian thought, we will examine how post-workerist and post-autonomist concepts and political strategies may connect to non-Western, indigenous, and decolonial ideas and concerns. In particular, we will imagine what demodernizing Italian thought may look like.

# 1 BIOPOLITICS IN POST-PANDEMIC TIMES

## Chapter Summary

The Covid-19 pandemic was a biopolitical crisis on a global scale. However, the term "biopolitics" did not feature prominently in the debates surrounding the pandemic. This suggests that the term has lost some of its conceptual relevance today. Roberto Esposito has described various problems surrounding the term "biopolitics," which we will explore in this chapter. According to Esposito and others, the discourse of biopolitical theory has become so broadly stretched that semantic inflation sets in. When everything becomes "biopolitical," the term loses some of the specificity required to grant it a political bite. Biopolitical theory has also lacked historical specificity. Historical case studies often form easy input for historical analogies that leave out much of the uniqueness of today's political conundrums. However, this methodology has led thinkers like Agamben, during the Covid-19 pandemic, to make unnecessarily hasty judgments about the politics of lockdowns and vaccination campaigns. Lastly, Esposito criticizes the lack of attention to the mediating role of institutions. Biopolitics never occurs in a vacuum but is the product of concrete institutional mediations. How institutions exactly foster or disallow life fundamentally affects the living conditions of populations. Exploring these institutions reveals how biopolitical power actually works in everyday practice. It allows us to determine which dimensions of biopolitical theory ought to be stressed in order to render the field relevant again for post-pandemic times. Biopolitics namely always creates divisions within the population that impose an unequal distribution of vulnerability. Some lives are more worthy of being lived than others, and policies like enforced lockdowns combined with enforced exposure to health risks for "essential workers" show how this distribution of vulnerability works in practice. Esposito subsequently allows us to connect "bios" and "politics" through his theories about the immunological paradigm and instituent thought. Institutions regulate the balance between fostering community and immunizing individuals and communities from foreign influences. Ultimately, Esposito's "affirmative biopolitics" will be situated within the Italian feminist tradition of focusing on care and the commons. However, the persistent human-centeredness of theories of biopolitics must be challenged to extend the reach of biopolitical theory to non-human life.

When the Covid-19 pandemic spread across the globe in 2020, various key topics in Italian thought became central issues in grand-scale politics and people's daily lives. Protecting the lives of the citizens and securing the health of the population, in other words "biopolitics," became the primary concern for governments. The medical world, and more specifically virology, had taken center stage in advising the policy measures taken by governments. The infection rates within the population were closely monitored with daily statistical updates, and taking immunological measures was the number one priority of nation-states. The draconian emergency measures imposed by various governments went along with rhetoric reminiscent of a state of war. The measures prompted concerns for the state of emergency becoming the new normal. The lockdowns imposed in various degrees of strictness forced many people to organize work, domestic duties, and leisure in their severely confined living spaces, causing the boundaries between life and work to blur more than ever before. Furthermore, the lockdowns accelerated the online organization of work, education, and domestic purchases, increasing the apparent "immateriality" of labor and giving even more power to platform companies and IT multinationals.

It seemed that the pandemic proved the relevance of various concepts and problematics that Italian thinkers had been discussing for decades, especially given that Italy was one of the countries most dramatically affected by the pandemic. Times had become "biopolitical" to a degree that even the most pessimistic scholar could not have foreseen. However, theories of "biopolitics" did not play a significant role in the academic nor the public debates and analyses of the pandemic. In the many op-eds and articles published in special online editions of academic journals to analyze the global crisis, Foucault's descriptions of the measures taken during the plague, leprosy, and measles epidemics were hastily evoked, and the term "biopolitics" was occasionally used, but this did not go much further than superficial historical analogies with the present time. One prominent Italian thinker who did draw a lot of attention was Giorgio Agamben. He initially dismissed the coronavirus as a mere flu and regarded the emergency measures as an attempt to impose totalitarian forms of control.[1] Agamben's one-sided views chimed well with the craziest conspiracies of the Covid-denialist and anti-vaxx crowds but rightfully sparked controversy among his fellow philosophers.

The Covid-19 pandemic was a litmus test for the relevance of Italian thought and for the relevance of the term "biopolitics" specifically. In various ways, the pandemic showed that certain concepts and theories associated with Italian thought were no longer deemed adequate to offer insightful analyses of the pandemic. Academics well-versed in Italian thought saw Italian theories of biopolitics confirmed every day, yet that circle of social theorists proved unable to demonstrate that relevance to the wider public. Compare that to the international sensation created by the divulgation of Agamben's *Homo Sacer* or Hardt and Negri's *Empire* in the 2000s. These books not only clarified the stakes of the American War on Terror and the recent shifts in neoliberal globalization but also spoke to new generations of activists and public commentators. These books and their articulations of biopolitical theory quickly became the standard for doing critical theory anywhere in the world. Not so with biopolitical theory during the Covid-19 pandemic. As Roberto Esposito formulates, "there has been a conspicuous distancing from the biopolitical paradigm in the cultural debate."[2] This seemed to show that the heyday of certain key concepts of Italian thought, which used to be popular even outside of academic circles, was over and no longer seemed suitable to comprehend the complexities of the present. The fact that the term "biopolitics" was so little used outside specialist discourse, when the world was experiencing a biopolitical crisis on a global scale, is particularly telling.

Taking mainly inspiration from the work of Roberto Esposito, who arguably wrote the most extensive critical reflections on the use of the term "biopolitics," we argue that the current hesitance to use the term is a consequence of the dilution of its meaning due to its popularity. Semantic inflation has granted biopolitical theory an overextended reach, resulting in a decline in strategic aptitude and political meaning. The use, or even overuse, of the term vulgarized its meaning to such an extent that it lost its analytical value for a wider public, even during a global pandemic. In this chapter, some of the issues with the use of the term "biopolitics" will be discussed and suggestions provided for how these issues which limit the potential of the term could be avoided.

In his recent books, Esposito too notices that there are problems with the term, which he traces back to conceptual and theoretical vagueness surrounding the term in Foucault's own writings. The fact that many scholars have proposed an alternative term instead of "biopolitics" (necropolitics, noopolitics, geontopower, alterbiopolitics, to name but a few)[3] shows dissatisfaction with the term as such. Besides conceptual unclarity, another recurring criticism is that theories of biopolitics tend to lack historical precision; various specific historical situations are flattened into varieties of one and the same dynamic.[4] Esposito, thirdly, criticizes the tendency among some recent scholars to regard biopolitics as the direct, unmediated effects of politics on life, bypassing the role of institutions.[5] This runs the risk of overlooking the various ways in which biopolitics is enacted concretely via various layers of institutionally mediated policies and political decisions while also mystifying the workings of biopolitics. In relation to this, certain uses of the term "biopolitics" can actually have de-politicizing effects, and this is probably the harshest criticism, because specific structural forms of inequality that run through society, such as gender, class, and colonial relations, are sometimes disregarded.[6] Esposito confirms that all these issues are indeed present in problematic instances of biopolitical theory, but he also tries to overcome them by addressing the theoretical problems surrounding the term.

The de-historicized use of the term was abundantly clear during the pandemic, when superficial analogies between seventeenth-century plague epidemics and today's lockdown regimes fed denialists' critiques of state power. Just like seventeenth-century doctors had locked families up in their houses under situations of extreme violence to prevent the spreading of the plague, today's lockdowns were supposedly ploys for governments to enforce quasi-totalitarian power schemes. This kind of analogy supported Agamben's unrelenting criticisms of government policies during the pandemic years. This was not the first time that Agamben had taken liberties in his historical readings of Foucault. Already in *Homo Sacer,* Agamben generalizes the scope of biopolitics to every kind of sovereignty, extending it as far back as the ancient Greeks. Agamben's perspective garnered international success because his version of the term "biopolitics" spoke particularly to the conjuncture of the post-2001 War on Terror, which included invasive measures such as the Patriot Act, and the plight of the prisoners of Guantanamo Bay. Theorists such as Foucault, Negri, and Virno, however, have turned to the term "biopolitics" for very different reasons. Foucault himself only referred to the plague prevention methods in *Discipline and Power* as a precursor to disciplinary power and not biopolitics. The paradigm for biopolitics, for Foucault, was rather the relatively benign vaccination campaigns of the eighteenth and nineteenth centuries. By the 2000s, Italian neo-Marxist thinkers had adopted the term to analyze a shift toward a post-Fordist economy in which life itself became the motor of production. All of these thinkers in their own way used the term "biopolitics" strategically to analyze particular historical conjunctures.[7] A biopolitical analysis of the present should not consist of discerning loose analogies between the present and phenomena described in Foucault's books and lectures, but it should serve to analyze specific aspects of the present historical conjuncture, which is different from the nineteenth century or the 1990s. If we want biopolitical theory to hold any meaning or relevance for the post-pandemic era, we must move beyond superficial similarities between the present and the past toward uncovering the biopolitical logic animating the continuity between the present and the past. In what follows, we will address the problem of biopolitics and inequality, the issue of institutional mediation and biopolitics, the question of affirmative biopolitics and a politics of the common, and, finally, the problem of the human-centeredness of the term "biopolitics." Addressing these issues will clarify for a large part some of the undesirable effects of the vulgarized use of the term and form a basis for its future use.

## Distributed Vulnerabilities

During the pandemic, the French philosopher Jean-Luc Nancy published a text in which he claimed that the Covid-19 virus "communizes" us all because it affects everybody: "It essentially puts us on a basis of equality, bringing us together in the need to make a common stand."[8] In a reaction against this claim, as well as against the vague use of the term "biopolitics" in op-eds, Daniele Lorenzini correctly remarks that a key feature of biopolitics is the creation of divisions within the population. Lorenzini describes biopolitics as a politics of "differential vulnerability": "Far from being a politics that erases social and racial inequalities by reminding us of our common belonging to the same biological species, it is a politics that structurally relies on the establishment of hierarchies in the value of lives, producing vulnerability as a means of governing people."[9] Foucault explained that the rationale of biopolitics was never simply to promote the health of entire populations equally but to protect the vitality of one part of the population at the cost of others.[10] Biopolitics implies that certain groups are structurally more exposed to health risks, exploitation, poverty, and bad living conditions in order to safeguard the health of more desirable populations. Foucault added that racism is used to create a caesura within the population between people whose lives are valued and those who do not count or whose lives are perceived to be a direct threat.[11] As Lorenzini clarifies, biopolitics creates "hierarchies between different human groups, and thus (radical) differences in the way in which the latter are exposed to the risk of death."[12] The population is not a single homogenous totality but an internally fractured collective differentially subjected to various risks and policies. In this sense, biopolitics is always about inequality. It largely reproduces and exacerbates existing forms of inequality based on class, gender, and race. We know now that, during the pandemic, for a part of the population to stay at home, work remotely, and minimize their risk of exposure to the virus, so-called essential workers had to keep on working, forced to risk their health. Some groups of people were also structurally more vulnerable to devastating health or financial consequences—from the inhabitants of Brazilian favelas to everybody without adequate health insurance in the United States. In some parts of the world, vaccines were not available, and the diffusion of the virus was barely monitored.

The role of racism for Foucault was to make the differential exposure to the risk of death governable and acceptable to its target populations. This condition seemingly justifies differential exposure to death in a society. In the words of Lorenzini, "racism, in all of its forms, is the 'condition of acceptability' of such a differential exposure of lives in a society in which power is mainly exercised to protect the biological life of the population and enhance its productive capacity."[13] However, Lorenzini also adds that biopolitics should not be reduced to the binary choice between life and death as Foucault tends to do, but concerns the "effort to differentially organize the gray area between them."[14] He mentions the management of migration, for example. Biopolitics in this sense is also a politics of governing mobility, which of course also differentially exposes certain people increasingly to risk and the possibility of death. Some individuals are hailed by receiving nations as desirable migrants, while others are allowed to die on dangerous journeys toward the Global North. A biopolitical analysis should not stop at saying that we live in "biopolitical times" in a generalized manner, or, as Agamben claimed, that during the pandemic the lives of everybody were reduced to bare life in a general sense,[15] but it should analyze and challenge the specific features of the distribution of vulnerability in society, including its constant normalization and re-articulation. A biopolitical analysis should expose the conditions that make differential exposure to risk possible and acceptable.

Tiziana Terranova has clarified that what counts as a "threat" to the population has become more diversified since the times that Foucault was describing. While in the beginning of the twentieth century the main biopolitical concern were endemics or hereditary diseases that could negatively impact the population, this later became a much wider set of potential risks:

> Risks of epidemics triggered by viruses spreading from distant countries; dangers posed by migrants to local jobs and ways of life; menaces to Western economies represented by booming ex-Third World countries; and, of course, the direct threat of sudden explosions and random deaths cast by the shadow of terrorism.[16]

What is threatened is more than the strictly medical health of the population but also the economic and existential well-being of the population, including its alleged social and cultural values, or as Terranova writes, the "cultural, economic and biological norms" dominant in a specific time and place.[17] Safeguarding these norms will go along with the multiplication of "differential racisms" along various axes. What counts as an alleged threat can also be the challenging of gender norms, migrants that come to fill in certain jobs, or the geopolitical dominance of certain nations.

To adequately grasp the full range of these differential racisms and the practices that they make possible, it is also necessary to overcome the limitations or blind spots of older theories of biopolitics, however rich and inspirational they may be for the present. Lorenzini too avows that, in order to understand how differentiated vulnerabilities are used as a tool of governance, we have to move beyond Foucault's descriptive approach of biopolitics to a more normative one.[18] In order to explore other forms of oppression and struggle, Foucault had to wrest himself away from the Marxism that dominated French intellectual life in the 1960s and 1970s, which was mainly focused on class struggle and worker emancipation. Consequently, Foucault somewhat neglected the role of class inequality in his studies. Esposito too observes that when it comes to biopolitics, Foucault's focus on an economy of life amounts to "overlooking equally important topics related to modes of production, class struggle, and constituent and constituted powers."[19] He also notices that the "term 'inequality' ends up disappearing from his vocabulary."[20] Similarly, various Foucault-inspired scholars have taken up the task to study the role of racism and colonialism in greater detail than Foucault had done. Achille Mbembe, to name one, argues that many of the most brutal events of the twentieth century were made possible by decades of colonial and racist dehumanization intertwined with class oppression.[21]

Though they have certainly paid more attention to various forms of global exploitation, we can nevertheless in hindsight find similar limitations in the focus of Italian neo-Marxist thinkers on the phenomenon of immaterial labor. In their analyses of post-Fordism as a shift from industrial mass production to a postindustrial economy based on immaterial labor, they have tended to neglect the fact that this immaterial labor has always been dependent on low-skilled and very material labor, both in the Global North and elsewhere. While theories of post-Fordism have very successfully described the rise of high-skill creative jobs, they have mostly ignored the simultaneous proliferation of deskilled jobs in, for example, the transportation sector, call centers, and logistics. These jobs are now increasingly organized according to the model of the gig economy and algorithm-driven platforms (see Chapter 3).[22] Negri saw in the shift to immaterial labor and the biopolitical production that characterizes the post-Fordist economy a potential for the multitude to develop forms of resistance, or a politics of life. This, however, underestimates new forms of differential vulnerability and certain labor practices that lead to a segmentation of the working population instead of bringing them together in a shared struggle. The rise of the gig economy at the center of the post-Fordist economy puts serious pressure on the multitude's capacity for collective resistance. The competitive and impersonal working conditions of a labor process run by algorithms make it difficult to organize collective labor struggles; the formation of unions is often explicitly discouraged, and collective bargaining for better working conditions is made near impossible.

A similar problem can be found in Agamben's use of the term "biopolitics." Though his theories became particularly relevant to understand the direct aftermath of the War on Terror and the 9/11 attacks, Agamben extended Foucault's use of the term "biopolitics" back to Antiquity. In *Homo Sacer*, he famously argues that biopolitics has always been the outcome of sovereignty: "*It can even be said that the production of a biopolitical body is the original activity of sovereign power. In this sense, biopolitics is at least as old as the sovereign exception.*"[23] Agamben follows Carl Schmitt's definition that the sovereign is he who decides on the state of exception.[24] Whenever life is governed under a legal order, there must be a sovereign to decide on the applicability of this order. The sovereign thereby decides whether individual subjects are in- or excluded from legal protection. The sovereign decision over life and death produces a caesura in life between *bios*, life in the fullest, most qualitative sense (including participation in social and political communities), and bare life, life stripped from its socio-political qualities and reduced to mere physical survival. Biopolitics reduces the lives of certain people to bare life, which leaves them at the same time included and excluded in society, or better, included by means of exclusion. The *homo sacer* is included into socio-political life, but not as a citizen enjoying the same rights and liberties as fellow citizens. The *homo sacer* is stripped of all juridical and social recognition so that nothing but mere life exposed to the unaccountable power of the *polis* remains.

Agamben, however, has the tendency to present his theories of biopolitics as one generalized dynamic, characterizing modern society as a whole. He certainly focuses on the particular plight of refugees (see Chapter 5), since he wrote *Homo Sacer* at the height of the Yugoslav Wars, when many refugees fled to Italy and were interned in refugee camps. Yet Agamben's approach runs the risk of not differentiating enough between various kinds of inequalities, which was apparent in his writings during the pandemic. Already in *Homo Sacer* itself, Agamben sees bare life in refugees, Holocaust victims, coma patients, and even sadomasochists. The Covid-19 measures imposed by the Italian government were for him the last straw in the process of undemocratically imposing totalitarian measures that unravel our common *bios* and reduce populations to the state of bare life. However, such monolithic statements miss the differential vulnerabilities exposed during a pandemic. Essential workers riding for goods-delivery apps like Deliveroo were operating under very different conditions and health risks than remote workers ordering food online. Arguably, not the remote workers under lockdown but the essential workers forced to withstand the risk of death by infection were the real *homines sacri*.

Agamben's theory of biopolitics has become exemplary for regarding biopolitics as a purely negative process, which has prompted others authors, such as Negri and Esposito, to counteract this one-sided negative view and argue that biopolitics can also be theorized in more affirmative or politically constructive ways. Both approaches, however, have insufficiently come to terms with the differential vulnerabilities produced by biopolitics and revealed during the pandemic, according to Lorenzini. The attempts to use the term "biopolitics" to analyze the dynamics of a particular past conjuncture have been inspiring, but they have also led to theoretical limitations and blind spots. To understand the various inequalities at work today, one should analyze the specific dynamics of the present situation and not reproduce the blind spots of influential authors writing about other times.[25] According to Esposito, one of these blind spots has been the role of institutions in the functioning of biopolitics.

# The Institutional Mediation of Biopolitics

For Esposito, the criticism that the term "biopolitics" can have de-politicizing effects goes to the heart of problems surrounding the term, which were already visible in Foucault's use of it. The term suggests the intertwinement of life and politics, but in Esposito's view, Foucault never adequately theorized the precise connection between both. This theoretical unclarity has haunted the use of the term ever since. The relation between life and politics alternates between two options: either life is completely subjected to the prevailing political powers, power over life, or life will always remain outside of it, acting as a source of resistance to the prevailing politics of subjection, a power of life. Instead of bringing the two terms together, life and politics always remain separated or even opposed to each other.[26] The term "biopolitics" is in this sense inadequate because it seems to omit the various layers of mediation that can explain the many intricate ways in which life and politics are interwoven.

To overcome the ambiguities that surround the term "biopolitics," Esposito proposes the "immunological paradigm," or the dialectic between immunity and community, as a better model to understand the need to protect the population, as well as the most destructive tendencies of the twentieth century. Esposito points out that etymologically community and immunity share the same root, namely *munus*. The Latin *munus* means both "gift" and "law," "more specifically ... the law of a unilateral gift to others."[27] In Roman society, *munus* referred to the tasks or obligations people had toward others, hence, as Esposito clarifies, a "process of gradual opening from self to the other."[28] Rich citizens were, for example, expected to fund public projects and festivals. In contrast, immunity is the negation of that openness. People who were "immune" in Roman times were freed from certain obligations toward others. It should be noted here that "immunity" was originally a legal term, long before the medical world adopted it. While communal life requires people to live with other people, even if this entails a challenge to the self or the values of the community, "immunity" refers to the various ways in which individuals will protect themselves against the dissolution of selfhood. The same occurs on the level of social groups: community dynamics bind groups together, yet immunitarian tactics protect the collective's identity against foreign intrusion. Esposito describes the tension between community and immunity in the following manner: "if community breaks down the barriers of individual identity, immunity is the way to rebuild them, in defensive and offensive forms, against any external element that threatens it."[29] In Esposito's view, this tension is the central problem of modernity. This immunological tendency will not only exclude people who are perceived as threatening or as not belonging to a certain community; beyond a certain threshold it will also become self-destructive, like an auto immune disease, and rob a community of the conditions for communal life.[30] Only in the light of this tension can we understand the seeming paradox that Foucault encountered: how can a politics aimed at preserving life, biopolitics, produce the most murderous regimes in the twentieth century, obsessed with murdering people on an industrial scale?

In recent years, Esposito has once again taken up the inadequacies of the term "biopolitics," but this time with a focus on the mediating role of institutions between politics and living beings. "It is often said that 'biopolitics' must entail a direct implication between politics and biological life that bypasses any institutional mediation."[31] Such an unmediated view on biopolitics, bypassing the workings of various institutions, is one of the main reasons why the term can have questionable political effects, according to Esposito. What is missing is a better understanding of the role of institutions. He argues that life is always in one way or another institutionally mediated or "instituted," as he calls it, from a newborn baby in the hospital to inmates in prison. Human life is always "inscribed in a historical and symbolic fabric from which it cannot be separated."[32] Esposito subsequently argues that there is no such thing as a bare life, opposing Agamben's use of that notion in his theories of biopolitics.[33] Human beings are always part of a web of historical circumstances, social codes and shared meanings, even in an extreme case such as a dehumanizing concentration camp. Furthermore, life is always instituted anew, and this is a political task of the highest importance, especially after something like a global pandemic: "we can never stop instituting life and redefining its contours and objectives, or its conflicts and opportunities: because human beings are instituted by life, which ushers them into a common world."[34] Importantly, Esposito sees any collective with a certain level of organization as an institution, so these could also be protest movements acting against government institutions. "As the masters of legal institutionalism teach, not only do there exist extra-state institutions but also anti-state institutions, such as protest movements that possess some form of organization."[35]

Just as life is always instituted, Esposito argues that, reversely, institutions must be regarded as living organisms, which change, grow, transform, and perish. Institutions only exist insofar as they are continuously put into practice in everyday social interactions. They are always open to transformation under pressure from popular demands, which persistently revitalizes institutional frameworks. This dynamic of exerting pressure on institutions is what Esposito calls an "instituent praxis."[36] However, institutions also tend to become stagnant, static, self-preserving, and generally indifferent to people's lives, concerns, and demands. Esposito had already ended his *Persons and Things*, written in the wake of protesters occupying squares in various places from Cairo to New York, with the images of the people demanding institutions to change. If the latter do not heed to popular demands, the institutions would collapse. "The living body of increasingly vast multitudes demands a radical renewal of the vocabularies of politics, law, and philosophy. In the coming years we will see whether these institutions will be able to respond, or whether they will shut themselves up in self-defense before definitively imploding."[37] Though they manage to exert pressure on institutions, the multitudes are also "still lacking adequate organizational forms," in Esposito's view.

In the writings of Foucault, Esposito notices not only that the connection between life and politics remains unthought, but he also notices a distrust of institutions as a whole, a reflection of a more general anti-institutional attitude among 1970s countercultures.[38] Some theorists and activists equate institutions too quickly with undemocratic hierarchies, as if human emancipation requires the abolition of all institutions. When Foucault analyzed institutions such as the prison, the asylum, or the hospital, these were immediately described in terms of suspicious power dynamics and nefarious processes of subjectivation. Consequently, the lives of people are often opposed to or at odds with institutions, which are regarded only in terms of dynamics of subjecting, disciplining, and control. Inversely, Hannah Arendt, another big influence on theories of biopolitics, wanted to protect institutions by keeping them free from both (private) life and politics.[39] Rethinking the role of institutions, or "instituent thought" as Esposito names it, is required to overcome the depoliticizing effects of regarding biopolitics as a direct, unmediated interaction between politics and life. Without adequately theorizing the mediating role of institutions, the "power of life" would also remain a relatively abstract idea lacking the potential for effective social change. As he writes, "just as a formalistic institutionalism, external to vital dynamics, is locked in a self-referential orbit destined to be soon depleted, so an unmediated biopolitics, crushed into the bareness of a formless life, loses any political effectiveness."[40] The opposition between life and institutions also explains, according to Esposito, the tendency of certain theories of biopolitics to end up developing overly defensive political strategies.[41]

Esposito's notion of "instituent thought" can be heard as a response to the notions of "constituent power" as developed by Negri and Agamben's "destituent potential."[42] Negri has argued that various protest groups can strategically align themselves to form a broader and more powerful protest movement, as happened in the 2000s alterglobalization movement and the various political movements of the early 2010s using public assemblies. Thus various grassroots groups can join forces into a wider movement and act as a form of "constituent power" exerting pressure on the existing institutions from below and even prefiguratively creating new counter-institutions to replace the currently constituted political order.[43] Negri has pleaded for thinking about resistance along two axes: horizontally developing a protest movement while at the same time vertically constituting new institutions that either break with the constituted order or radically transform existing institutions, like the European Union, so that they can become democratic forums for the self-government of the multitude.[44] Though he tends to avoid an explicit theoretical confrontation, Esposito's "instituent thought" emphasizes the intertwinement of our lives and various institutions more than Negri does. Instituent praxis is less a matter of clear-cut revolutionary breaks and more of continually re-enacting and transforming institutional orders until they have morphed into something quite different than before.

Agamben, however, explicitly rejects Negri's "constituent power." In his view, the workings of power can only be rendered inoperative by a negative strategy of disruption, a process that he calls "destituent":

> access to a different figure of politics cannot take the form of a "constituent power" but rather that of something that we can provisionally call "destituent potential." And if to constituent power there correspond revolutions, revolts, and new constitutions, namely, a violence that puts in place and constitutes a new law, for destituent potential it is necessary to think entirely different strategies, whose definition is the task of the coming politics.[45]

According to Agamben, constituent power can only create a new legal order that, yet again, has to be backed up by a sovereign power that decides on the state of exception. Replacing one sovereign power with another, however, does not help us escape the logic of sovereignty itself. If the rights and liberties granted to citizens via a constitution depend on sovereign power, which can suspend these legal guarantees in the name of national security or public health, then simply founding a new legal order with a constituent power will not liberate people from the threat of being reduced to bare life.

In his controversial commentaries on the pandemic, Agamben actually referred quite regularly to various institutions, which tellingly reveal the difference with Esposito's instituent thought. In one of the texts that caused the most commotion, "Requiem for the students," Agamben condemns online university classes as the end of the university as a social form of life.[46] The debates between students about cultural and political matters, the verbal exchange between students and lecturers, and the general social life of students in university towns are purportedly erased by online education. The university as an institution would stop being a shared space for common reflection and learning, and would instead become a mere distribution mechanism for information and diplomas to atomized, isolated individuals. The text caused commotion because Agamben compares professors agreeing to give online classes to fascist collaborators, but he also displayed a deep nostalgia for the traditional institution of the university.[47] One could even say that he romanticizes the university as an institution of free-spirited academic pursuits and ignores all its problematic aspects, such as the elitism and inequality that it often perpetuates. Even more suspicious is the assumption of universities as in a state of irreparable decline: "It is certain that our universities had reached such a level of corruption and specialistic cluelessness that it is almost impossible to mourn their loss."[48] Problems with universities are presented as an irrevocable endpoint of decline. Agamben refuses to entertain any hypotheses to counter this decline. In Agamben's mind, institutional reform does not resolve the problems of the logic of sovereignty and is hence ultimately pointless. The response seems to be a turn away from institutions like the university rather than a political struggle for their rearticulation. Referring to this piece, Esposito aptly observes that Agamben is right that there is a danger of de-socialization in online education, but that Agamben's analysis fails to propose strategies for resocializing or repoliticizing institutions like the university.[49]

Esposito's critique that there is a danger that life and politics remain separate or even opposed in theories of biopolitics, and that institutional mediations should not be overlooked, is an important intervention. One indeed risks ending up with a rather mystified "politics of life," in which the political potential of subjectivities, bodies, and multitudes remains quite powerless to bring forth lasting structural changes in society if institutional mediations are ignored. However, in all his works, Esposito is at his best when he offers a genealogy of the use and transformations of a certain notion. When it comes to making concrete suggestions for the future, Esposito mostly limits himself to evoking inspiring yet loose exemplars that lack the same level of astute practical strategizing. Similarly, his recent writings about institutions leave many questions unanswered, including how Esposito sees the role of institutions in dynamics he described in his other works. In his other books, he pleads, for example, for regarding life as indeterminate, impersonal, and singular, not reducible to legal categories such as the person.[50] What would institutions look like that can avoid biopolitical mechanisms of exclusion or making divisions within the population? How could institutions guarantee the singularity of all life, avoiding problematic legal categories, and protect the lives of all? Especially when it comes to national or transnational institutions, such as governing, legal or military institutions, the organization of these seems very far removed from Esposito's ideals. In practice, would people not be forced into a never-ending process of perpetually demanding reformist change to institutions incapable of responding to popular challenges?

## Noopolitics: New Media as Institutions

Despite the unanswered questions and the fact that Esposito does not offer reflections on crucial institutions such as the media, Esposito's emphasis on the institutional mediation of life offers advantages for the development of theories of biopolitics relevant for the present. Whether one wants to analyze the management of the health of populations, the organization of labor, or the extraction of value from our daily activities, it is clear that these processes are now mediated by complex layers of digital technologies, datafication, automation, and various kinds of algorithmic governance. Any analysis of the ways in which life and politics are mutually implicated in the present would be incomplete without confronting these various forms of mediation that will shape what counts as "life," including the contradictions and inequalities that run through it. Various scholars have shown how algorithmic governance reproduces racial biases and that the automation of labor—for example, in artificial intelligence (AI)—reproduces social hierarchies and commodifies social competences.[51, 52] These technological mediations are the consequences of the commercial strategies of powerful companies, the policies and decisions made by transnational and national governing bodies and local forms of organization, including the development of alternative uses of these technologies by collectives. In short, they are the locus of struggle between various institutions, as described by Esposito, including unions, platform collectives and precarious workers challenging government policies and corporate strategies.

That the population is internally fractured and differentiated, as well as strongly mediated by the prevailing media technologies, is central to one particular contemporary theoretical transformation of the term "biopolitics"—namely, the notion of "noopolitics" as used by Maurizio Lazzarato and Tiziana Terranova.[53] Lazzarato proposes the term "noopolitics" as a supplement to the biopolitics of the species theorized by Foucault, influenced by the work of Gabriel Tarde. Tarde, as opposed to authors such as Gustave Le Bon, who regarded the masses or the crowd as the prime forces of his time, argued that from the end of the nineteenth century, the masses were not the main problem in society but the formation of the *public*, or more accurately, *publics*.[54] The formation of various publics disperses and fragments the population in ways that do not entirely coincide with social stratification along lines of class. As Terranova clarifies, "The same individual cannot belong to two different classes, but can belong to two or more different publics."[55]

Terranova points out that when Foucault's interests shifted from biopolitics to neoliberal governmentality, he also pointed out the importance of publics and public opinion as a key concern for the government of the population.[56] For Foucault, both the public and the health of the species in a bio-medical sense are part of one continuum:

> The population is therefore everything that extends from biological rootedness through the species up to the surface that gives one a hold provided by the public. From the species to the public; we have here a whole field of new realities in the sense that they are the pertinent elements for mechanisms of power, the pertinent space within which and regarding which one must act.[57]

However, Tarde already knew that publics tend to be the product of forms of affective capture and Terranova adds that "tele-technologies such as television or the Internet are fundamental mechanisms of capture and control of new segmented, undefined subjectivities operating as publics."[58] Distributed networks and the proliferation of social networks have increased the segmentation and "micro-segmentation" of publics. Controlling these processes of the formation of publics will be a central concern for the governance of the population and in this the "public opinion" plays an important role. Following Lazzarato, Terranova writes, "public opinion is thus, for Lazzarato, the first institution of control societies—as quantified and measured by opinion polls and surveys," but she adds that "a public does not necessarily coincide with the institution of the public opinion."[59] The fact that publics are not entirely captured within the public opinion offers according to Terranova the possibility for the constitution of publics acting as "counter-weapons."[60]

Lazzarato and Terranova were writing in the wake of the War on Terror following the 9/11 attacks in 2001, with all the circulation of anti-Muslim affects and fear of terrorism. By now, the capacities of media technologies to capture sentiments and form and reform publics have been amplified massively with severe consequences, from Brexit to "alternative facts"— spewing populists and publics firmly hooked on the same conspiracy theories. It is clear that the liberal governing institutions have the greatest difficulties with controlling the formation of new publics, and so far, it is mainly the far right that has been able to weaponize this situation (see Chapter 4). Even though Lazzarato and Terranova call the domain of noopolitics a "second *bios*," involving "a politics of memory and attention," future theories of biopolitics will have to take into account that populations are fractured along lines continuously formed and reformed.[61] These are vulnerable to capture but also contain the potential of forming counter-hegemonic publics. The "life" of the population is now more than ever mediated, as well as fragmented, by various "institutions" in the broadest sense.

## Affirmative Biopolitics: Care and the Common

As the previous sections have already made clear, various theorists of biopolitics also reflect upon which forms of resistance are possible either against biopolitics or from within the conditions created by specific variations of biopolitics. Esposito argues against exclusively negative interpretations of biopolitics: biopolitics cannot be reduced to strategies of governance and domination. Biopolitics always already assumes the *munus*, the potential of our openness toward the other, community as mutual entanglement, donation, and obligation; it implies that both the individual and the collective body are "naturally challenged, infiltrated, and hybridized by a diversity that isn't only external, but also internal."[62] This entails the potential for an affirmative biopolitics. Esposito often ends his books with pleas for developing such a more affirmative kind of biopolitics, which is precisely a politics aimed at overcoming the divisions in the population that biopolitics installs. As he writes in *Common Immunity*, "one part of the world cannot be saved without saving all of it at the same time."[63] This more affirmative alternative, which should be a politics based on other principles and grounds, is mostly referred to as an "affirmative biopolitics," but it also appears in his work as "co-immunity"[64] or "common immunity." A "common immunity" no longer cuts through the community, dividing people who matter from those who value less, but aims to protect all. While in some of his books, such an affirmative biopolitics is something that still must be developed, because it would require transforming deeply entrenched metaphysical and legal categories, in some texts and interviews he nonetheless points out concrete examples of what an affirmative biopolitics could be. He first pleads for more investments in health care facilities, especially in the wake of the pandemic.

> An affirmative form of biopolitics would instead focus on heavy investments in public health facilities, building hospitals, making medicine affordable or giving medications free of charge, maintaining comfortable living conditions for the population, and protecting doctors and nurses who have died during the epidemic.[65]

Besides such social policies, he also adds that "affirmative biopolitics also means, for instance, de-privatizing the water supply, reclaiming and protecting forests." Esposito is strongly inspired by experiments with commoning as a basis for affirmative biopolitics. He repeatedly mentions the struggle against the privatization of water in Italy, but also the fight against commercial pharmaceutical patents on crucial medications, driving up the prices and limiting their availability.[66] And, indeed, in *Common Immunity* he was placing a lot of hope in making the patents of the vaccines against Covid-19 free and commonly available, demanding that they would be distributed freely across the entire world, as a beginning of a truly "common immunity."[67]

With his pleas for an affirmative biopolitics, Esposito situates the notion of "biopolitics" within an often overlooked but central aspect of Italian thought, the rich tradition of feminist theory and activism in Italy. Italian feminism has always placed reproductive care and interdependence at the heart of political struggles, criticizing the lack of attention for those concerns in the prevailing neo-Marxist theory. In the 1970s, The Marxist–feminist movement criticized both capitalism and its workerist opponents for neglecting domestic labor and the sphere of social reproduction.[68] While orthodox Marxism tends to focus on exploitative relations inside the factory's relations of production, feminists noted that male workers' labor-power was itself produced in the hidden abode of social reproduction. Women in the household are often tasked with taking care of their working-class husbands, raising children, sustaining community life in the neighborhood, and so on. These activities are crucial to the production of labor-power: male workers' bodily and mental energy sold on the labor market. However, whereas male workers still receive a wage for their labor, women receive nothing but ephemeral gratitude. The Marxist–feminist movement in Italy subsequently campaigned for housework wages, a wage for women who disproportionately bear the burden of domestic labor.

In *Caliban and the Witch,* Silvia Federici documents the genealogy of the housewife by pointing to early modern transformations in capitalist biopolitics.[69] According to Federici, the scientific revolution and its struggle against folk medicine, often the domain of female healers, intersected with a dearth of servile workers on the labor market. The emerging state apparatus in Western Europe responded by articulating a gendered division of labor in which male workers would offer their obedient labor-power to capital in exchange for a female servant at home, while instigating witch hunts against the women who resisted their domestication. The capitalist wage-system thereby became a vector of a patriarchy that supported capital accumulation.

Adriana Cavarero, who in recent years has engaged more and more in a theoretical dialogue with Esposito,[70] challenges the dominance of an individualistic ontology in the history of philosophy, valuing personal autonomy and independence. She does not go along in the Marxist-feminist identification of care with exploited labor but articulates a philosophical anthropology that renders care fundamental to the human condition. Cavarero traces examples of a more relational ontology in *Inclinations,* such as the figure of the Virgin Mary reclining toward her infant in a relation of care.[71] A relational ontology presumes a fundamental vulnerability in people, who are all dependent on other people for care. Careful not to reproduce varieties of the male/female binary, nor conflating care work with the domestic labor often imposed on women in society, Cavarero also does not see the individualistic and relational ontologies as complementary: "It is rather to think the relation itself as originary and constitutive, as an essential dimension of the human."[72] Irrespectively of one's gender, all human life is vulnerable, and everyone is called upon to care for others. That this dimension has historically been identified with the feminine is not only an injustice to women but also to men who have been missing out on a crucial aspect of their humanity. As opposed to a politics based on autonomous individuals who engage in a social pact with each other, emphasizing a fundamental vulnerability and interdependence marks us as creatures that live "in greatly unbalanced circumstances, consigned to each other."[73]

The "commons" have also taken up an important place in feminist thought, especially in Federici's work.[74] She notices that the interest in the commons has become so widespread that the terminology of the commons is now even adopted by the United Nations and the World Bank, which she regards as an attempt to appropriate the commons within a capitalist framework.[75] She also questions the political role of the commons in the work of Hardt and Negri and especially the role of the internet and the capacity for sharing information by online communities in the constitution of the multitude. Federici even remarks that the way digital technologies are now organized is both ecologically and socially destructive. She also adds that Hardt and Negri overlook the role of commons in the reproduction of everyday life, and more specifically the "potential to create forms of reproduction enabling us to resist dependence on wage labor and subordination to capitalist relations."[76]

To develop a politics of the commons, one has to keep in mind that women all over the world have historically depended on access to communal resources. They often relied on attempts to collectivize reproductive labor "as a means to economize on the cost of reproduction, and protect each other from poverty, state violence and the violence of individual men."[77] This should not be seen as mere "tradition" or as the naturalization of forms of labor generally imposed on women but as active strategies of survival to avoid starvation, slavery, and exploitation. Such commons are based on other principles than the policies pushed by, for example, the World Bank. Federici gives the money commons in certain parts of Africa as an example. These are women-run credit associations in areas where people have no access to banks and are purely based on trust. They operate on an entirely different basis than the micro-credit systems promoted by the World Bank, which often resort to shame tactics when women cannot pay off their debt.[78] Federici also points out that commons such as the urban gardens in North American cities have been important for the strengthening of the community cohesion for immigrant communities from Africa or the Caribbean.[79]

Most importantly, a politics of the common requires the reevaluation of the role of the community. Most people tend to ignore the connection between their food, clothes, and technological devices and the immense suffering of others in the world. As Federici writes, "no common is possible unless we refuse to base our life, our reproduction on the suffering of others, unless we refuse to see ourselves as separate from them."[80] Commoning presumes first and foremost the production of a "common subject." Such a common subject is not a secluded group refusing solidarity with others: "'community' not intended as a gated reality, a grouping of people joined by exclusive interests separating them from others, as with communities formed on the basis of religion or ethnicity."[81] Importantly, this "common subject" does not consist only of humans or inter-human solidarity for Federici, though this is obviously a key component of commoning. It also involves the responsibility for the lifeworld we all inhabit and are dependent on. "Community as a quality of relations, a principle of cooperation and responsibility: to each other, the earth, the forests, the seas, the animals."[82]

Federici situates the politics of the commons that Esposito sees as a key component of an affirmative biopolitics within global practices that have always existed as a means of survival and resistance to capitalism. For Federici, it is important not to forget the history of practices developed by women relating to the reproduction of daily life as an essential part in the struggle against capitalist exploitation. The commoning that Esposito turns to requires the constitution of a community that does not operate on the basis of exclusion, and which implies not only solidarity and cooperation with other people but also a general responsibility for the world, including non-human life.

## The Life of All?

Whether the *bios* of biopolitics refers to human life only or also includes non-human life has often remained somewhat underdeveloped in theories of biopolitics, though it is sometimes implied (see Chapter 2). In his writings about the pandemic, Esposito adds that the climate crisis too demands a transition to a more common world. As he writes, "in this case, too, the ecological transition that it demands and makes inevitable will either be global or not happen at all."[83] Because the term "biopolitics" was strategically used to describe the management of the life of the (human) population, as well as the exploitation of (human) skills in the transition from Fordist to post-Fordist labor, biopolitics is implicitly understood as a politics that puts human life at the center of politics. Now, when Esposito ends *Common Immunity* with the phrase "the life of each is protected only by the life of all,"[84] can life truly be restricted to human life only? Is it not an important feature of the differential vulnerability created by biopolitics that the health of a part of the (human) population is safeguarded at the cost of the vast and systematic exploitation of millions of species of non-human life, whose lives are regarded as commodities to be freely exploited? Even with a focus on human life, is there not a differential between the well-being of a part of the global population and the vast number of people exposed to depleted resources, natural disasters, heavily polluted lands, or lands extracted to the point of being completely barren? Even when one studies only the immaterial labor that has become characteristic for post-Fordist economies, the environmental impact of the technologies that creative labor often relies on is only beginning to get the much-needed attention.

When Foucault discusses the role of what he calls the milieu in *Security, Territory, Population*, under the influence of Georges Canguilhem, this can refer to both the social and the environmental context. Foucault calls the milieu "the medium of an action and the element in which it circulates."[85] As examples he mentions the following: "The milieu is a set of natural givens—rivers, marshes, hills—and a set of artificial givens—an agglomeration of individuals, of houses, etcetera."[86] It is interesting that in these brief moments Foucault does not talk about environmental factors as such, but always the close intertwinement of environmental with social factors. In a response to the theories of Cavarero, Judith Butler too remarks that our "singular existence" "is in fact sustained by various social relations and infrastructural conditions, by the environment, shelter, food, modes by which life itself is coproduced with agents both human and technical. So there is no sustaining of singularity without ecology."[87] And just as Foucault did, Butler wants to emphasize that the social and the ecological should not be regarded as separate: "And by listing sociality and ecology in that way, we do not mean to separate them absolutely as separate spheres, since the social is embedded in the ecological at the same time that the ecological is defined by the social."[88]

Esposito ends *Bios* by pointing to Deleuze's last text, *Pure Immanence: Essays on a Life*. In the notion of "a life," as described by Deleuze, Esposito finds "all the threads that we have woven to this point under the sign of affirmative biopolitics,"[89] though he also adds, "while still not tracing the figure of an affirmative biopolitics."[90] This indeterminate life cannot be ascribed to a single individual, and precisely because of this it can be regarded as common. Life in this sense is not the life of an individual human being; it is at the same time generic and singular, just like a newborn baby is at the same time similar to all the other babies and singular, with its own features.[91] *A life* is not the life of a person, but, reversely, *im*personal. This life is in common precisely because it is not *the* life of one individual human. Furthermore, citing a phrase from Deleuze's *The Logic of Sense*, this indeterminate life, which Esposito calls "an impersonal singularity (or a singular impersonality),"[92] can also not be reduced to *human* life only: "[It] traverses men as well as plants and animals independently of the matter of their individuation and the forms of their personality."[93] The impersonal life that for Esposito traces the figure of the affirmative biopolitics he pleads for is not only a human life but also the life of non-human beings, such as animals or plants, together forming a more encompassing common web of life.

Obviously, managing the health of the population or organizing forms of labor will require manipulating environmental factors. We would argue that it is a key factor of biopolitics that it consists of dispositifs that make people systematically and structurally nót realize the close interdependence between human life—whether this concerns health, labor, pandemics, technologies—and non-human life. Here the theories of biopolitics developed by Esposito have something important to offer. In the increasingly popular Environmental Humanities, there is a tendency to be focused on unmediated, direct, and localized relations between human and non-human life. Naturalist observations of ethological phenomena serve as the impetus to rethink political action. To give one example, in the recent works of French philosopher Baptiste Morizot, he describes the ecological crisis as a "crisis of sensibility"—namely, the fact that people do not pay attention to the non-human life around them.[94] In *Ways of Being Alive*, he pleads for another way of relating to non-human life on the basis of his own experiences of tracking wolves in the Vercors region in France. When tracking wolves, one needs to place oneself in the perspective of a wolf to predict how it would act. He also describes practices in the south of France where shepherds learn to adjust to co-exist with the wolf packs in the area.[95] In such cases, people who are skilled in interpreting wolf tracks and behavior, such as Morizot, can act as "diplomats" to mediate between the various living beings involved. The point is that a direct, localized attentive practice allows for the development of another relation to non-human life. In *L'inexploré*, Morizot argues for the development of an "alterpolitics" which is inspired by the politics of animals, or "ethopolitics," as he calls it.[96] Animals have always engaged in subtle behavior, such as emitting signals, sounds, or scents, to communicate with other species. Morizot argues that animals do not only relate to other species in aggressive terms or in a predator–prey relation, but by emitting signals they seek a *modus vivendi* with other living beings that they share the habitat with. Human beings too could engage in such a practice of finding a modus vivendi with other living beings, which requires attention to the presence and behavior of other species. However, most people do not have direct interactions with, for example, wolves; their relation to wolves is mediated by films, documentaries, media coverage, online clips, books, political communication, information campaigns, stories told by others, etc. Furthermore, one does not need to have a direct relation with a wolf, a bear or a snow leopard (to name some animals that have drawn extensive fascination in ecological literature)[97] to develop more ecological awareness and a better way of relating to non-human life. And, as Iwona Janicka and Sarah Vanuxem soberly observe, Morizot's diplomatic approach would already be quite a lot more difficult if one replaces wolves with mosquitoes.[98]

What is often not included in popular texts in the Environmental Humanities is the fact that human/non-human relations are inevitably mediated by various levels of institutional policies, various layers of media technologies, and multiple levels of, not only local, but also trans-national, political decision-making, lobbying, commercial interests, and other factors. Or as Esposito would say, life, including the human/non-human relations, is always institutionally mediated. If the term "biopolitics" still has a relevance in the analyses of our present and future conjunctures, a biopolitical analysis should be sufficiently historically situated, focus on specific distributions of vulnerability, take into account the various institutional mediations, and include the close the interdependence of human with non-human life in its analysis.

# 2 BEYOND BIOPOLITICS? ITALIAN THOUGHT, POSTHUMANISM, AND ENVIRONMENTALISM

## Chapter Summary

The concept of "life" takes center stage in Italian thought, particularly in the painstaking analyses of biopolitics in Agamben, Esposito and others. The distinction between *bios* [human cultivated life] and *zōè* [naked life] is foundational to much of Italian thought. In this chapter, we discuss contemporary Italian theorists, like Braidotti, Barca, Coccia and Luisetti, who question and venture beyond this distinction. Their thinking is rooted in a materialist and Spinozist–Deleuzian paradigm which is radically different from the Foucauldian genealogies of Agamben or Esposito's archaeologies of biopolitics. Rather than focusing on the history of governments controlling and steering human populations, they draw attention to the potential of living and even non-living beings to form webs of entangled connections. On the one hand, we will explore how this alternative trajectory for Italian thought allows us to move *beyond biopolitics*; for example by privileging *zōè*, as raw living matter, over *bios* (Braidotti), by considering "earth-beings" as part and parcel of a new political ecology (Luisetti), and by radically expanding our view of politics towards a "atmospheric" or true *cosmopolitics* (Coccia). On the other hand, by reading these recent theories in dialogue rather than against biopolitical philosophies, we will highlight the potential for a different reading of biopolitics in Agamben and Esposito. This chapter also shows how these new readings of and beyond biopolitics allow Italian thought to resonate with ecological and environmental, posthuman and decolonial theories.

In the introduction to this book, we noted how, for Roberto Esposito, Italian thought is part of a new "turn" in continental philosophy, which follows the so-called linguistic turn that gave rise to poststructuralism. This new turn, he claims, "as a whole belong[s] to the paradigm of *life*."[1] In his aptly titled *Living Thought: The Origins and Actuality of Italian Philosophy*, Esposito presents much of contemporary Italian philosophy as the collective endeavor of developing and rescripting Foucault's writings and seminars on the history and mechanics of biopower—the power over living bodies—and biopolitics. For Esposito, but also others like Gentili and Stimilli, Italian thought, as a more-or-less coherent constellation of philosophical and political concerns, is both the product *and* an important if not *the* principal vector of the biopolitical turn in contemporary theory. This biopolitical turn reputedly supersedes the linguistic turn: "rather than being examined in its autonomous structure, language is [now] situated within a broader horizon, described in terms of biology, or of ontological realism," Esposito claims.[2] If, in (post) structuralism, the human subject finds itself the product of linguistic structures or, on the contrary, highly unstable signifying chains, and thus radically limited in its autonomy, Italian thought pushes this unsettling realization even further by considering language itself as just one part of the general phenomenon of "life."

However, as we have seen earlier in this book, Italian thought is not a philosophical Darwinism in which the concept of "life" would act as a master-signifier that would comprise and explain, once and for all, major philosophical fields, such as language, subjectivity, humanity, or politics. On the contrary, Italian thinkers such as Giorgio Agamben, Rosi Braidotti, Roberto Esposito or Franco "Bifo" Berardi, despite their epistemological or ideological differences, underline in their work the "impurity" of life. Life is not only an immanent force that cannot be easily contained by reason, science, language, or politics but is also always already mediated by and entangled with, for example, technology, politics, or the law. With Nietzsche, Esposito affirms that "at the same time … life has a constitutively political dimension and that politics has no other object than the maintenance and expansion of life."[3] Life falls both within *and* outside of historically defined legal, political, or scientific practices and categories: "our life does not lend itself to an absolute naturalization or to an absolute historicization ...," we read in *Living Thought*.[4] In Italian thought, life is both a biological given, an ontological constant *and* a product or construct of history. The concept of biopolitics perfectly encapsulates this tension between the biological and the political. As we affirmed with Esposito in this book's introduction and in Chapter 1, the nexus between life and history is *politics*.[5] According to Esposito, the central insight of Italian thought, which he traces all the way back to Machiavelli, is "the immediately biological characterization of the political order."[6] Biopolitical theory teaches us the interpenetration of life and politics; the decisive lesson of Italian thought for contemporary philosophy, political and critical theory is that power and knowledge, whose combined forces constitute politics, must "establish a biunivocal, productive relationship with the world of life. They must make life their object, but equally, their source."[7] Italian thought thus offers a notion of life that is fundamentally impure and porous, as what we understand to constitute life is partly constituted by historically contingent phenomena like technological inventions, new forms of governance, political revolutions, or developments in jurisprudence. This emphasis on the porosity of life is a crucial contribution of Italian thought to contemporary theory, in particular in a context in which, on the one hand, environmental catastrophes multiply and intensify at breathtaking speed, to the point of effectively dealing the final blow to anthropocentrism, and, on the other hand, (human) life gets more and more enmeshed with all sort of technologies (medical-, nano-, or communications technology and artificial intelligence). The insistence in Italian thought on the impurity of a life open to history sets the scene for a conception of life exposed to non-life, and of human life as ontologically exposed to non-human life.

In their book *Animality and Contemporary Italian Philosophy*, Felice Cimatti and Carlo Salzani claim that Italian philosophy has always been characterized by a certain "anti-Cartesianism,"[8] as it refuses Descartes' "neat separation between human beings and the rest of the natural world."[9] For Cimatti and Salzani, "Descartes cannot but be a dualist, because he wants to save the metaphysical status of human beings" against the rising influence of Galilean science, which, in stark contrast, "would soon equate human beings to any other animate being."[10] The Italian tradition, on the other hand, at least since Saint Francis of Assisi, assumes that the difference between human and non-human life is not metaphysical but a mere matter of *difference*. At stake is not dualism but pluralism. This emphasis on the diversity of life profoundly challenges the implicit and not-so-implicit hierarchies that result from Cartesian dualism. As Cimatti and Salzani write, "the principle of diversity is 'naturally' egalitarian."[11] A profound equality marks all human and non-human forms of life that evades the human exceptionalism pervasive in most of modern philosophy.

In this chapter, we will explore how, from Agamben to Emanuele Coccia, and from Braidotti to Federico Luisetti, we step further and further into the entanglements between life and non-life, human and non-human life. Consequently, in contemporary Italian thought, we also move further and further away from biopolitics as theorized and made famous by Esposito and Agamben into new *posthuman* political ecologies. In what follows, we will see how, for contemporary theorists such as Braidotti or Coccia, the domain of "life" is gradually expanded from the general category of "living matter" to the (literally) astronomical proportions of a "cosmopolitics." As we mentioned in the previous chapter, if we want the defining concept of Italian thought, biopolitics, to retain its relevance for our era of the Anthropocene, we should include the many entanglements of human and non-human life in our analyses and uses of biopolitics. Most of the thinkers scrutinized in this chapter express this criticism of the traditional biopolitical theories of Agamben, Negri, or Esposito. Instead of taking sides, we prefer to read both approaches in dialogue as we believe that the resonances that emerge in such a dialogue allow us to both seize the limitations of biopolitical thought *and* affirm its continued relevance as a critical tool in the Anthropocene and the posthuman theories that have emerged with it.

## Leviathans and Chthulus: In and Beyond the "Anthropological Machine"

In the previous chapter, we discussed Esposito's critical genealogy of biopolitics. He stresses that we cannot fully grasp the logic of Foucault's discovery and its immense significance for the history of Western politics and political philosophy if we fail to read it alongside the intimately related tension between community and immunity. Political modernity, both in its catastrophic aspects (totalitarianism, genocide) *and* in its utopian side (the welfare state, social democracy), needs to be understood as the inevitable but highly ambivalent outcome of the dynamics within the triad community-immunity-biopolitics. Esposito agrees with Foucault that biopolitics is the determining form of politics in modernity, but in contrast to Foucault, he insists that biopolitics operates as a process of *immunization*.[12] The ultimate aim of biopolitical strategies, ideologies, governance, and statecraft is to protect the organic body against the threat of alien bodies, either the micro-scale of the individual body or the macro-scale of the collective body of the ethnic community. Considering the totalitarianisms of the past century, but also the current rise of populist and nativist political ideologies, we can easily imagine how the protection of the alleged purity and sovereignty of the organic or collective body—the immunization of "life"—can reverse into the destruction of divergent bodies, into the extermination of vulnerable forms of life.

A recurrent figure in Italian thought, most notably in Agamben, Marramao,[13] Esposito, Negri, and Luisetti, is Hobbes' Leviathan. In Hobbes' eponymous political treatise, published in 1651, the Leviathan quite literally embodies the modern state. On the iconic frontispiece of Hobbes' treatise, the gigantic body of the Leviathan, wearing its crown and holding scepter and sword, consists of a multitude of individual human bodies, ascending toward the giant's head. The Leviathan offers these individual living bodies protection by incorporating them into a collective, closed-off and hierarchically organized social body—a social body that remains clearly anthropomorphic as well as anthropocentric. It is the collective body of human life-forms in need of protection from other human bodies. For thinkers such as Agamben, Negri, and Esposito, Hobbes' Leviathan represents the logic of immunity par excellence: modern politics promises immunity against outside threats and, in return, molds individual bodies in all their differences into a single organism. The figure of the Leviathan represents how immunity, community, and politics are inextricably linked in political modernity; the paradigm of biopolitics, which dominates political modernity, is the product of their interdependence with the Leviathan as their emblem. However, as Esposito carefully unpacks in several of his books, there is something paradoxical about this relationship: if *communitas* entails a fundamental openness (a "being-together" or "being-with"), *immunitas* signifies the exact opposite (shelter, closure, protection, "being-against").[14] Hence Esposito's hesitation vis-à-vis exclusively negative interpretations of biopolitics, such as Agamben's. Biopolitics cannot be reduced to strategies of immunization premised on ethnic domination or biomedical sanitization. Negative biopolitics always already contains the potential for an affirmative biopolitics. As Federico Luisetti argues, it is this recognition of the fundamental porosity of bodies living in common—to which immunization will always be a belated and failed response—that makes Italian biopolitical theories highly relevant for politically and philosophically coming to terms with the Anthropocene.[15] For Luisetti, the Leviathan, as the embodiment of negative immunitary biopolitics, can no longer be emblematic for politics in the Anthropocene, as it fails to shelter us on today's unruly Earth—an Earth that presents us with the consequences of centuries of industrialization, colonization, and extractivism in the form of climate change and subsequent environmental catastrophes.

In the Anthropocene, the living human body cannot be immunized against what we now realize to be a *living earth*, an assemblage of life-forms, human and non-human, to which we are inevitably exposed. As Luisetti argues, to replace the Leviathan and its implied anthropomorphism and -centrism, we need to look for alternative mythological beasts and forces [*altre potenze mitologiche*] that capture an affirmative biopolitics for the Anthropocene;[16] for example, by reading Italian theories of biopolitics alongside Donna Haraway's Chthulucene and James Lovelock and Lynn Margulis' Gaia.[17] Luisetti proposes to align the Italian biopolitical turn with the biological turn of Euro-American critical theory in the work of, among others, Donna Haraway, Elizabeth Povinelli, Isabelle Stengers, Elizabeth Grosz, Bruno Latour, and Philippe Descola. Italian thought thus invites us to rethink "community" in the Anthropocene as a more-than-human collective, as reciprocal donation and obligation of care between humans and non-humans alike; it offers us refined conceptual tools to avoid the pitfalls of immunitary reason—a regress into promethean anthropocentrism—and to rethink the political consequences of the fundamental openness of the human subject from which it may include both human and non-human others.

Despite the relative absence of environmentalist themes in most Italian thought and traditional biopolitical theory, we do not need to start from scratch.[18] With his notion of "the anthropological machine," Agamben shows that the paradigm of biopolitics itself already includes a potential opening toward non-human otherness. As we will see, other thinkers like Braidotti, Coccia, and Luisetti are addressing the concept of life from very different philosophical perspectives, relying predominantly on Spinoza and Deleuze rather than on Foucault and Heidegger. However, at the same time, Agamben's thought does offer a segue out of a narrowly anthropocentric biopolitics into posthuman political ecologies. Especially, his book *The Open* incisively criticizes the role of the human/animal distinction in Western political thought, revealing how Western politics and metaphysics have over millenia converged in a biopolitics that pursues the good life by radically demarcating human *bios* from animal *zōè*. According to Agamben, the socio-political life (*bios*) of human communities has repeatedly had to define what it means to count as a human being worthy of subjecthood (and, for example, subsequent citizenship). This process of demarcation, however, has not only produced human subjects and citizens but also animal *zōè* outside socio-political life and the bare life of human beings deemed unworthy of full subjecthood and condemned to a zone of indistinction between humanity and animality, like the Jew under Nazism or the enslaved non-Western others in colonialism.

In *The Open*, Agamben provides a rather pessimistic assessment of our times. Modern biopolitics has reduced politics to the governmental management of humanity's bare animal survival. Since Hobbes, the aim of politics is not to elevate citizens beyond their base biological instincts but to ensure the population's security, and facilitate the pursuit of self-interest. However, "the total humanization of the animal coincides with a total animalization of man."[19] Seemingly, for Agamben, the porosity of the human subject—the openness of humankind toward his others, human and non-human—has taken a turn for the worse. Our post-historical predicament, Agamben argues, has left us with one single final task, "the total management of [humanity's] own animality."[20] Biopolitics, as *the* paradigm of political modernity, leaves humanity with little more than the management of "life" itself and thus ushers humanity into "post-history." Biopolitics, in Agamben's negative understanding of it, no longer allows for a politics that offers grand narratives of progress, be it religious narratives of salvation or various ideologies of emancipation. As the pure management of living bodies, biopolitics sees no need to take humankind beyond the bare necessities of mere survival. In Agamben's eyes, biopolitics may propose to *optimize* human life by regulating it (to strengthen or lengthen it), but it does not have a historical *telos*, a goal or horizon for life (i.e., an eternal afterlife or some kind of political revolution). In our stage of the biopolitical paradigm, all that we are left with, is the technocratic management of living bodies:

> The traditional historical potentialities—poetry, religion, philosophy— … have long since been transformed into cultural spectacles and private experiences and have lost all historical efficacy. Faced with this eclipse, the only task that still seems to retain some seriousness is the assumption of the burden—and the "total management"—*of biological life, that is, of the very animality of man.* Genome, global economy, and humanitarian ideology are the three united faces of this process in which posthistorical humanity seems to take on its own physiology as its last, impolitical mandate.[21]

In our post-historical condition, human life, by means of highly sophisticated medical technologies and post-ideological forms of governance, is optimized for an animal-like existence of pure, passive consumption, an intricate form of mere survival, a life in the passive tense devoid of a form or project. Agamben underlines the seemingly irresolvable contradiction of this contemporary *conditio humana*: "It is not easy to say whether the humanity that has taken upon itself the mandate of the total management of its own animality is still human."[22] Post-historical man has slipped into a state of indistinction between human and animal. At the pinnacle of technocratic advancement, humanity has reduced itself to a state of quasi-animality.

How is this possible? How can human self-realization reverse into its animalistic opposite? According to Agamben, our current predicament results from what he calls "the anthropological machine"—a recurrent mechanism in Western thought and politics that differentiates between humanity and animality, the human and the non-human. As we will see, for Agamben, paradoxically, the "anthropological machine" is both an instrument to determine the fundamental difference between man and animal *and* the very mechanism that effectively produces the *anthrōpos* [the human]. It is by introducing a caesura in life itself that something distinct like human life can emerge. Agamben's key example in *The Open* is Martin Heidegger's discussion of the human/animal distinction in *The Fundamental Concepts of Metaphysics*.[23] Heidegger argues that animals are "poor in world" (*weltarm*) in the sense that they do not relate to their surroundings as *Dasein* (human subjectivity) but only react to so-called "disinhibitors" (*das Enthemmende*) that trigger instinctive responses. A bee instinctively reacts to a flower insofar as the latter triggers visceral responses, but it cannot reflectively experience the flower as flower. It cannot distance itself from its own immediate and automatic responses. Human beings, on the other hand, possess the potential to suspend the enactment of these instincts. In experiences like boredom and anxiety, nothing in the world triggers an immediate response, which grants human *Dasein* the capacity to relate to the world as such. While Agamben pays much attention to Heidegger, structurally similar anthropological machines operate in other metaphysical and political apparatuses. The production of human life often hinges on the suspension of animalistic instincts in favor of some uniquely human vocation or other. Many religions have even built vast disciplinary apparatuses to fight sinful bodily instincts to realize the full potential of human life. Those instincts never truly disappear, however, but remain present in a suspended state, continuously haunting human identity. Human socio-political life (*bios*) is formed through discursive operations that identify particular qualities that define belonging to that community, while other qualities that contradict this collective identity must consequently be sidelined.

As the previous example shows, the peculiarity of this differentiation, according to Agamben, is that it occurs *within* humanity. Animal instincts do not disappear but remain dormant in humanity. Rather than presupposing that there are the two antithetical ontological facts of human versus non-human life, the anthropogenesis produced by the anthropological machine entails the forging of humankind by and *within* itself. The separation between human and non-human life results from a rift inside life itself. Agamben underlines the inherently political character of this "anthropological machine," which is foremost a *bio*political machine, as it divides human coexistence into "proper" and "improper" forms of life: those who are worthy of humanity and those who are not.[24] If individuals are somehow identified as human yet fail to enact the qualities specific to their human community, their lives are often associated with untamed animality and a dangerous animalistic force from which the human community must be allegedly immunized. From the Nazis' dehumanizing remarks about Jews to white-supremacist American panics about the sexuality of Black enslaved males, the inherent instability of anthropological machines has provided the discursive infrastructure for pogroms, lynchings, and mass murder throughout history.

The division between the human and the non-human, for Agamben, is not simply a natural phenomenon; it results from the joint articulation of knowledge and power provided by philosophy and theology, science, and the law—a peculiar knowledge-power that, at the same time, *produces* what it claims to objectively study. As such, the divide between human and animal is absolutely foundational for Western thought, Agamben argues: "If animal life and human life could be superimposed perfectly, then neither man nor animal—and, perhaps, not even the divine—would any longer be thinkable."[25] The separation between human and non-human life produces the fundamental binaries of our thinking. For example, language and thought (human) versus instinct (non-human), a sense of time and history versus complete immersion in the present, anticipation of a "world" beyond our immediate field of vision versus immediate presence in the environment. Therefore, the question of the non-human, coinciding in much of Western thought with that of the animal, goes at the heart of Western philosophical, scientific, and political traditions. As we noted earlier, the "anthropological machine" that churns out humans and non-humans is a biopolitical device, a "device for producing the recognition of the human"[26] *within* the human, for separating the animal, non-human part within humanity. Western "human*ism*"— the study and defense of the human—always already entails a *decision* establishing what and who counts as properly "human." This is a *political* decision in that it determines who is recognized as a member of the family of humankind and who will be subject to the "animalization of man," and consequently excluded from humanity.[27] In Esposito's terms, the anthropological machine is an instrument of immunization against the non-human. "In our culture," Agamben claims, "the decisive political conflict, which governs every other conflict, is that between the animality and the humanity of man. That is to say, in its origin Western politics is also biopolitics."[28] Agamben stresses that the operation of this anthropological sifter machine is not some aberration of nineteenth- or twentieth-century racism; it is in fact *the* fundamental logic of Western thought. Over the past decades, Agamben has painstakingly unpacked the ambivalence of the "anthropological machine" as it recurs throughout the history of Western thought:

On the one hand, we have the anthropological machine of the moderns. As we have seen, it functions by excluding as not (yet) human an already human being from itself, that is, by animalizing the human, by isolating the nonhuman within the human ... The machine of earlier times works in an exactly symmetrical way. If, in the machine of the moderns, the outside is produced through the exclusion of an inside and the inhuman produced by animalizing the human, here the inside is obtained through the inclusion of an outside, and the non-man is produced by the humanization of an animal ... Both machines are able to function only by establishing a zone of indifference at their centers, within which—like a "missing link" which is always lacking because it is already virtually present—the articulation between human and animal, man and non-man, speaking being and living being, must take place. Like every space of exception, this zone is, in truth, perfectly empty ... What would thus be obtained, however, is neither an animal life nor a human life, but only a life that is separated and excluded from itself—only a bare life.[29]

At its core, the anthropological machine resorts to a paradoxical operation of "inclusive exclusion." The non-human is never simply an "outside," something fundamentally alien vis-à-vis humanity; the non-human is identified, isolated within humanity, and finally expelled from it. In Western thought, the meaning of "humanity"—and who gets to participate in it—is based on this two-step process of first including the non-human as that part of humanity that does not take part in the human *bios*.[30] Against this animality, the human species must subsequently be immunized. Again, we can see why, for Agamben, this is not simply a matter of biological nomination but a political decision: in particular in the past two centuries, the horrendous examples of colonialism, racism, and totalitarianism, culminating in the Holocaust, have demonstrated the inhumane and genocidal consequences of such biopolitical decisions rooted in the urge to distinguish between human and non-human.

In works such as the *Homo Sacer* series and *The Use of Bodies*, Agamben shows how the mechanism of "inclusive exclusion," which lies at the root of Western anthropogenesis, is repeated throughout the Western history of thought, from the foundations of politics to determining who gets to count as human to refining techniques of governance: "The strategy is always the same: something is divided, excluded, and pushed to the bottom, and precisely through this exclusion, it is included as *archè* [ground] and foundation."[31] In this light, anthropocentrism and anthropometrics [taking humanity as the measure of all things] are anything but static. In Western thinking, humankind has never been able to simply assume their centrality in the web of life, but this privileged status needs to be realized and confirmed *over and again* by repeating the operation of inclusive exclusion. Crucially for Agamben, as he stresses in the passage from *The Open* quoted above, the anthropological machine creates a zone of indistinction within humanity, an exception within the norm, as it needs to actively "animalize" or "humanize" life-forms. Because the distinction human/non-human is the product of a decision, of a designation in which politics and science are articulated together, there is a moment of indistinction, a moment of inclusion prior to any exclusion, in which the human and non-human are not-yet differentiated, a life without form. As Agamben reminds us: "it is this bare life … that functions in the juridico-political machine of the West as a threshold of articulation between *zōè* and *bios*, natural life and politically qualified life."[32] Neither human nor non-human, but a formless "bare life" which is nonetheless not a biological given but the result of complex political as well as epistemological processes; a bare life that ranges from the life of the enslaved, the victims of the Holocaust to refugees stranded on Lampedusa, but also that of the animal in and beyond the bioindustries.[33]

Agamben sees different paths leading from this zone of indistinction. On the one hand, the path that directs us toward the total subjection of (human) life, be it in the excesses of modern totalitarianism or in the kind of cynical, post-historical consumerism Agamben discusses in *The Open*. In this light, the reduction of human life, in the age of globalization, to mere post-historical survival—even if this involves highly sophisticated forms of medical technology, an abundance of commodities to be consumed and unprecedented freedom of movement—goes hand-in-hand with the degradation of any other form of life, through extractivist exploitation, drilling for fossil fuels, and industrial agriculture at a planetary scale, resulting in innumerable non-human holocausts and extinctions.[34] Life becomes a mere resource for governmental projects having no higher aim than bare survival.

On the other hand, Agamben proposes a path that would lead us right to the heart of the indistinction. Rather than generating "new articulations between the animal and the human," we should sabotage and deactivate the anthropological machine "so that an inseparable life, neither animal nor human, can eventually appear."[35] If we manage to bring the anthropological machine to a standstill, to render it inoperative, we may be able to imagine a radically new relationship between the human and the non-human, man and animal, nature and history.[36] If the aim of the anthropological machine is to "produce the human through the suspension and capture of the inhuman,"[37] putting to a halt the process in which the human and non-human are identified in the very gesture that separates them means that we can no longer distinguish between these two terms. As a consequence, Agamben writes, "in the reciprocal suspension of the two terms, something for which we perhaps have no name and which is neither animal nor man settles in between nature and humanity."[38] To break the anthropological machine does not mean that we should be looking for new definitions of the human and non-human, including those that recast man as the "human animal" or those that seek to conflate the human and non-human into a universal notion of "life." On the contrary, it means to stay with(in) the indistinction, within the gap that was already at the heart of the anthropological machine, and to not interpret this hiatus negatively as lack: to no longer seek to define humanity or animality in their opposition but to consider the suspension of their determination as the liberation of potential for newly imaginable forms of life and their coexistence. If the Anthropocene, ironically, heralds the end of *anthropo*centrism, Agamben's meticulous disassembling of the anthropological machine points us toward a new way of thinking, beyond the biopolitics inherent in Western thought and its nefarious separation of forms of life.

Building on Agamben's work, Carlo Salzani argues that overcoming the rift that divides the human from the animal is neither a matter of granting "rights" to animals or offering them a seat at the table of humanity. There is little to gain from "elevating" animals into humanity and thus affirming the latter's inherent superiority. But reducing human beings to their biological animalistic existence is equally counterproductive, as it often entails projecting rather simplistic and dangerous versions of Darwinism onto human societies, for example.[39] Both options would leave the anthropological machine, and the fundamental hierarchies it produces, firmly intact. In contrast, to de-activate the very structure of the machine would release both the human and animal body from any historical and metaphysical baggage. The deconstruction of the foundational structure of inclusion-exclusion of the animal would effectively make the distinction between *zōè* and *bios* meaningless, and, consequently, its catastrophic dehumanization of human lives into bare life. This would effectively transform both human *and* animal life into forms of pure potentiality, "completely unmarked and finally free from any determination."[40] As such, it would transform "life," from a (bio)political instrument of governance and oppression into life as "pure immanence": life for and by itself, "returned to pure potential."[41] As Massimo Filippi claims, what results from the destabilization of the anthropological machine and the categories it produces is "no more 'post-human' than it is post-elephant or post-murine": it simply "restores to bodies the fluid sets of relations that constitute them."[42] It is this push for a thinking beyond biopolitics but nonetheless in search of new political ecologies and ontologies that we find in the work of Rosi Braidotti.

# From *Bio-* to *Zōè*-politics

Although the work of Rosi Braidotti does not share a genealogy with that of Agamben—Braidotti resolutely prefers Spinoza over Heidegger—her recent work on posthuman subjectivity gives us a sense of what thinking (or *a* thinking) beyond biopolitics might look like.[43] Key to such a novel way of thinking is a radical overhaul of the concept of *zōè*. In his *Homo Sacer* series, Agamben opposes *zōè*, the general category of "life," to *bios* as socio-politically cultivated life. Braidotti is highly critical of Agamben's rendition of *zōè* and his predominantly negative vision of biopolitics. As she points out, in Agamben, *zōè*—a notion of life that transcends human life alone—is only negatively defined. Either one interprets it as a kind of pre-politicized life entirely outside the clutches of politics and the anthropological machine, which renders *zōè* completely unknowable and unsayable, or one identifies *zōè* with bare life, i.e., life defined by its violent exclusion from *bios* and stripped of its socio-political qualities until nothing but naked matter remains. The latter emerges only as the product of a politics of domination which inflicts suffering and ultimately death. In both interpretations, *zōè* is predominantly defined through its opposition to *bios* but lacks any positive content of its own. *Zōè* does not exist in any meaningful way prior to the anthropological machine. Only when the machine is made inoperative can something like "life" in a positive sense emerge. But even then it has to remain eternally suspended, it can only "exist" as potential, and is thus never fully affirmed.

For Braidotti, Agamben's conceptualization of *zōè* remains severely restricted by the Heideggerian legacy in his thinking, which "consists in taking mortality, or finitude, as the trans-historical horizon for discussions of 'life.'"[44] Living beings are always already understood in their relationship toward death (their *sein-zum-Tode* in Heideggerian parlance). Life is *negatively* understood in its "constitutive vulnerability,"[45] and as secondary vis-à-vis death, rather than as a primal, affirmative, and generative force. In the wake of Heidegger, Foucault, and Agamben (or even Esposito), life is seen in light of its *finitude*, as inherently limited, and making us subject to all sorts of domination that precisely exploit our inherent vulnerability. As a result, to Braidotti's ears, the tonality of current conceptions of biopolitics, such as Agamben's, is too melancholic and pessimistic. "This over-emphasis on the horizons of mortality and perishability is characteristic of the 'forensic turn' in contemporary social and cultural theory, haunted by the specter of extinction and by the limitations of the project of western modernity. I find the over-emphasis on death as the basic term of reference inadequate to *the vital politics of our era*,"[46] she writes.

In contrast to Agamben, Braidotti advances a *vitalist* biopolitics, a radically affirmative or *zōè-centered biopolitics*. Such a fundamentally *zōè*-centered politics would be truly post-anthropocentric and *posthuman*. It would also be radically different from much of contemporary environmental political activism, for which movements with names like *Extinction Rebellion* or *The Last Generation* tellingly set the apocalyptic tone.[47] More often than not, environmental politics assumes and promotes "a shared form of vulnerability, that is to say a global sense of inter-connection between the human and the non-human environment in the face of common threats."[48] In opposition to "the reactive bond of vulnerability," Braidotti proposes "an affirmative bond that locates the subject in the flow of relations with multiple others."[49] As mentioned above, this would foremost imply rethinking the concept of *zōè* itself. In Braidotti, *zōè* is recoded as "the non-human, vital force of Life."[50] Braidotti's *zōè* refers to the generative force that is life, and that refuses to be separated into human and non-human life, man and animal, animal and vegetable life, and even living matter and technology. "*Zōè* [is] the dynamic, self-organizing structure of life itself," Braidotti writes, "[it] stands for generative vitality. It is the transversal force that cuts across and reconnects previously segregated species, categories and domains."[51] In Braidotti's posthuman perspective, life

> is posited as process, interactive and open-ended. This vitalist approach to living matter displaces the boundary between the portion of life— both organic and discursive—that has traditionally been reserved for

*anthrōpos*, that is to say *bios*, and the wider scope of animal and non-human life, also known as *zōè*.[52]

The human subject cannot claim any privileged relation to life at the top of a hierarchy of living beings, as life is the ever-changing, radically open-ended and dynamic assemblage of all living matter. In Braidotti, life is neither a holistic unity, as it constitutes a relentless *becoming*, nor is it a paragon of finitude that is ultimately modeled after human mortality. Crucially, "life" here is not a master-signifier or metaphysical notion to encapsulate and determine all others: "it expresses itself in a multiplicity of empirical acts: there is nothing to say, but everything to do. Life, simply by being life, expresses itself by actualizing flows of energies, through codes of vital information across complex somatic, cultural and technologically networked systems."[53] To the predominantly negative concept of biopower as an exterior governing force to which we are subjected and that is productive or empowering only in so far as it shapes us according to its own norms, Braidotti opposes the affirmative notion of "*zōè*power,"[54] which is literally empower*ing*, as it allows the subject to tap into the generative potential for transformation shared across all living matter. As the vital force of life, *zōè* plugs the human subject into a complex and unending assemblage of energies and flows, into a multiplicity of ecological but also socio-political, psychic, and techno-scientific environments. These entanglements transform it into a posthuman subject whose relational capacity now "includes all non-anthropomorphic elements"[55] and not just those who compose the community of human beings, the Leviathan. A potential posthuman ethics or politics would proceed from a kind of Nietzschean *amor fati,* "a way of accepting vital processes and the expressive intensity of a Life we share with multiple others, here and now."[56] In turn, we may sense Agamben's or Esposito's skepticism toward Braidotti's call to embrace all living matter. In their conception of biopolitics—or perhaps better still, from the perspective of biopolitics *tout court*—there can only be *mediated* matter and life, that is to say, life given sense and form by historically specific forms of power and knowledge. The latter, at least, seems to imply a crucial role for emphatically human institutions to mediate between living matter and socio-political agency.

For Braidotti, any post-anthropocentrism or posthumanism must necessarily consist of *zōè-centred egalitarianism,* a radical horizontality between human and non-human life, between organic and non-organic environments, as we plug ourselves into technology while navigating a world co-inhabited by innumerable species. *Zōè*-centered egalitarianism assumes "that all matter is one, that it is intelligent and self-organizing (autopoietic); it takes 'living matter' as *zōè*-centered process, which is geophysical but also psychic and nowadays interacts productively with the technosphere."[57] Whereas in Agamben the deconstruction of the anthropological machine results in a kind of infinite suspension of affirmation, a pure potentiality for letting alternative forms of life coexist into being, in Braidotti, the unconditional affirmation of a shared materiality and equally distributed living matter comes first.[58] For Braidotti, such an affirmative approach is extremely timely in our contemporary, global socio-political, economic, and even geological context. In the Anthropocene, capitalism has become a geological or natural force in itself, causing climate change, species extinction and leaving countless pollutants to form geological layers. "Contemporary capitalism is indeed 'bio-political' in that it aims at controlling all that lives,"[59] Braidotti argues. Capitalism nowadays extracts both physical, cognitive and affective resources from our lives, completely subsuming our existence under the iron-clad laws of capital (see Chapter 3). The same goes for life itself, as capitalism now intervenes in every aspect of living matter, from genetically modified crops and artificially produced animal life-forms, such as Dolly the sheep and the OncoMouse,[60] to fracking for the last drop of fossil fuel on a living planet, life itself is turned into an extractable resource for the global economy.

Crucially, for Braidotti, this means that "because Life is not the prerogative of humans only, it opens up a *zōè*-political or post-anthropocentric dimension."[61] Hence, in the Anthropocene, the human finds itself connected to "the fate of other species," opening up new horizons for a "transversal alliance."[62] Such an alliance would cut horizontally through a multitude of species and would build upon a vitalist-materialist "political ontology of radical immanence" that would engender "a transversal relational ethics to counteract the inhuman(e) aspects of the posthuman predicament."[63] Braidotti warns against focusing on the purely negative aspects of our current environmental and geo-political issues, on looming catastrophes like rising sea levels, forest fires, loss of biodiversity, or nuclear meltdowns. That project risks once more separating the human from the non-human and elevating humankind above nature, this time around by designating humankind as the all-powerful culprit of environmental disasters alienated from "nature."

Braidotti urges us to recognize *zōè* as a nature–culture *continuum*. The response to the cynical commodification and exploitation of life itself in the Anthropocene has to be met with an equally radically materialist, post-anthropocentric politics, a *zōè-centered* politics in which human and non-human life alike are subject to and powered by the radically generative force of *zōèpower*. In what follows, we will see how Emanuele Coccia and Federico Luisetti propose a similar radically horizontal, post-anthropocentric perspective while departing from Braidotti's vitalist materialism by including non-living "earth beings" (Luisetti) into a new political ecology, and its infinite expanse into a *cosmo*politics (Coccia). We thus move far beyond biopolitics.

## Beyond the Human: From Geo- to Cosmopolitics

Emanuele Coccia and Federico Luisetti offer a radical effort to imagine a post-anthropocentric politics, which taps into *zōèpower*, and even *geopower*. Though both Coccia and Luisetti are skeptical of the term "Anthropocene," they acknowledge that the contemporary planetary condition has radically changed the relationship between the human subject and its environment. More specifically, both point out that the bitter irony of our age is that, in the *Anthropo*cene, the *anthrōpos* no longer has a monopoly on subjectivity. Coccia stresses that "the climate crisis is the sensitive emergence of Earth as a subject, one that acts freely beyond any possible control. We are no longer masters of its behavior, either cognitively or pragmatically. Earth has begun to do what it wants again."[64] For Coccia, "climate crisis" can be a misleading term. The current transformations of the Earth's climate, which negatively manifest in the form of storms, fires, and floods, reveal that "climate" is a highly effective denominator for a complex arrangement of atmospheric, geophysical, and biological elements. "Climate should be defined," Coccia writes, "as the place where all living species and nonliving matter on Earth define their compatibility with each other, with no one having total control over the other."[65]

In turn, Luisetti notes how:

In the new millennium, the notion of the Anthropocene has popularized this sense of being-acted-upon by uncontrollable environmental forces. Greenhouse gas emissions and the exploitation of natural resources have altered the Earth's metabolism … climate change and the environmental catastrophe have caused a crisis of presence of planetary proportions, which is *reframing the experience of being a subject in the age of global ecological disruption.*[66]

Commentators love to use the term "Anthropocene" because it captures humankind's oversized impact on Earth's ecosystems, but it may indeed be another misnomer, as humanity now finds itself overwhelmed by the new-found subjectivity of a hyperactive unruly Earth. The latter's "misbehavior" is precisely triggered by humanity's overconfidence in its self-assigned role as master and commander, not only of other living beings but ultimately of the Earth itself. The discovery of the Earth's agency shatters a centuries-old confidence of human exceptionalist superiority, and raises fundamental ethical, political, and epistemological questions. If humankind now finds himself enmeshed in an intricate web of seemingly infinite life-forms as well as meteorological and geophysical forces, how to conceive of humanity's position within this mesh? "The ecological crisis is an incredible cognitive and political obligation,"[67] Coccia claims. What happens when the human subject is no longer Leonardo da Vinci's Vitruvian Man, the measure of all things?[68] What new names and concepts do we need to make our current predicament simply imaginable and thinkable? Where does this leave the hallmark of Italian thought, biopolitics, which now finds itself entangled with the newly found power of *geo-* [from *gaia*: earth] or *atmos* [air or climate] or even *cosmos*? As Coccia urges, "none of the political devices invented so far will help us solve the climate crisis. We need to invent new ones."[69] For both Coccia and Luisetti the point is not to concoct yet another solutionism, a politics that would allow man to effectively govern the climate crisis and thus to regain his monopoly on subjectivity and domination of life and planet. We need a politics that does not "prevent or avoid the storm: on the contrary, it must accompany and protect it,"[70] an atmospheric politics that does not seek to combat bad weather but sees in it a new imagery for a non-anthropocentric politics, a politics for an ungovernable Earth which may no longer even call itself "politics."

In a critical assessment of Agamben's archaeology of biopower, Luisetti points out a cardinal blind spot: Agamben "fails to recognize the *environmental nature of contemporary governmentality* and the emergence of geopower."[71] According to Luisetti, Agamben and a host of other theorists of biopolitics repeat Foucault's failure to grasp the radical implications of his own pioneering analyses of biopower. The subjects of biopower in Foucault, Luisetti reminds us, are not abstract individuals but, crucially, "biological collectives managed, through the mediation of political economy, by state-coordinated techniques of bioregulation."[72] Biopower implies a certain naturalness of the population. Populations appear as a natural phenomenon and not, for example, as the artificial collective body of citizens offered shelter in the Leviathan that is the State, brought into being by a social compact among individual rational agents. The regularities of the population, revealed by biopolitical power-knowledge, have an agency of their own that cannot be reduced to the conscious will of any human collective. However, the population is "not a primary datum but the result of a series of variables such as climate, material surroundings and the intensity of commerce."[73] Biopower then, in its most unsettling interpretation, signifies "the securitization of the *milieu*, the emerging features of *a form of power centered on the ecological environment*, in which human populations are simply variables among others."[74] For Luisetti, the Foucauldian archaeology of biopower at the heart of Italian biopolitical theory contains the seeds for the fundamental repositioning of the human subject as part of an ecological milieu.

In response to the rise of neoliberalism as *the* dominant form of governmentality today, and the ever-rational *homo oeconomicus* as its subject, Foucault and thinkers like Agamben and Esposito narrow the discursive field of biopolitical theory down to "the anthropological dimension of the population," that is to say: the human species in isolation from its milieu.[75] According to Luisetti, Foucault not only shifts his attention to the birth and lineage of the neoliberal *homo oeconomicus,* the calculating subject of rational economic choice, but the latter also comes to prefigure Foucault's definitions of biopower and biopolitics. The emphasis on subjectivity in the guise of the individual agency and responsibility of the *homo oeconomicus* in neoliberalism leads Foucault to marginalize the role of the environment and to restrict biopower to "the government of the *bios* of the human species, the behavior and physiology of human agents."[76] In seeking to understand the sources and consequences of neoliberalism, Foucault replicates its emphasis on *human* capital. Tragically, Foucault thus ignores how neoliberalism, at the precise moment when he was delivering his lectures on governmentality in the 1970s, already constituted a form of *geopower*. Governmentality heralded a seismic shift in politics, as it embedded the governance of populations in "the thick network of environmental affects … species, ecosystems, biogeochemical and physical processes"[77] that constitute their milieu. Under neoliberalism, these non-human processes are indelibly commodified, marketized, privatized, financialized, and speculated upon on a planetary scale. As geopower, neoliberal governance "regulates the planetary environment, marginalizing human capital and thus setting the stage for the Earth politics of late capitalism."[78] In this sense, neoliberalism, as the preferred mode of governance of contemporary capitalism, turns *bio*politics into a subdivision of sorts of *geo*politics, now understood as the exercise of *geopower*.

In the Anthropocene, we are confronted with what Luisetti calls a "neoliberal state of nature."[79] Neoliberalism has not only pushed the exploitation of natural and human resources beyond the already dramatic record of the Great Acceleration under Fordism, through new forms of commodification, modes of production and extraction, technologies, and modes of transportation. It also manipulates the mitigation of the catastrophic effects by introducing new forms of governance and monetization for our damaged environments. With Green New Deals, carbon emission markets, net-zero emissions reductions, and energy transitions, "capitalism has responded to the environmental crisis of presence with a toolbox of … flexible governance that strives to combine the management of ecosystems with marketization and dispossession."[80] Moreover, neoliberalism presents the global marketplace as an "ecosystem in its own right," albeit one ruled by (wrongly understood) Darwinian natural selection, relentless competition, and resilient adaptation.[81] "In the green neoliberal planet," Luisetti writes, "the *homo oeconomicus* merges with the *homo biologicus*; economic and species survival are one and the same thing. Malleable green citizens are asked to save the planet and themselves from extinction by conforming to corporate agendas and state-led energy regimes."[82]

This ecological critique of contemporary capitalism resonates with Marxist concerns. Stefania Barca, for example, dubs the discourse and politics of the Anthropocene as "eco-capitalist realism: considering industrial growth as the only valuable form of human existence, [this discourse] induces one to wonder how [capitalism] can be saved by making it compatible with the earth's biophysical limits."[83] Eco-capitalist realism finds it easier to imagine global environmental catastrophe than the end of capitalism and subsequently promotes the further commodification of non-human life as the sole strategy for getting us out of the mess capitalist commodification has produced. According to Barca, this tendency threatens the "forces of reproduction," i.e., the elements required to reproduce life on Earth as we know it.[84] Barca thereby expands the concepts of "working class" and "forces of production" to argue that the ecological working class consists of all living beings who deploy the forces of reproduction to produce and sustain life on Earth but have been dispossessed of these forces in the name of capital accumulation. Capital has captured the forces of reproduction to make them serve the end of further capital accumulation, even if this cannibalizes the underlying conditions of possibility for human and non-human life alike.

For Luisetti, the neoliberal state of nature, however, is Janus-faced. On the one hand, we have the cynicism of neoliberal geopower, which disavows its own dependency on non-human ecosystems. It ignores its own entanglement in a milieu, a thick planetary network of human and non-human life, by centering the human subject as the sole agent of political governance, now reinvented as the eerily hybrid economic/biological man. On the other hand, the tacit imposition of geopower has also liberated, since the 1970s, new ways of thinking through alternative visions of symbiotic planetary life. Luisetti identifies two opposing conceptual personae embodying "the divergent trajectories of subjectivization fostered by the environmental crisis of presence … the *homo oeconomicus* and the *symbiont*, alternative modes of being subject, rooted either in competition or collaboration, ecocide or livability."[85] The recognition of the fact of universal symbiosis, of which neoliberal geopower is the negative incarnation that perverts radical interdependence into competition and survival, has inspired an array of concepts that attempt to capture the abundance of relationships, collaborations, entanglements, and distributed subjectivities of the era of geopower. The latter embody the political potential for a kind of affirmative geopower for which "nature and culture, geochemical and biological processes are different aspects of the continuum of life, an ecological plane of transformations, punctuated by hybrid selves of various degrees of mobility and animation, consciousness, and sentience."[86] In this light, Luisetti reconsiders Lovelock and Margulis's Gaia hypothesis, which imagines the Earth as a scene of universal symbiosis, urging us to rethink human exceptionalism, personhood, and individual subjectivity.[87] In this political ecology, "life forces converge creatively in human and other-than-human bodies."[88] However, for Luisetti, the emphasis on "life" obfuscates the full and radical meaning of geopower, which would allow us to take a decisive step beyond Foucault's as well as Agamben's biopolitical theory. With theorists such as Elizabeth Povinelli and Kathryn Yusoff,[89] Luisetti argues that *geopower* includes geological *non-life*, as it depends, for example, on the extraction, management, and governance of fossil fuels and the environments where these are "found," as well as the people who relate to these environments. Desert- and seascapes as well have in the meantime become crucial parts of the global production of green energy, implying that even the least inhabited places on Earth are now significant vectors of geopower. The latter manages life and non-life in their interdependence. In contrast to Braidotti and Coccia, Luisetti asks how we can conceive of an ecology "that does not interpret other-than-human forces as an expression of life?"[90] Can we imagine bodies that are not living bodies but *geobodies*? And, if these geobodies are to be included in a new political ecology, how can they be "subjective as well as nonliving?"[91]

## Geobodies and Earth-Beings

To grasp the socio-political and epistemological significance of geobodies, Luisetti reaches beyond the confines of Euro-Italian theory to indigenous Andean thought. From the anthropologist Marisol de la Cadena, he borrows the concept of "earth-beings," by which de la Cadena captures the convergence between "social processes and nonliving beings … geobodies caught at the intersection of divergent forces."[92] Earth-beings are geobodies, like rocks, lakes, springs, rivers, mountains, or deserts, that become subjects because we engage with them ritually, economically, or politically. They are co-constitutive of a variety of world-making practices, from their exploitation through mining or deforestation in our neoliberal world to Andean symbolic practices that rupture the divide between humans and the landscapes, the world of non-life in which indigenous populations find themselves enveloped. Earth-beings are subjects without personhood. They emerge as subjects only insofar as they participate in a complex dynamic between material and immaterial practices as we living human beings engage with them in "creative relationships with their divergent existence."[93] However, they do not constitute recognizable personalities with their own psychology or legal recognition. Their subjectivity is measured in their operative agency vis-à-vis other entities rather than through the *dispositif* of personhood. In defiance of their irreconcilable strangeness in terms of scale or material composition, geobodies "inhabit narrative worlds in which they can be animated and switch places with the universe of living beings, acquiring movement, growth, emotions, social skills, and death."[94] To fully acknowledge the pivotal role of earth-beings for a new political ecology, Luisetti proposes:

> a decolonial ecology that disentangles geobodies from the language of life and the dispositif of Western personhood. My hypothesis is that stones, valleys, air, ice, and waterbodies are revealed as ecopolitical subjects by the current crisis of presence. And their nonliving subjectivity cannot be contained anymore by anthropological constructions of animism and totemism that, from colonial times, have confined them in Indigenous life worlds.[95]

The fact that the Earth is now speaking truth to human power through climate change and is throwing our self-assured apex presence on the planet into crisis demonstrates the limitations of Western thought. Therefore, we need to decolonize Western thought, Luisetti argues, by reading it alongside other ways of knowing, such as indigenous Andean thought and practices. If we manage to value non-Western indigenous thought beyond colonial clichés and their residual presence in the humanities, decolonial epistemologies offer highly significant tools to confront our current planetary predicament.[96] The glaciers, rivers, lakes, valleys, and seas of Europe and North America should also be conceived of as earth-beings if we are to engage with them on terms other than those of the neoliberal subsumption of all that exists.

Non-Western thought can foremost teach us how to disentangle personhood and subjecthood. Revisiting Esposito's reflections on personhood (see Chapter 1) vis-à-vis indigenous and decolonial thought, Luisetti's work seeks to "extricate the subjectivity of non-living earth-beings from the living selves of multispecies ethnographies, which hinge on the bio-anthropological language of other-than-human personhood."[97] However, theories of Gaia as a living planet, on which humanity dwells within a multispecies assemblage, Luisetti argues, remain tacitly anthropocentric, as they continue to privilege language, even if this language is that of trees communicating or our interaction with companion species.[98] They identify language as the marker of agency and personhood, and subsequently look for non-human languages to elevate non-human species to a form of subjectivity that remains modeled on human personhood. Earth-beings may be mute, but they are not simply passive. "Earth-beings are not swayed by desires and cognitions but they are affected," Luisetti writes, "they move or stand still, they linger, pollute, or weather away, experiencing the forces of the Earth as variations of their existence."[99] Their subjectivity escapes the Western sense of personhood, which ultimately upholds *logos* over *zōè*. In Agambenian terms, earth-beings remain excluded from the anthropological machine. The alleged epistemological and political shift from *logo*centrism to *bio*centrism to *zōè*-egalitarianism may simply cover up intransigent *anthropo*centrism. Moreover, as Luisetti reminds us, the equivalence between being endowed with personhood and being the proprietor of *logos* has historically been a pillar of colonial ideology. Those in whom *logos* was deemed absent saw themselves dispossessed of both personhood and lifeworld, and relegated to the realm of *zōè*.[100] In Western thought and colonial history, both clearly running in parallel, personhood "is the outcome of multiple exclusions."[101]

In contrast, to bring earth-beings into the world and co-create a plurality of worlds with them means to engage with beings whose temporality, consistency, scale, and materiality defies personification. For Luisetti, current attempts to grant geobodies such as rivers or lakes "rights" by turning them into legal personae misses the point.[102] Though tempting, the crux is *not* to personify geobodies into human law, so as to force them to "speak the language of litigation"[103] while ignoring their unique ontologies. That strategy forecloses the potential of them becoming earth-beings. However, Luisetti does not simply want to reduce humankind to animals or non-living matter. At stake is not our capacity *to be like* the river or the rock but rather *to be with* the river and the rock, to recognize that, as a living species, we share a "terrestrial condition" with non-living geobodies, and that earth-beings emerge at the point of intersection between different living and non-living bodies. A new political ecology for the Anthropocene would be "concerned with the scenes in which nonlife stages its own political subjectivity and confronts humans … with its modes of existence, redefining regimes of inhabitation of the Earth, altering distributions of natures, identities, bodies, and humanity."[104] Moreover, like the geobodies that surround us in the Anthropocene, our state of being is that of a product of planetary forces beyond our control. In this sense too, we must urgently engage earth-beings, including those in the Northern hemisphere, as ecopolitical subjects. For Luisetti, such a (geo-)political economy, for inspiration, would turn to "naturalistic thought, art practices, philosophies, religions, and social movements that have redesigned the perception of the world from the perspective of geobodies: Japanese Shinto rituals, Andean *tirakuna*, Deleuzian 'bodies without organs,' pluriversal, ecofeminist, and multispecies ecopolitics."[105]

In the remainder of this chapter, we will see how, according to Emanuele Coccia, we need to become aware that "(the) Earth" and the beings that populate it do not exist in isolation from what surrounds and encapsulates them on a cosmic scale: the air and the atmosphere, the stars and the sun. With Braidotti and Luisetti, we left anthropogenic biopolitics for new radically materialist and inclusive political ecologies, but with Coccia, we take off far beyond geocentrism for a radical *cosmo*political posthumanism.

## "The Earth is Not a Home": Coccia's Cosmopolitics

Coccia calls for a new political ecology that would allow us not so much to sustainably inhabit the Earth but that would let us "inhabit every non-human entity."[106] It would allow in and let ourselves be undone by a multitude of different perspectives. "All animals, plants, fungi, and viruses will appear to us as subjective entities, lifeforms, and perspectives on the world; rocks, mountains, hills, wind, rain, storms, seas, and rivers will open up as spaces of subjective play and existence."[107] Much like Luisetti, Coccia proposes an ecology of all forms of existence, living as well as non-living, and the often alien worlds they allow us to participate in. Our thought should be "the playground of all the elements of Earth."[108] For Coccia, the inclusion in our political thinking of *all* the elements necessitates a critique of a lingering *geocentrism* in environmental thought and political ecology. In *The Life of Plants: A Metaphysics of Mixture*, Coccia insists that "geocentrism is the delusion of false immanence: there is no autonomous Earth."[109] Just as biopolitics risks regressing into biocentrism, the new emphasis on geopower narrows down our political and philosophical vision to what lies beneath us. In fact, Coccia claims, "we should stop calling our planet 'Earth.'"[110] The proper name "Earth" flattens the boundless multiplicity of living and non-living beings it contains. It also obscures Earth's fundamental relation to what lays outside its surface, from the atmosphere that envelops it to the Sun. Without both, the Earth would effectively be nothing but a lifeless rock. If the Anthropocene forces us to observe our planet, but also its climate, atmosphere, and place among the stars as a complex whole, "Earth" and its derivatives, like "Gaia," may only be partial names. These terms privilege *geo-* over *atmos*, ground and soil over air. Coccia objects to the term "Earth," as it "suggests that the planet is primarily soil, the lithosphere, which is equivalent to saying that we define our identity by our feet … We could have chosen other organs and the world would have had a different face, a different name."[111] For Coccia, naming the pluriverse is *the* political task for today, even if this task is seemingly impossible. Political action depends on a shared reference, but this does not mean that the reference has to be a monolith of sorts. We have to redefine our planet "in the sense of a space in which everything—plants, animals, lichens, fungi, stones, winds, clouds, etc.—is perceived as an actor, as capable of acting, as a subject."[112]

In *Metamorphosis*, Coccia urges us to abandon the image, as comforting as it may be, of Earth as our "home." Geopower is ultimately still rooted in the tangible materiality of our environment, which requires this imaginary of planetary homeliness to exert power over the Earth. Who gets to own this land, this rock, this house made of stones? Who gets to call this soil their "home"? The idea of Earth as our "common home" perpetuates geopower rather than weakening it. It is precisely the chimera of "home" that "structures our political experience" and "defines the way in which we continue to think about the relationship between living beings, and between living beings and the space that surrounds them."[113] Coccia reminds us that the Greek term *oikos* [home] is at the root of not only *ecology* but also *economy*. The Greek *oikonomia* refers to "laws of the household" that Greek families, headed by the father of the household, were supposed to obey in order to secure their material sustenance. Political ecology, according to Coccia, tends to regard the planet itself as a household subject to human government. For ecological thought, "the biological world is structured like the most basic social order that obtains between humans: the household."[114] Yet Coccia sees at least two major political implications of turning Earth into a home, ecology into economy. First, "home" suggests familiarity that prefers sameness over difference, "a childish nostalgia for the idea of nature as an immense, natural, welcoming, benevolent home, a family where there are only sisters, brothers, fathers, friends, and never any real strangers."[115] In this sense, the geocentric notion of Earth as a shelter, cave or home, wheels anthropocentrism back in.

Second, if nature is akin to a household, it becomes "a system within which everything and everyone must have a meaning and a function. Everything in this economy is defined according to its utility."[116] The imaginary of a common *oikos* suggests that the non-human world must be managed. The image of the household imposes a sense of ownership and hierarchy as well as a demand for utility and productivity of the non-human world as a resource for humans. According to Coccia, the domestic paradigm has resulted in a colossal, ironic double-bind. "In trying to safeguard the non-human, ecology has ended up as one of the world's greatest agencies for the anthropomorphizing and humanization of the non-human. Thanks to ecology, the world is like an immense allotment garden where all life forms politely respect the boundaries."[117] As long as we cling to the image of Earth-as-home, "political ecology" remains an oxymoron. If *politics* means conflict and contestation, *ecology* means stagnation, order, and invisible guiding hands.[118] Ecology-as-economy assumes there is some kind of natural balance of planetary ecosystems that we must restore and govern like a good father. But what if such equilibria do not really exist and there is nothing but human and non-human entities mutually affecting each other in beneficial *and* destructive ways with no pre-ordained balance in sight? Even Darwinian evolution draws on the image of home as natural selection steers species' strategies of finding the milieu they can inhabit as a home. The competition among all that lives optimizes strategies of adaptation: evolutionary struggle is "a ruse to make the great House yet more powerful and robust than ever."[119] Yet, as Coccia affirms, "ecology is impossible, because nothing can ever remain in place: beings never have a home, and no place will ever be a home for a single owner."[120] A true political ecology would imply a radically new relation to the spaces we inhabit and in which we dwell. This relationship cannot be geophilic or -centered, and it must withstand the allure of the home. In fact, for Coccia, such a political ecology is more readily accessible to us than philosophy, ecology, and politics have made us think:

All living beings make their relationship to space a means of metamorphosing themselves and the world they inhabit. Settling in a place means transforming it: a house is only a scar left by some metamorphosis of the world that we have forgotten. Any relationship of prolonged and frequent use of a place and the beings that live there entails a profound change in its nature. Every dwelling is a twofold invasion: we invade the space we inhabit and that space invades us.[121]

Like Braidotti and Luisetti, Coccia proposes a political ecology that actualizes a mode of being that was ours all along. All beings, living and non-living, are engaged in a relentless process of *heterogenesis*: they are mutually affected and transformed, brought into being time and again by their living and non-living environments. Once more, we are continuously undone and remade by whatever surrounds us and co-exists with us. Rather than being a ground in which a hierarchy of beings is anchored and a home in which this hierarchy is managed. "*Planet Earth is nothing but the life of metamorphosis*, the drift of all living things: its nature is such that everything must change places and every place must change its contents," as "metamorphosis operates against all houses."[122] Central to Coccia's thought is the idea that "every metamorphosis is evidence of the relationship between disparate forms that defines the being of every living thing. This relationship is not something that lies outside our bodies. It is their very physiology."[123] Every single being is animated by metamorphic forces. The stone is polished by the river, human beings transform the stone into a tool that transforms the tree into a plough, the land they plough becomes the domain of a variety of vegetable and animal life, domesticated or otherwise. All these forms are transformed by one another, engaging one another in a never-ceasing process of shared world-making. "Each species relates to others as an architect of the world,"[124] Coccia writes.

A new Leviathan would not be composed exclusively of human bodies nor would it take the shape of a human body. Today's body politics is a metamorphic web of stones, fungi, bacteria, moss, clouds, swamps, glaciers, crops, cows, and lice, all outnumbering by far any recognizable human shape.[125] To accept metamorphosis as the driving principle of any ecology is to make ecology truly political in the sense that it now becomes *a matter of collective world-making*, of the project, intentional or not, for the modification of other beings.[126] There can be no natural hierarchy, equilibrium, or "sustainability," as the world is built and rebuilt over and again by and for infinitely different species and geobodies. "This is why relations with the world are never simply physical or natural, but always political," Coccia writes. "For each species, being in the world means living in space designed and built by others. To live is therefore always to occupy, to invade a foreign space and to negotiate what a shared space could be."[127]

Coccia strongly opposes the idea that there is something like a *soil* or a territory in which one may take *roots*, an idea that has determined much of modern political history with all its human and non-human catastrophes. No living being can claim a territory as its own, and any soil is a living soil, always already occupied by an infinity of other species. Any territory is always already populated and sculpted by geobodies. "The soil then ceases to be an autonomous reality," Coccia claims.[128] Moreover, in *The Life of Plants*, Coccia puts forward an equally subversive concept of "roots" that has far-reaching implications for the political use of this term, still eagerly tossed around these days by populist and nativist political fractions. We have never truly grasped the significance of roots from the perspective of vegetative life itself. While the metaphor of roots is ubiquitous in politics, nobody really bothers with investigating what roots can do. Roots are not unidirectional, solely directed downwards toward the soil beneath our feet, like some kind of foundation. On the contrary, Coccia argues that roots are mediators, connectors between worlds, conductors for metamorphosis. Contrary to the imagery of political modernity, roots are the marker of *hybridity* and not of belonging of any kind. "Thanks to its roots, the vascular plant, alone among all living organisms, inhabits simultaneously two environments that are radically different in their texture, structure, and organization and in the nature of the life that inhabits them: earth and air, sun and sky."[129] The political lesson to be learned from attentively studying plants and their roots is that life—including that of the human *zōon politikon*— is "never cloistered in a single environment, but it radiates through all environments."[130] Roots act as cosmic mediators: they connect radically different environments, like earth and sky or soil and sun. Roots coalesce these elements into a world, "a *cosmos* whose unity is atmospheric."[131]

With Coccia, crucially, we leave Earth behind as the sole carrier for politics. The plant is living proof of the "synergistic communion" of all forms of life and non-life. From nourishing minerals in our soil to the animals that eat them to the air we breathe, plants process, alternate, produce, and ultimately reunite all of these things into a thick living web. "Already in the body of the plant, everything is in everything," Coccia affirms, "the sky is in the Earth, the Earth is pushed toward the sky, the air makes itself body and extension, and extension is nothing but an atmospheric laboratory."[132] Coccia proposes a *cosmo*politics that exceeds and includes both *bio-* and geopolitics insofar as he sees not only an interdependence between all life-forms, or between life and non-life, but also how these are dependent on what exceeds the surface of our planet: the atmosphere, the Sun, the cosmic matter that constitutes everything.[133] The emblem for Coccia's cosmopolitics is neither Gaia nor the procession of earth-beings, but a radically re-imagined root:

> The root is what allows plants to implicate in this cosmic mediation the Earth, in its planetary dimension. If the Earth rotates physically around the Sun, it is in plants and thanks to them that this connection produces life and matter, which always exists in new forms. Plants are the metaphysical transfiguration of the rotation of the planet around the Sun, the step that transforms a purely mechanical phenomenon into a metaphysical event.[134]

Coccia's new radical ecology opposes the delusion of geocentrism: the Earth was never autonomous, life was never autarchical.[135] Plants teach us that the Earth was never separable from other celestial bodies, least of all from the Sun. All life emerges from the highly complex dynamic between cosmic matter, the energy radiated by our nearest star, with the atmosphere acting as a membrane between the Earth and the cosmos. "The core of our world is not a stable point, forever frozen,"[136] Coccia states. At the same time, if our entire world results from this dynamic, there is a material continuity between the Earth, with all its earth-beings and life-forms, and the rest of the cosmos.[137] Coccia explains how, every time we feed ourselves with plants, we feed ourselves with the processed energy of the Sun. In this light—the bright and nourishing light of the Sun—"the human world is not the exception in a nonhuman universe; our existence, our gestures, our culture, our language, our appearances are celestial."[138] A politics of the Anthropocene, Coccia urges us, should look both up toward the stars in the sky and below our feet to what continuously connects them. A cosmopolitics for the Anthropocene, therefore, will be light-years from bio- and geopolitics.

In this chapter, we argued how Agamben's and Esposito's conceptions of biopolitics contain openings toward a posthuman *bio*politics. We also noted how Braidotti proposes a radically horizontal *zōè*politics, which found itself including non-living geobodies in Luisetti, and expanded well beyond earth as its dwelling place in Coccia's *cosmo*politics. As we mentioned in the introduction to this chapter, the point is not so much to read Agamben and Esposito as representatives of "canonical" Italian biopolitical thought against Braidotti, Luisetti, and Coccia but rather to read all of them critically and in dialogue. It is from the affirmative political ecologies and ontologies of the latter three that we can discern openings toward a posthuman biopolitics in Agamben and Esposito as well; in turn, Agamben and Esposito may show that the workings of human biopower cannot be so easily overruled by affirming the primacy of all living and non-living matter. The Chthulu may well prove to be a new Leviathan.

# 3 THE GENERAL INTELLECT: THE DIGITALIZATION OF WORK AS CLASS STRUGGLE

## Chapter Summary

New digital technologies are continuously transforming the workplace. Today, artificial intelligence (AI) and algorithmic management in sectors like platform work are causing major social upheavals. Companies like Uber, Deliveroo and Amazon increasingly use technological innovations to unilaterally determine the future of work. In the 1960s, workerist Marxists already revived Marx' *Grundrisse* and his reflections on the so-called "general intellect" to conceptualize the role of technology in class struggle. According to Marx, capital invests in technological development to extract workers' collective intelligence from living labor and embody it in machines privately owned and operated by capital itself. Across multiple generations, the tradition of workerist and post-workerist Marxism has fruitfully used the concept of general intellect to theorize contemporary developments in the workplace. Today, AI and algorithmic management are performing a mental subsumption process, i.e., an integration of the human mind itself in the automatisms of an online network at the service of capital accumulation. However, while reflections on the general intellect often lead to pessimistic conclusions about the automation of human intelligence itself, they also point to moments of resistance and renewed worker autonomy. By reappropriating the general intellect, workers can repurpose all this computing power to serve their own needs and ends.

Domingo was a gig worker for Uber, driving around Los Angeles in 2023.[1] One night, the app promised him a $100 bonus if he completed ninety-six rides. At ninety-five rides, he decided to keep driving for the bonus but … it took 45 minutes to receive a new request. There were enough customers looking for Ubers, but none of these orders went to Domingo. The platform's algorithm had kept him driving for as long as possible to boost its supply of available drivers. It had calculated the odds that drivers like Domingo would log off despite the promised reward, and the outcome was to keep him waiting to extract more value out of their availability. Algorithmic management constitutes what Matteo Pasquinelli has called "the eye of the master," a technological infrastructure that absorbs information about workers' habits and social conducts in order to better subject them to capitalist surveillance.[2] However, Uber's use of new platform technologies to undermine workers' interests and render them dependent on the fickle decision-making of an app is not unique. The digitalization of work has generally been a Big Tech strategy to reconfigure power relations in the workplace in their favor.[3] AI threatens to automate people out of their jobs, GPS-enhanced tracking perfects managerial control over increasingly mobile workforces, and digital rating and review systems grant consumers unchecked power to make or break precarious workers' careers. As Karl Marx wrote in the first volume of *Capital*, "it would be possible to write quite a history of the inventions, made since 1830, for the sole purpose of supplying capital with weapons against the revolts of the working class."[4] Introducing new workplace technologies is a common strategy for capital to increase its power over the labor process, but it is also a stake in a class struggle for control over this process. Workers are not passive victims of technology-induced power grabs. They fight back by breaking the machines, evading managerial control, and reappropriating power over workplace technologies from their bosses.

The centrality of class struggle within the workplace over technological changes forms a key insight of 1960's workerist Marxism. In a 1964 issue of the *Quaderni rossi* journal, Raniero Panzieri and Renato Solmi translated and published a section from Marx's *Grundrisse* that they tentatively called "The Fragment on Machines."[5] In those pages, Marx took the concept of "general intellect" from British political economist William

Thompson to denote how workers' collective knowledge about their labor was being subsumed under managerial control via factory technologies.[6] By putting industrial machines in control over the labor process, skills-based human intelligence was increasingly transferred to machines, rendering it redundant among workers. Why hire expensive craftsmen if the technological precursors to the assembly-line could centralize the coordinative know-how of the labor process in the hands of managers and engineers while putting the execution of the production process in the hands of deskilled and cheap workers? The self-propelling general intellect of the machinic factory system subsumed and determined every single gesture of the human body until workers were reduced to mere "living accessories" for automated production processes. By separating the intellectual work of coordinating the labor process from the manual execution of labor, capital managed to concentrate power in its own machines while reducing workers to mere cogs in a system beyond their control.[7] Highly specialized artisanal workers with the bargaining power to resist capitalist control could subsequently be fired and replaced by a deskilled industrial reserve army eager for employment at any cost.

The fragment constitutes a hallmark text for multiple generations of Italian Marxists. As Virno writes,

> Often in westerns the hero, when faced by the most concrete of dilemmas, cites a passage from the Old Testament … This is how Karl Marx's 'Fragment on machines' has been read and cited from the early 1960s onwards. We have referred back many times to these pages … in order to make some sense out of the unprecedented quality of workers' strikes, of the introduction of robots into the assembly lines and computers into the offices, and of certain kinds of youth behavior. The history of the Fragment's successive interpretations is a history of crises and of new beginnings.[8]

Through critical readings of Marx's "Fragment on Machines," Italian post-workerists today show that the power relations animating the digitalization of work are not too dissimilar from the impact of then-novel industrial technology in the nineteenth century. However, post-workerists' preference for Marx's "Fragment on Machines" does not just derive from the desire to unravel the insidious forces of the twenty-first-century workplace. In contrast to Marx's pessimistic account of the machinery question in *Capital*, the *Grundrisse* brings a surprisingly optimistic message. Marx does not solely describe workplace technologies as weapons against the revolts of the working class. They also represent an emancipatory potential, once workers succeed in reappropriating the general intellect. If the working class seizes the means of production, they can redesign capitalist technologies to, among other things support non-alienating working conditions or even automate unpleasant work and increase free time for all. For Marx, the increasing automation of the production process constituted not only a catastrophic abstraction of living labor but also a political opportunity. The general intellect could become a force of liberation, a thought that became central to (post-) workerist imaginary of "new beginnings."[9] As Negri and Hardt write, "biopolitical weapons, such as digital algorithms, might in fact be the most important focus of contemporary struggle."[10]

But to uncover the emancipatory potential of digital technologies, we must first move through the purgatory of technological dispossession. Digitalization, algorithmic management, and AI herald a new stage in the so-called subsumption of labor under capital. Living labor's capacity for self-direction and wealth-generation becomes increasingly integrated in the capitalist accumulation process, and machines are crucial tools for the absorption of these potentialities into the capitalist production system. While Marx studied the transition from "formal" to "real" subsumption, meaning that nineteenth-century industrialization moved from putting not just the product of labor but also the labor process itself under capital's ownership and control, Italian post-workerists study digital algorithms as tools for "mental subsumption."[11] As Pasquinelli observes, digitalization develops "an extensive algorithmic modelling of collective knowledge, a social calculus that aims to encode individual behaviors, community life, and cultural heritage under the form of vast architectures of statistical correlations."[12] Human thought itself becomes a closely coordinated vehicle for capital accumulation once it is mined for data. In the nineteenth century, the general intellect subsumed workers' *manual* labor in the factory's machinic systems, but their mental life evaded capitalist control. Workers could think about whatever they pleased, as long as their bodies performed the movements the assembly-line required. With contemporary algorithmic management, however, workers' inner psychology becomes a direct target of capitalist control. The subsumption of living labor under capital has reached a new stage in which the human subconscious mind has become a living accessory to the self-accumulation process of capital. Labor platforms like Uber use psycho-medical research about workers' psychological biases to subtly nudge human behavior in favor of the platform's business model.[13] By designing an interface that mimics a video game, for instance, where you can win symbolic tokens for completing tasks, workers are surreptitiously seduced to work harder and longer than they might have originally intended. Even the mere presence of push notifications whenever new tasks appear shows how digital platforms have conditioned the mind into being permanently available for work.[14] On the other hand, mental subsumption under capital could also spark a liberating potential. As theorists such as Lazzarato and Negri ceaselessly argue, capital is now directly dependent on human mental input for its continued survival. If workers' minds resist or are even merely exhausted from constant overstimulation, it threatens the sustainability of capital itself. If the accumulation of capital halts at the refractory minds of platform workers, opportunities for resistance emerge. From these moments, the image emerges of a digital general intellect under democratic control.

## The Becoming-Rent of Profit

Workerists like Panzieri and Romano Alquati popularized the use of Marx's concept of general intellect in the 1960s. They mainly critiqued factory technologies and Taylorist management techniques as threats to working-class autonomy. They repeated Marx's analysis of the real subsumption of labor under capital but applied it to the new production methods of Fordist capitalism. Capital deployed workplace machinery to not only appropriate the products of human labor but also to intervene in and restructure the labor process itself to make labor more productive for capital. Workerists, however, advocated workers to use the hidden affordances of factory technologies to fight back against capital. In their view, not the USSR or China but the high-tech factories of Fiat were at the forefront of socialist activism. They had witnessed a mass migration of impoverished and precarious workers from the Italian South to the factories in Turin, Milan, and Venice, who were not unionized or represented by the mainstream left-wing political parties. These workers felt frustrated with the factory discipline imposed through assembly-line production methods but had few available channels to protest their unfair treatment. Instead, they turned to a hidden transcript of tactics like sabotage, absenteeism, and subversive factory slowdowns to reclaim their autonomy.[15] Workerists applauded these tactics of resistance as first steps toward the takeover of the production process and its technological infrastructure itself.[16] If workers could, through their own grassroots self-organization, appropriate control over the assembly line and its rhythm, then they could also displace management entirely and run the factory autonomously.

In the 1990s and 2000s, the original workerists and a younger generation of post-workerist thinkers, like Lazzarato, Carlo Vercellone, and Yann Moulier-Boutang, rekindled 1960s reflections on the general intellect to study the advent of immaterial labor and cognitive capitalism.[17] At first, they did not have in mind algorithmic management, digital platforms, or AI, as these only rose to prominence in the 2010s–20s. Nonetheless, the post-workerists theorized the first instances of the digitalization of work already in these earlier decades, taking their cue from computerized just-in-time production methods and the techno-scientific knowledge economy. They moved the application of Marx's theory out of the factories by arguing that the extra-economic human lifeworld—human cognition, linguistic interaction, and affective bonding—were becoming new direct sources of economic value. Today, generative AI software like ChatGPT illustrates this development in its most extreme form by using vast swathes of online written language as training data for its own algorithms, but already in the 2010s the dominance of digital platforms showed us what was to come. Digital platforms are online spaces where algorithms rearrange human interactions according to the economic model of supply and demand.[18] While people usually cultivate friendships, for instance, in the offline world, via vernacular practices like meeting for dinner at someone's house or going out together, social media platforms integrate these social interactions in a virtual space governed by its own proprietary algorithms that determine how these friendships are given shape. Facebook's algorithm, for example, collects data about people's online habits to curate a newsfeed of messages especially designed to cater to the demands of every single social media user. To generate profits from this service, Facebook incorporates advertisement space into the newsfeed and auctions off this space to external companies wishing to target specific audiences.[19] This development gives new meaning to Marx's notion of real subsumption: not only do technologies intervene in the labor process to steer employed workers' actions in ways that increase capitalist profit-making, digital platforms like social media intervene in individuals' free time to stimulate them to produce more valuable personal data for Big Tech companies. Not only our working time but also our leisure activities have been subsumed under capitalist control.

Labor platforms like Uber, Deliveroo, or Airbnb have a slightly more complicated business model than social media: they do not only curate online socialization tools but also connect supply and demand in a labor market. Some city dwellers are looking for a taxi ride, while others are looking for a driving gig, so Uber's algorithm matches the demand for rides to a supply of workers. Consumers and workers are thereby integrated into a network of information streams governed through Uber's algorithms, the new shape of the general intellect. By gathering and analyzing masses of data about people's riding habits, these algorithms calculate the most economically efficient manner of coordinating supply and demand in the market for taxi rides. While individuals used to hail taxis haphazardly through physical proximity— by walking down the street and raising their hand or by calling another human being in charge of dispatching—people now log in to an app that algorithmically rationalizes their coordination without embodied interaction. As Bifo writes, "labor has lost any residual materiality and concreteness, and the productive activity only exerts its powers on what is left: symbolic abstractions, bytes and digits, the different information elaborated by productive activity."[20] Of course, Uber drivers and other platform workers still perform physical labor, and customers are still flesh and blood living beings, but the coordination of the labor process involves less these embodied encounters and more the manipulation of the digitalized abstractions that manage these embodied encounters. Uber's algorithm first reduces embodied individuals to online profiles with anonymized data points and then guides them across the urban landscape with the help of push notifications, GPS-location software, and monetary incentives. The general intellect of Uber's algorithmic software coordinates via the analysis and manipulation of data points in real-time, a fleet of drivers according to the swings and sways of the urban transportation market. From the standpoint of the platform, the workers only exist as pieces of information ready to be algorithmically steered into the direction that maximizes Uber's earnings. This grid of connectivity abstracts from workers' concrete bodies, recomposing them into disassembled time fragments that can be coordinated at will depending on where market demand is coming from. According to Bifo, "the worker no longer exists as a person. He or she is only an interchangeable producer of micro-fragments … that enter into the continuous flux of the net."[21] Bifo even explicitly identifies the mobile phone as the ideal tool for this fragmentation of concrete workers into abstract data points that the corporate general intellect can algorithmically coordinate at will. He argues that, thanks to everyone having a smartphone, companies no longer need to hire workers for at least eight hours a day, because now they can just design an app that sends micro-jobs whenever the market demands them. Platform companies like Uber prefer not to hire workers as employees because then they would have to pay them wages also for the time no consumer requests come in. Hence they prefer to identify workers as independent contractors, who receive one-task contracts whenever the app registers consumer requests. Thanks to the availability of the smartphone, "capital no longer recruits people, but buys packets of time, separated from their interchangeable and occasional bearers."[22]

However, platform companies not only deploy technological interferences in the labor process to increase workers' productivity but also to extract personal data from human interactions. Stimulating productivity at low labor costs is a central task of algorithmic management. That was already illustrated in the case of Domingo in the introduction, but, for instance, digital ratings and reviews also serve to render platform workers more productive. Drivers are encouraged to work harder and offer extra benefits to customers in order to acquire good ratings and reviews. Since the algorithm distributes tasks according to these ratings, any negative evaluation results in fewer future earnings. Algorithmic surveillance thereby directly ties workers' income opportunities to their voluntary servitude to the Uber business model. But, secondly, labor platforms like Uber also generate revenue from amassing ownership over an online infrastructure and database. Like social media companies, Uber also sells targeted advertising space to other companies, and it leverages its ownership over data concerning people's transportation habits to generate rent elsewhere. This data, in turn, is used to minimize the role of labor: Uber has famously invested in self-driving car technology.[23] By extracting knowledge about workers' driving habits as training data for AI machine-learning algorithms, Uber had attempted to get a first claim on self-driving cars. If the latter ever became the norm, Uber would have had the first initiative to monopolize this sector. With its extensive database for instructing self-driving car technology, no other company would have been able to compete with

Uber. Drivers are, in other words, not only creating revenue directly through their job performance but also indirectly by generating a database of collective human intelligence owned and operated by Uber, with which the latter expands its hold over social life from urban transportation to all car-based transportation.

A major debate among post-workerists concerns how to theorize platform companies' techniques of exploitation on the side of data production. While the algorithmic techniques of real subsumption in platform workers' labor process align with the classical Marxist theory of exploitation, how the capture and accumulation of people's personal data exploits platform users is more mysterious. Terranova has pushed for the so-called free-labor thesis, which interprets the production and expropriation of personal data as analogous to workplace exploitation.[24] Traditional factory workers, according to Marx, are exploited insofar as they do not receive in wages the full value of their labor-power during the commodity production process. A capitalist manufacturer of shoes, for example, might extract a certain quantity of surplus value from the production of shoes by establishing labor contracts with workers that offer wages at subsistence levels, even if the value of the shoes these workers produce is much higher than the workers need to reproduce their own bare life. According to Terranova, social media users produce personal data, but when they sign the terms and conditions of social media platforms, they sign away all ownership over these data without receiving any wage at all in return. The production of personal data on digital platforms hence constitutes free labor.

But does this approach adequately describe what takes place in the process of data production and expropriation?[25] Terranova, for example, identifies this process as one that ends in selling the commodity of data to advertisers, but companies like Facebook, Amazon, or Uber rarely sell any of their data. Their profit model is rather focused on the exclusive ownership of their own curated databases, which they do not wish to share with other companies. Instead of selling personal data, they prefer to auction off advertising space. Facebook, for example, leverages exclusive ownership over a unique database of consumer information to charge other companies rent for access to targeted consumer markets. British political economist Brett Christophers makes a helpful comparison between social media and shopping malls: a shopping mall does not "sell customers" to shops, but it rents out space in an area where it guarantees significant consumer traffic, increasing shops' chances of attracting potential customers.[26] In the same way, social media companies make money from licensing advert space in online areas with lots of consumer traffic. Labor platforms like Uber similarly not only use algorithmic management techniques to make individuals work harder and faster but also use their exclusive ownership over a database as a rent-seeking opportunity. They rarely sell data about their users, but they own a digital network to which people need access for acquiring social goods, like transportation, and charge rent to whomever wants access to these consumer markets. Uber licenses this access by charging a fee for every transaction conducted on its platform, similarly to how a shopping mall could ask shops to pay a fee every time they sold something.

Carlo Vercellone has therefore turned to Marx's theory of rent extraction rather than traditional exploitation to make sense of Big Tech's business model.[27] He calls this hypothesis the "becoming-rent of profit." Big Tech companies do not directly mobilize human labor-power to produce commodities they can sell at a profit. They rather build a technological infrastructure that responds to social needs and over which they have sole ownership. Whenever people look for friendship, Facebook offers a platform through which they can connect with friends; whenever people need a taxi ride, Uber offers an infrastructure that matches them to a driver; whenever people go on holiday, Airbnb and Booking.com offer curated lists of lodgings ready to be booked. Ideally, platform companies monopolize all traffic in a particular social activity so that they become the sole mediator of that particular service. Once such a monopoly is established, platform companies use people's dependence on their mediating role to extract more personal data from them, and they demand rent from other companies wishing to access these potential consumer audiences, as when Facebook auctions off advertising space or Uber rents out its database of workers' driving know-how to companies that design self-driving cars. Platform companies produce value from claiming ownership over a potentially abundant resource—people's social relations and desires—and renting it out for profit. Surplus value comes not from the unequal exchange between labor-power and the wage but through the exclusive ownership of data assets and the renting out of digital infrastructure on the basis of these assets. As Javier Moreno Zacarés writes, "accumulation is now less about *making anything* and more about simply *owning something*" to which others need access.[28] Big Tech's profit model is, in fact, a rent-extraction model.

# The Mental Subsumption of Social Conduct

The digitalization of work and human social conduct in general has significant consequences for the form and impact of the general intellect. Post-workerists no longer use the term to refer to the assembly-line machinery of large-scale industry but to the digital communicative networks that support cognitive capitalism and the becoming-rent of profit. Marx's general intellect was physically located in the workplace, and workers had to gather at its sites to generate surplus value by physically operating machinery. The business model of many platform companies hinges not on employing workers at a particular site and exploiting their labor like a traditional employer does but on owning and expanding an ephemeral general intellect, an assemblage of codes that coordinate human interactions online and extract valuable data from these interactions. This ephemeral general intellect still has geographical anchoring in data centers and computing hardware, but these are usually invisible to workers that interact only with virtual traces of this hardware inscribed on their smartphone screens. From the perspective of Italian post-workerism, the technological infrastructures that absorb human knowledge to better coordinate the production of economic value have shifted from the realm of manual labor in the factory to data centers in remote places that gather and process digitized information streams. With theorists such as Lazzarato and Bifo we may claim that, as a platform, Uber owns and operates a general intellect derived from drivers' and customers' personal data with which they can establish ride-hailing services in any city across the globe without ever physically moving there. Its success is built on the technological capacity to translate people's transportation habits in a data-driven coordinative network for ride-hailing services. By monopolizing the general intellect that operates these digital networks, corporations like Uber turn ownership of the general intellect itself into a business model.

Bifo theorizes this shift as a move from real to mental subsumption: human thought itself becomes a direct object of control for capital via the digital technologies that manipulate our deepest desires and vulnerably exposed brains. "Automation today is invading the very sphere of cognition (memory, learning, and decision), so paving the way for the ultimate form of subsumption … Power at this point takes the form of biopower, as it is embodied in the neurofabric of social life itself."[29] Nineteenth-century factory workers were subjected to meticulous disciplinary control over their bodily movements, but their minds were usually off limits. The assembly line disciplined workers' bodies but left their thoughts untouched. Under conditions of mental subsumption, however, the mind itself becomes an object of control. Addictive interfaces, constant push notifications, and opaque algorithmic decision-making wire the human brain directly into a digital general intellect that connects a worldwide web of networks. This process entails, first, technological devices adapting to the human mind and its psychological biases to maximize data extraction. Facebook software engineers invented the Like button, for example, in order to better track users' interests and desires by offering a button that translates these inner thoughts into outwardly traceable behavior.[30] Second, human beings must also adapt their behavior in order to generate legible input for their digital devices. They must train their fingers for text messaging, unlearn their local dialects and accents to activate speech recognition software and fit their political opinions into 140-character slogans to debate politics on X. According to Bifo, power takes the form of techno-linguistic automatisms, i.e., human conduct and machinic operations become so intertwined that they constitute self-propelling automatisms coordinated through algorithmic control.

In the words of Italian philosopher of technology Luciano Floridi, the distinction between offline and online experiences is in the process of being suspended. Techno-linguistic automatisms produce a general intellect in which human and machinic parts are so deeply interconnected that both can no longer be separated. Human life online and offline blurs into what Floridi calls "onlife experiences."[31] Airbnb hosts, for example, must carefully curate an online profile to attract potential tourists *and* build the offline personality to match it if they wish to receive good ratings and turn their guest room into a profitable side-hustle.[32] The personal identity of any single Airbnb host is thereby distributed across online and offline spaces. The Airbnb host's existence and behavior expresses not only the offline reality of hosting a stranger in one's own home but also the digital realities of an online avatar and the data points Airbnb gathers about this avatar. Airbnb's platform translates offline human encounters into data about hosts' hospitality, friendliness, cleanliness, etc., and compares this data with information about other hosts to determine which lodgings and hosts appear highest on the search engine result lists. Since tourists usually only look at the first few results of a search for lodgings on the

Airbnb website, any negative datapoint can bankrupt an Airbnb host's business. And whenever Airbnb changes the metrics of its rating system or the questionnaire for customer reviews, Airbnb hosts must alter their offline conduct to retain a good online reputation. The onlife experience of hosting an Airbnb lodging thereby seamlessly intertwines digital and non-digital conduct into a hybrid subjectivity. If Airbnb hosts fail to internalize the platform's evaluation norms, bad ratings will push their lodgings down on the company platform until tourists will no longer see these lodgings appear among their search suggestions.

## Resisting Mental Subsumption

Bifo's presentation of the general intellect and mental subsumption is extremely pessimistic, but this apocalyptic approach is not unique in contemporary political theory of technology. Shoshanna Zuboff's *The Age of Surveillance Capitalism* is probably one of the most influential critiques of Big Tech today, and it likewise warns for the complete automation of human conduct in the pursuit of profits. Surveillance capitalism "has taken us from automating information flows about you to automating you."[33] According to Zuboff, Big Tech companies render human conduct legible for data collection and analysis and subsequently deploy "means of behavioral modification" to manipulate these conducts.[34] In more Foucaultian terminology, we could argue that surveillance capitalism performs an algorithmic governmentality or conduct of conducts.[35] The means of behavioral modification are not tools that directly negate subjective freedom or force them to enact any specific command. Airbnb does not force hosts to adapt their profiles, yet it indirectly influences their income streams to nudge them in the appropriate directions. Likewise, Uber leaves drivers the nominal option to refuse certain tasks, yet if drivers want to make a living they must make their "free" choices align with the imperatives network Uber's algorithms advances. Algorithms manipulate the *milieu* or choice architectures in which individual subjects freely determine their own conduct.[36] They also use knowledge about the subconscious dimensions of the human mind to create subtle interventions that indirectly influence people's behavior. Smartphone apps send push notifications not because these *force* individuals to engage with social media, but because the human brain has been psychologically conditioned to automatically respond to its buzzers and lights.[37] The outcome is an algorithmic governmentality of "certainty without terror": Big Tech companies can exactly predict and steer the conduct of populations without the need for direct violent intervention.[38] Subtle subconscious cues influence human desires and subjectification until people have spontaneously internalized the conducts expected of them in the surveillance capitalist business model.

However, an ambiguity haunts Zuboff's portrayal of the techno-linguistic automatisms that subsume and coordinate human conduct. While she starts with arguing that Big Tech merely governs our nominally free human conducts, she concludes that these forms of behavioral modification are so advanced that any space for human freedom is at risk of irredeemably disappearing. Taken to its utmost extreme, mental subsumption reduces human individuals to automated conduits for capital accumulation. Similarly, Bifo sometimes calls the rise of mental subsumption "neuro-totalitarianism" and writes that "individuals cannot resist the capture that occurs when change happens in the field of communicative devices."[39] While such grand statements find an avid audience in the age of doomscrolling, we should still question whether this diagnosis adequately reflects reality. Are Zuboff and Bifo not victims of Silicon Valley's hype machine that overpromises the possibilities of Big Tech in order to attract venture capital and financial investments? Big Tech companies often rent out advertisement space to other companies that want to target specific consumer demographics, but empirical research has often shown that people do not actually click on these ads and are very rarely influenced by them.[40] Are we then truly automated by the Big Tech profit machine at all? Human beings seem very capable of avoiding techno-linguistic automatisms and ignoring the means of behavioral modification. To quote Marx again, the machines of the general intellect "are henceforth an industrial perpetuum mobile that would go on producing forever, did it not meet with certain natural obstructions in *the weak bodies and the strong wills* of its human attendants."[41] Italian workerism and post-workerism continuously stress these residues of human autonomy. As Negri and Hardt profess in *Empire*, "the multitude, in its will to be-against and its desire for liberation, must push through Empire to come out the other side."[42] There is no need for nostalgically reminiscing the good old pre-digital days. The process of mental subsumption enacted by today's general intellect constructs a new terrain for political struggle in which we must merely look for new weapons. Workers impose limits on the general intellect's capacity to accumulate value through algorithmic governmentality insofar as they either organize and resist their subsumption under capital or collapse and burn out under the weight of algorithmic domination. In Pasquinelli's terminology, a "collective counter-intelligence" combats the extraction of human knowledge and sociality.[43] Both tactics of active refusal and exhaustion are pervasive in the digitalized world of work.

Gig workers regularly organize to demand better pay and working conditions. Since 2016 for example, food delivery couriers at, among others, Deliveroo and Uber Eats have regularly organized mass strikes across the UK.[44] In 2014, clickworkers of Amazon Mechanical Turk (AMT) organized on online forums like Reddit to flood Jeff Bezos's email account with complaints about horrible workplace treatment.[45] Previously, Bezos had said in a *Business Insider* interview that he was easily reachable for all his employees at Amazon. However, he must not have counted the Amazon Mechanical Turk workers as his employees, given that the opacity and unaccountability of the algorithmic management techniques governing their labor was a major source of contention among clickworkers. It was almost impossible for workers to reach a human staff member whenever the algorithm made mistakes or blocked payments. AMT workers subsequently organized online and took up Bezos's implicit invitation to flood his account with horror stories from AMT. Such tactics are reminiscent of the activism of the factory workers studied by Italian workerists in the 1960s. Romano Alquati, for example, highlighted the invisible self-organization of workers as a crucial force of working-class resistance.[46] Alquati saw that many factory workers in industrial cities like Turin and Milan were not integrated into official bargaining institutions and trade unions, which made them look like easy targets for capitalist exploitation. However, these workers created their own forms of organization by discussing workplace politics at lunch, at afterwork drinks, in their neighborhood, etc. Invisible solidarities emerged through these informal practices as resources for workplace activism. Workers would, for example, instigate wildcat strikes or sabotage the assembly-line to slow down the production process. Today's platform workers similarly use informal meeting places on the streets or online forums for building political solidarity against digital power.

Unfortunately, platform workers' weak bodies often resist algorithmic control when they can no longer cope with the pressure of constant availability and structural overwork.[47] This is the only form of resistance Bifo is still able to imagine. "Resistance" names then not the organized revolt of the oppressed but a kind of electrical resistance in which human bodies simply fail to channel capital's endless pursuit of surplus value. Mental subsumption overstimulates human beings to such an extent that sheer exhaustion forces the body to resist through simple breakdown. In Bifo's own words, "the human organism cannot take endless chemical euphoria and productive fanaticism: at some point, it begins to surrender. As happens with patients affected by bipolar disorder, euphoria is replaced by long-term depression."[48] Amazon fulfillment centers, for example, have dispensing machines that sell painkillers so people can keep working, but still their bodies are unable to keep up with the working pace, forcing most to stop within a matter of months. Uber drivers also often suffer from sleep deprivation due to constant push notifications, and food couriers regularly die in traffic accidents because algorithmic management pushes them to take risks to get to your door as quickly as possible. As Bifo predicted, the integration of human bodies and minds in algorithmic networks that disregard the biological rhythm of human life leads to contradictions in which workers either revolt or falter. "The coming European insurrection will not be an insurrection of energy, but an insurrection of slowness, withdrawal, and exhaustion."[49] Strong wills and weak bodies constitute the limits to growth for contemporary capitalism.

The theory of labor under algorithmic management should reflect these possibilities of resistance against mental subsumption. While the general intellect might try to reduce workers and their "free choices" to the living appendages of its own machinations, the appendages sometimes revolt in subsumption struggles.[50] The process of subsuming human conduct under the operations of capital is a refractory development with many setbacks and changes in direction. While capital can design technologies as strategic devices for exerting control over human conduct, human collectives can invent insurgent tactics that subvert these strategies and escape their grasp. Labor is a rebellious power that resists its instrumentalization for capital accumulation. Techno-pessimists seemingly forget that human–machine interactions in the onlife experience are usually a two-way street, not a frictionless one-way integration of living labor into the general intellect. Whereas Bifo and Zuboff stress how the general intellect co-opts human conduct into pre-established systems of algorithmic governmentality unilaterally dominated by Big Tech, they fail to describe how individuals evade these tactics of instrumentalization. The governed can resist their subsumption under surveillance capitalism, and they often do. Anytime you do not click on a targeted advertisement, you have successfully resisted mental subsumption.

Lazzarato's theory of subjectification offers a counterweight to the pessimistic account of mental subsumption. In his view, subjectification is a conflictual process in which subjects and the technologies that govern them struggle over the norms and goals of the conduct of conducts. Lazzarato distinguishes between two mechanisms of subjectification that each contain their own form of resistance. First, "social subjection" denotes processes in which meaningful discursive representations are addressed to conscious individuals as interpellations to modify their behavior. So-called signifying semiotics, i.e., languages composed of signifiers linked to meaningful signifieds, construct subjective representations with which individuals identify. Platform companies like Uber, for example, diffuse advertisements that interpellate potential workers as entrepreneurs. With slogans like "Become your own boss," "We believe in doers," or "Uber wants you as a partner," platform companies identify workers as self-possessed entrepreneurs for whom the gig economy presents an empowering opportunity for financial independence.[51] They directly address workers as micro-entrepreneurs with meaningful statements that put forward representations of the self that encourage workers to interpret their real conditions of existence through the lens of entrepreneurship. With Lazzarato we see how, once workers accept this semiotic address, they think and act like one-person businesses. When, for example, revenues go down due to an update of the app's terms and conditions, micro-entrepreneurs do not respond in employee-like fashion, by contacting a union or going on strike. They rather spontaneously react as entrepreneurs, working longer hours or combining multiple apps to boost their income. The ideology of entrepreneurialism offers a repertoire of interpretations and actions with which gig workers constitute their immediate interactions with the world.

Mental subsumption, however, not only influences workers' conscious sense of self but also manipulates the subconscious parameters within which workers make conscious decisions. This perspective aligns with Lazzarato's second mechanism of subjectification, "machinic subjugation." Apart from the circulation of meaningful discourses with which individuals can consciously identify, Lazzarato indicates the prevalence of "asignifying semiotics," languages not meant to communicate conscious representations but to directly intervene in the real. The digital codes constituting the algorithms of Uber's matching process or its rating and review system are not mental representations with which individual workers can identify. The binary system of ones and zeros underlying algorithmic management is a linguistic code that coordinates flows of electricity in digital networks. These signs coordinate flows of information traffic by issuing commands to either stop or continue electrical circuits. They directly impose certain actions on reality without first addressing reflective consciousness. Lazzarato gives the illuminating example of driving a car: the experienced driver sees traffic lights on the street, feels resistance from the gas pedal, hears the horn of cars behind him, and acts quasi-instinctively upon these signals to generate a smooth *agencement* of human and machine elements that cooperatively get the car to drive. These signals do not trigger conscious reflection but quasi-automatic responses. "Often as we drive, we enter 'a state of wakeful dreaming', 'a pseudo-sleep', 'which allows several systems of consciousness to function in parallel, some of which are like running lights, while others shift to the foreground'."[52] Only when an unexpected event disturbs the automatic flow of traffic does conscious reflection re-emerge. The asignifying semiotics of the traffic *dispositif* coordinate the conduct of humans and machines in quasi-instinctive ways. Drivers are so immersed into the activity that the conscious yet slow interpretation of signs becomes redundant. Rather than conscious individual subjects, they act as human elements within the car as a human–machine assemblage.

Nonetheless, Lazzarato uses the notion of machinic subjugation to clarify the workings of the general intellect and algorithmic governmentality.[53] The binary ones and zeros of computer coding are not meaningful representations of a reality outside the code but directives for the passing or cutting of electrical currents. They do not modify reality through individual consciousness but change existence itself by managing flows of electricity, data, ratings and reviews, labor-power, etc. These codes constitute algorithms that subsequently govern the conduct of conducts among human individuals. The algorithms coordinating the work of Uber drivers or Deliveroo couriers employ mathematical formulae as asignifying semiotics to regulate flows of online information and translate these into flows of labor-power in the offline world. From the perspective of the algorithm, workers are not addressed as conscious individuals expected to identify with binary codes. These codes establish worker profiles, however, that structure the income opportunities offered to workers via the platform. If the algorithm spots Airbnb hosts whose customer ratings are dropping or Uber drivers highly likely to wait for any ride offered to them, like Domingo from the opening section, then it will automatically hold back on potential task offers. The general intellect sets up an impersonal government of labor-power operated on asignifying semiotics that first translates workers' performance into data and subsequently coordinates the workforce in turn by analyzing and acting upon these data.

Lazzarato stresses how social subjection and machinic subjugation are dialogic, conflictual processes of subjectification. Explaining the workings of social subjection, Lazzarato highlights the example of former French president Nicolas Sarkozy calling the youth of the Parisian suburbs "scum" [*des racailles*].[54] Sarkozy made this statement as a discursive tactic to distinguish French collective identity from allegedly foreign elements. Sarkozy's listeners were expected to interpret this utterance as a negative definition of Frenchness as not being an immigrant from a poor urban neighborhood. "*La France profonde*" was allegedly composed of white, middle-class, law-abiding families, whereas individuals that failed to conform to this image were relegated to the (non-)identity of "scum." However, the youth from the *banlieues* did not simply accept their relegation to second-rate citizenship status. They heavily protested Sarkozy's statement and his urban policies. They thereby showed their identity as French citizens by participating in national politics and forcefully broadened Sarkozy's limited conception of French identity. While signifying semiotics communicate *attempts* at performatively structuring subjective identities, whether those attempts succeed depends on the reception of these utterances among their audience. One can similarly interpret Bezos's statements in *Business Insider* and the ire it stirred among AMT workers: he praised his accessibility to all Amazon workers, implicitly suggesting that AMT workers were not genuine members of the workforce. Workers subsequently opposed this discursive demarcation of the workforce by actively claiming worker status through their protest.

Lazzarato argues that social subjection is always a dialogic process in which multiple subjects attempt to influence each other's conducts with the representative claims they make. While Bezos relegates AMT workers to second-rate status, these workers reclaim their subjective agency through counter-conducts. Lazzarato stresses that an exclusively linguistic or semiotic perspective on social subjection misses this potential for responsive agency. Every utterance implies the audience's "ethico-political self-positioning": subjects must inevitably articulate their own stance vis-à-vis the representative claims made in signifying semiotics before we know whether social subjection has successfully taken place.[55] Audiences can receive a representative claim and accept it at face value, but they could also reject it or subvert its meaning to something other than what the speaker intended. As Lazzarato argues, "the response is always a self-positioning, a self-affirmation, and it is only through this positioning that one can respond, speak, and express oneself … Every speech act is a 'question' asked of others, oneself, and the world."[56] When Bezos renders the plight of AMT workers invisible, he invites his audience to forget about the shadow work of clickworkers Bezos once called "artificial artificial intelligence."[57] Given the poor working conditions on AMT, it is better for Amazon's marketing to keep this clickwork in the shadows and pretend it is performed by AI, even if there is really human labor hidden inside the machine. But workers, in Lazzarato's perspective, do not have to accept this regime of invisibility. There is always room for deviation from the norms of subjective conduct. The constitution of the self always already entails the subject's capacity to break with the dominant meanings of the ruling signifying semiotics and affirm alternative modes of conduct.

The same applies to labor platforms' techniques of machinic subjugation. While the asignifying semiotics of algorithmic governmentality attempt to steer subjective conducts by mentally subsuming the latter under a data-driven business model, platform workers can always resist this attempt. When Uber offers increasingly low pay through algorithmic wage discrimination, as in Domingo's case, workers can react and contest these mechanisms. They can surreptitiously subvert algorithmic management techniques by "gaming the algorithm." For example, drivers for Amazon Flex, an Amazon subsidiary that allocates Amazon package deliveries to self-employed drivers, are known for fooling Amazon's GPS tracking system by using multiple smartphones. They know they get allotted more tasks if the algorithm identifies their location as close to a distribution center. Workers hence hide extra smartphones in trees close to the center to attract more offers. The nudges and prompts of the general intellect are, at best, invitations for the enactment of particular subjective conducts aligned with platform companies' business model. They regulate a *milieu* in which subjects are immersed in a data-driven assemblage geared toward the production of more data and economic value for labor platforms. However, whether this *milieu* actually succeeds in predetermining subjective conducts depends on the ethico-political self-positionings of workers. Just like platform workers can reject CEOs' signifying semiotics in newspapers, they can obfuscate or evade the asignifying semiotics of algorithmic management through counter-conducts. For example, by confusing the algorithms' geolocation systems, workers resist their instrumentalization at the service of labor platforms. They tactically use the general intellect's operations against the platform itself to pursue their own interests at the platform's expense. Living labor thereby detaches itself from its subordinate role as agent for capital's self-accumulation.

# Toward a Republic of the General Intellect

With Lazzarato, we see how the mental subsumption of living labor under the general intellect is, in fact, a conflictual process. The general intellect instrumentalizes workers' conducts through social subjection and machinic subjugation, while workers retain their autonomy through tactical counter-conducts. Labor platforms use algorithmic management, gamification techniques, or discursive representations of micro-entrepreneurship to align worker desires with algorithmic dynamics, but workers establish individual or collective interventions to keep their desires independent from Big Tech's manipulations. If we want to theorize the potential for a democratization of the general intellect, getting a sense of collective strategies for worker control over digital technologies is vital, as demonstrated by Lazzarato and Bifo. Platform workers have created impromptu social movements to demand better working conditions.[58] The aforementioned UK delivery courier strikes, for example, start in WhatsApp groups workers maintain to share tips and tricks or offer emotional support to each other. But they sometimes grow into extensive social networks for large-scale social protests. While such initiatives are often ephemeral and vanish once political momentum subsides, more formalized institutions have also emerged from these struggles. Indy unions, like the British Independent Workers' Union of Great Britain, have grown through worker struggles, and traditional trade unions have also shifted significant attention to working conditions in the digital gig economy.[59]

Some of these worker-centric initiatives have taken their resistance a step further and have started recoding the general intellect to serve worker interests rather than co-opting their minds to reduce living labor to capital's living appendages.[60] Activists from the 2015 Nuits Debout protests in Paris, for example, decided to combat platform companies directly by creating a cooperative food delivery platform called CoopCycle.[61] Today, it is a global federation of locally owned and managed worker cooperatives with many member organizations. CoopCycle itself has designed the basic protocols for running a food delivery app and grants local cooperatives free access to this software and technical support from its data specialists to adapt the platform to the specific needs of the member organizations. CoopCycle thereby produces a general intellect at the service not of capital accumulation but collective worker self-determination. Workers themselves can decide how their labor is coordinated, how they are paid, and by which standards they are evaluated. Another example is the American platform for collective action called Coworker.org.[62] It rose from the Occupy Wall Street movement as an online tool for workers to propose and deliberate on workplace injustices and demands. By establishing an infrastructure where workers can meet online and discuss workplace politics, Coworker.org facilitates the formation and sustenance of worker collective action. The platform was, for instance, crucial in mobilizing Starbucks workers in the United States, first for smaller actions like dress code updates but later for larger actions like better parental leave. Coworker.org as well constitutes a general intellect, a technological infrastructure, that supports rather than undercutting worker autonomy.

Such initiatives point to an alternative future of work in which the general intellect constitutes a *res publica,* an object of public deliberation. Just like the traditional workerists celebrated the self-organized tactics of factory workers to announce an age of worker self-management, today's post-workerists call for a reappropriation of the digital general intellect. As Virno observes, "the general intellect, or public intellect, if it does not become a republic, a public sphere, a political community, drastically increases forms of submission."[63] If there is no social movement pushing for the democratization of workplace technologies, the latter will be used to reduce living labor into a moment of capital's self-accumulation. Today, capital mostly determines the design and inner workings of the general intellect that manages the workplace. The specific form workplace technologies take hence reflect this politics: these technologies extract economic value from workers and deploy means of behavioral modification to undermine their capacity to autonomously coordinate their own labor. They gather and analyze worker data to more effectively instrumentalize their labor-power. However, establishing the general intellect as a workplace republic implies that workers themselves decide how technologies are designed and operated. There is nothing inherent to these technologies themselves to restrict their services to capital only. As Negri asserts, "the fact that the mathematical models and algorithms are at the service of capital is not a quality of their own, is not a problem of mathematics—it is just a problem of power."[64]

According to Negri, there are also good reasons to retake and recode the technologies of algorithmic management. In his view, algorithms are "nothing more than a machine, a machine that is born from the cooperation of workers and that the bosses then impose over this cooperation."[65] Big Tech's business model depends on the extraction and privatization of personal data about our human social cooperation. Without these data inputs, these algorithms are blind. Uber's algorithm does not know how long it takes to drive any particular route, nor does Airbnb's search engine know which are the most valuable lodgings in a city. They first need to extract this information from human social cooperation in the form of data in order to train the algorithms to make effective decisions. The value of Big Tech's general intellect is, in other words, derived from the privatization of social cooperation as data. The business model of these firms depends on translating personal sociality into actionable information that can be used against workers' interests to maximize profits generated from their labor-power. Pasquinelli has called this observation the "labor theory of machines": the machinic assemblages that manage the workplace are mostly objectifications of workers' labor and know-how in mechanical or digital form.[66] Just like twentieth-century Taylorism first documented workers' actions in the factory to subsequently construct assembly lines that dispossessed workers of their firsthand knowledge to grant management more control, today's digital devices extract workers' knowledge about their jobs into data to algorithmically control their labor. Negri and Hardt argue that "the primary role in the social organization of production tends to be played by the living knowledges embodied in and mobilized by labor rather than the dead knowledges deployed by management and management science."[67] Living labor produces data, and the latter constitute a general intellect under capitalist control, alienated from its original makers. However, if human social cooperation is the source of the economic value embodied in the general intellect, then labor ought to retake control over this infrastructure. The algorithms animating the innards of Big Tech are but the mirror reflections of the social interactions that inform these algorithms with actionable data. Without human social cooperation, these algorithms would be empty and decisionless. For the post-workerists, it is high time for workers to reappropriate the general intellect.[68]

However, instituting the general intellect as a democratic republic is no utopian project aimed at delivering the ideal organization of labor once and for all. Democratizing workplace technologies does not put an end to all workplace conflicts or hierarchies, nor does it eliminate all possibilities of algorithmic domination. As Lazzarato stresses, human–machine interactions are dialogic processes in which human and non-human agents form assemblages for common action. These non-human technological elements still retain agency, and this can be used against the interests or desires of workers. Even in an ideal labor platform run as a worker-owned cooperative, algorithms might still make decisions that workers fail to understand or find unfair. The only advantage of the republican general intellect is that it grants workers the right to reform *their* general intellect accordingly. It democratizes the workplace by bringing back together the moments of coordination and execution in the labor process. While the capitalist general intellect expropriates workers of the know-how to organize their own labor in order to empower managers and engineers, the republic of the general intellect puts workers themselves in charge of designing and coordinating the machines that govern their labor.

Nonetheless, technologies are not mere passive conduits for human projects; they offer friction to which humans must adapt as well. There remains an irrepressible ambivalence to the general intellect, leading to conflicts even in democratically run platform cooperatives. Giving subjects power over the technologies that govern their labor also opens up debates about the design and governance of these technologies that reveal conflicts of interests and values within worker collectives. CoopCycle, for example, has experienced fierce debates about the use of motorcycles in food delivery. Because of its environmentalist commitments, CoopCycle wishes to promote the bicycle rather than motorized vehicles, but when South-American cooperatives wanted to join, a rift emerged.[69] The South Americans argued that, in cities like São

Paulo or Buenos Aires, bicycle-driven delivery was not practically feasible, while European cooperatives wanted to stick to the sustainability agenda. The South-American cooperatives eventually refused to join CoopCycle. Such internal rifts display the recurrence of workplace conflicts in the republican general intellect. Whereas previous conflicts took place along a capitalist hierarchical line between the management in control of the general intellect and the workforce subsumed under its operativity, conflicts in the republican general intellect ideally democratize this conflict on an equal playing field. Different groups within the workforce can still deeply disagree about how to govern workplace technologies, but at least they can stage this disagreement among equals rather than one faction occupying the locus of power and subjugating the other to its will.

# 4 CYBERFASCISM: THE ELECTIVE AFFINITY BETWEEN FASCISM AND SOCIAL MEDIA

## Chapter Summary

The far-right has proven itself surprisingly successful in popularizing itself on social media, leading to an upsurge of right-wing populist movements across the globe into the centers of power. We use Italian diagnoses of fascism and the fascist public sphere to explain the success of the far-right and the difficulties for the political left to counter this development. Based on the writings of, among others, Alberto Toscano, Umberto Eco, and Giorgio Agamben, we uncover an elective affinity between so-called "cyberfascism" and the communicative dynamics of social media. Cyberfascism feeds on the negative affects associated with social atomization, and responds to these resentments with promises of fulfillment and community. It offers this feeling of community empowerment by staging plebiscitary rituals in which individuals momentarily experience a sense of belonging through their common submission to a fascist leader. However, fascism never actually empowers individuals to become self-organizing political collectives but rather prefers to keep them submissive to the aforementioned leader. Social media excellently provides a platform for this style of publicity. It likewise assumes the atomization of social crowds and promotes affectively charged messages to keep people glued to their smartphone screens. This business model favors the rise of influencers who manipulate their audiences' affective mood swings to foster a loyal follower base. As Paolo Gerbaudo analyzes, the left has tried to mimic this online strategy with their own brand of influencer-leaders. However, since the left aims to actually empower the people rather than rendering it submissive to authoritarian leadership, these attempts fail to establish long-term hegemonic political formations.

In early March 2024, Donatella Di Cesare commemorated the recently deceased ex-Red Brigades activist Barbara Balzerani, tweeting that they had shared the same revolutionary aspirations, even if their methods diverged dramatically. The Italian far right did not take these words lightly. Di Cesare became the victim of an online smear campaign and disrupted lectures, while politicians tried to revoke her professorship at La Sapienza. Bullying dissenting voices into submission is a common tactic among the far right. By damaging the reputations of their opponents, alt-right activists not only discredit these individuals to mainstream audiences but also generate a chilling effect on others who would otherwise speak up against them. Examples like Di Cesare's predicament show that the public sphere has become a lot scarier since the advent of social media and online clicktivism. Social media platforms originally promised to reinvigorate the global public sphere. They offered opportunities for transnational communication, tools for expanding democratic values and practices across the globe. However, our current everyday reality is an incessant struggle for attention among mortal enemies, where the only winners are platform companies profiting from online traffic. The alt-right war machine is, in this context, a social movement that has adapted to the terrain of online reputation wars in order to establish right-wing hegemony.[1]

While there are ideological similarities between different national iterations of the far-right, it is difficult to identify a "fascist minimum" of ideological elements that all movements allegedly share, *pace* Roger Griffin's standard theory of fascism.[2] The online far right is composed of white supremacists, a resentful manosphere of incels and gaming geeks, edgelord New Atheists, and even trolls without ideological commitment who are there only "for the lulz."[3] Lazzarato calls this patchwork, loosely kept together through the viral dynamics of social media, "cyberfascism."[4] According to Lazzarato, critical theorists often focus too much on the role of technical machines like social media, to explain the far-right politics, downplaying the importance of these movements' political strategies. Technologies only become effective weapons once they are inserted into a war machine. In Lazzarato's view, "Bolsonaro and Trump have utilized all the available technologies of digital communication, but their victory doesn't come from technology."[5] Empirical research as well stresses that popular discourse often overemphasizes the causal influence of social media. It is, for instance, questionable whether YouTube's recommendation algorithm feeds consumers increasingly extreme content, or whether it just channels them to videos with higher production value.[6] Even so-called echo chambers or filter bubbles are quite rare, because algorithmic newsfeed curation regularly pushes the lowest common denominator of mainstream content as well.[7] While it would be preposterous to deny social media's role in mainstreaming the alt-right entirely, blaming social media directly for the radicalization of their users is equally unconvincing. Right-wing influencers cannot simply rely on algorithms doing their bidding. Strategic choices determine whose influence goes viral.

Cyberfascism is, in other words, a strategy to capture online attention and bring it into the orbit of fascist influence. It names a style of establishing public spheres that rivals the traditional liberal public sphere. Cyberfascists generate a war machine that responds to offline affects of disillusionment, anger, and resentment, and mobilizes these affects online to generate viral moments. *What* they specifically say does not matter, as long as their statements successfully *mobilize* online armies of angry individuals, isolated radicals, and trolls. When anti-environmentalists launch an online hate campaign against climate protesters like Greta Thunberg or Extinction Rebellion, they are not interested in rationally deliberating one agenda of environmental policy in favor of another. They use hate speech, alternative facts, and downright bullshitting to mobilize affects of misogyny, resentment toward the educated classes, and fear of being left behind, to push their adversaries out of the online attention market and ultimately the public sphere. The technical machine of social media constitutes the terrain for a struggle for attention, likes and clicks, not a liberal public sphere for the critical exchange of opinions. Successful cyberfascist war machines figure out how to use the features of this terrain to monopolize the attention market. If social media encourage affectively charged posting with snappy and one-sided messaging, then the cyberfascist war machine will produce exactly that to "win the argument" against environmentalists. When done successfully, dominance in the online attention markets helps cyberfascism to mainstream their tactics in the offline world as well.[8] The more people get to see a steady supply of far-right content, the more the Overton Window of mainstream political debate shifts toward the right and marginalizes left-wing perspectives.[9]

In this chapter, we argue that there is an elective affinity between fascism and social media that becomes visible in the formation of a cyberfascist public sphere.[10] Using the interpretations of fascism from Italian post-workerism, Umberto Eco, Alberto Toscano, and Agamben, we claim that fascist public spheres display three key features. They rely on the breakdown of working-class collective institutions and subsequent mass atomization, respond to people's sense of loneliness and disenfranchisement with empty promises of belonging, and foster that belonging by establishing plebiscitary rituals in which individuals become one by swearing allegiance to a common leader. Social media, on the other hand, also rely on mass atomization, possess a business model that intensifies the communication of affectively charged utterances, and they promote social dynamics circling around influencers that mimic the plebiscitary relationships of fascist leadership. These affinities make cyberfascism and social media ideally suited for each other. Social media constitute a unique terrain in which some political tactics operate better than others. According to Michael Hardt, digital media constitute a technological *a priori* that shapes the kinds of online communication that can take place on these media.[11] The technological affordances of social media are particularly apt for the spreading and intensification of a fascist public sphere. If, for example, YouTube promotes content based on clicks, subscriptions, and attention retainment, then videos will go viral that specifically generate clicks, subscriptions, and audience retention. If Reddit generates rapid successions of threads with anonymous posts, it becomes ideal for inventing and spreading conspiracy theories like Pizzagate, where anonymous accounts upvoted attention-grabbing delusions about the US Democrats running a child molestation ring from pizza restaurants.[12] In this context, the infrastructural logic of social media and the political logic of the cyberfascist war machine are exceptionally compatible.

## Mass Atomization Under Neoliberalism

In the 2000s, social media emerged as promising new tools for progressive politics and the diffusion of a global liberal public sphere.[13] They exhibited specific qualities that aligned with progressive hopes for deliberative democracy, individual freedom, and spontaneous association. On the internet, individuals could freely explore new forms of subjectification, and they could immediately organize with like-minded individuals across the globe without having to submit to the centralized authority of pre-established institutions. The conservative love of social hierarchy and identitarian traditionalism seemed incompatible with the technological *a priori* of social media. The latter became major organizing tools for the Occupy Wall Street movement, the Arab Spring, and the Alterglobalization movement. However, the progressive narrative has shifted dramatically since the late 2010s. The rise of fake news, the alt-right, and online hate speech in conjunction with Brexit and the 2016 US presidential elections showed how the far right could imitate and subvert the tactics of the left. According to Hardt and Negri, right-wing movements have appropriated "elements of the leadership, organizational structures, and protest repertoires of liberation movements of decades past."[14] While progressive movements successfully mobilized the technical machine of social media in the 2000s and early 2010s, reactionary forces learned from these successes and adapted themselves to promote cyberfascism.

The rise of social media as a political organization tool did not happen in a vacuum. Italian post-workerists stress the role of neoliberalism in shifting popular protests from traditional political institutions, like political parties and unions, to online activism. Already in the 1960s, Mario Tronti predicted in *Workers and Capital* that the Fordist social compromise between labor and capital in Europe would trigger a crisis of authority in the capitalist welfare state.[15] Under Fordism, capital granted workers higher wages, better working conditions, and political representation in exchange for social peace and high labor productivity in the factories. However, by forcing capitalist and working-class institutions to bargain over the spoils of economic growth, the welfare state would encourage workers to keep demanding more, which would in turn lead to a crisis of profitability for capital. Mediating working-class institutions would first channel protest energies into social bargaining, but this energy would eventually spill over into society in general. When cheap resource imports from the colonies halted and oil prices from the Middle East spiked, Fordist capitalism entered a deep crisis. In *Marx beyond Marx,* Negri studies the aftermath of this crisis. He notes that capitalism first responds to increased working-class antagonism by reforming itself in line with working-class demands.[16] If workers demand more room for individual creativity, autonomy, and cooperation at work, post-Fordist capitalism responds with flexible jobs, entrepreneurial freedom, and networked workplaces rooted in social cooperation. However, the side-effect of this unbundling of traditional labor organizations and the erosion of Fordist safety nets is the unmediated exposure of workers to the vagaries of labor markets. Workers gain individual freedoms but lose the mediating institutions that protect their collective interests. Capital comes to a new agreement with labor not based on a social compromise between the requirements of industrial profitability and workers' need for security and purchasing power but on the exchange of workers' desire for personal authenticity and freedom for precarious working conditions. Mediating institutions, like trade-unions and welfare provisions, slowly crumble. Money becomes the directive subject of capitalist development, while workers are forced to adapt to the determining force of capitalist markets.[17]

In *Assembly*, Negri and Hardt reconceptualize the decline of the Fordist social compromise through the lens of neoliberalism. They mostly agree with Michel Foucault's genealogy of neoliberalism as a governmentality that imposes competition and entrepreneurship on the population to stimulate economic growth, but they highlight the unfreedom coming from this governmentality more than Foucault himself did.[18] The latter optimistically stressed how neoliberal governmentality would erode the grip of disciplinary power over individuals in favor of a "theme-program of a society in which there is an optimization of systems of difference."[19] Foucault naively bought into the new social compromise of individualist freedom in exchange for precariousness. Neoliberalism promised to dismantle the social institutions responsible for normalizing people's conducts, because the free market would spontaneously coordinate populations allegedly without the need for top-down interventions. Rather than imposing one uniform mode of existence on all individuals alike, neoliberalism promotes diversity and free choice.[20] However, the erosion of disciplinary institutions has not fostered freedom but exposure to market imperatives, according to Hardt and Negri. Individuals are now expected to voluntarily conform to the fluctuations of free market competition without direct disciplinary coercion. Negri and Hardt argue that the neoliberal promise of governmental restraint even turned into its opposite.

Although neoliberal administration appears to be a kind of liquid governance that moves fluidly from one crisis point to the next, it is not really liquid at all. It is more like a durable fabric woven of disparate and disordered connections that are effectively aligned towards a unified project: to empty out the public powers and impose economic logics over administrative functions.[21]

Neoliberalism dismantled the channels through which people could voice their demands *within* the official political system, leading to mass atomization. Under Fordism, the working class possessed collective institutions to articulate its interests and constitute the class as a single and uniform political subject. Neoliberalism, on the other hand, renders individuals personally responsible for securing their own success. Unions lost members and bargaining power, socialist parties uncoupled themselves from working-class demands, social security services turned into disciplinary apparatuses. By immunizing the market from democratic regulation via working-class mediating institutions, neoliberalism exposed populations directly to the rule of international markets. If governments would even want to accommodate for social demands, constitutional breaks and pressure from financial markets would currently make these reforms practically impossible to implement.[22]

As Bifo concludes, "workers do not perceive themselves anymore as parts of a living community: they are rather compelled to compete in a condition of loneliness."[23] Once the economic and political infrastructure that gathers workers together in the same factories and neighborhoods disappears and the institutions voicing their demands fade, individuals are left isolated and denuded from political agency. The latter is reduced to the ability for passive clicktivism, a politics reduced to sharing and liking political agendas formulated elsewhere. According to Bifo, others abandon all hope in collective politics entirely and withdraw into suicidal solitude, like the Japanese *hikikomori*.[24] These are young, lonely individuals who give up on offline social interactions because they cannot cope with the neoliberal pressure to succeed. They lock themselves up in their apartments and pursue an exclusively online existence, living off unemployment benefits or precarious online gigs. They see this lifestyle of self-imposed social suicide as the only way to retain some sense of personal autonomy against the cutthroat competition pervading society.

In her genealogy of contemporary populism, Nadia Urbinati concurs that the decline of national mediating institutions in favor of global economic forces constitutes the ideal breeding ground for populist social movements.[25] When global markets are increasingly deregulated and social-democratic political parties are captured by corporate interests, ordinary citizens lose influence in the institutions that usually communicate public opinion to formal decision-making institutions. According to Urbinati, modern representative democracy is fundamentally "diarchic," meaning that it relies on an interplay between the diverse perspectives of public opinion and the more uniform formulation of the collective will within political institutions.[26] When mediating institutions lose their credibility, the public becomes suspicious of political elites, who are seen as monopolizing political decision-making for their own corrupt goals. Urbinati references the Italian context, where the popularity of Berlusconi and Beppe Grillo would only have been possible because of the preceding public outcry at large-scale corruption among the Italian political elite. Berlusconi rose to prominence in 1994 after the *mani pulite* affair that revealed mass financial fraud among the leaders of the social-democratic and center-right parties. Grillo's Five Star Movement reached national acclaim in the 2000s by railing against "*la casta*," the politicians and technocrats that ran the Italian government. In this context of generalized distrust, populist movements put forward an anti-establishmentarianism that distinguishes between "good, ordinary citizens" and "corrupt elites" with the promise of putting the people directly in charge with as little constitutional constraints as possible, as these restraints are reformulated as ploys of the elites to thwart the will of the people. Ideally, public opinion merges with the formal collective will of the people. Since any elitist representation is inherently suspect, the opinion of the people must directly rule over formal decision-making. Whatever the people desires must be enacted into law with as little mediation as possible.

While moralistic dualism is not unique to populism, Urbinati argues that populism, firstly, rejects all pretense to universality or impartiality when formulating its political claims.[27] Political movements usually formulate their aspirations as beneficial to the common good of all, even when they are actually factionalist demands, but populists cynically deny that politics can be anything but factionalist pursuits of private interests. It is only a matter of representing the *correct faction*, i.e. the ordinary people, rather than the false faction, the establishment. Secondly, populist parties reject mediating institutions like political parties or civil society organizations, as these retain an elitist aura that renders them suspicious in the eyes of the crowd.[28] That is why populist parties often champion social media as tools for circumventing the need for representative officials. Nonetheless, populism does not equal direct democracy. As we will see, it rather puts forward a strategy of "direct representation as incarnation":[29] the many do not directly participate in decision-making but invest their faith in a leader who embodies public opinion and enacts the will of the people in government. Opinion and will, the two poles of the democratic diarchy, are thereby united in the figure of the populist leader. To avoid becoming part of "the corrupt elites" themselves, however, populist leaders must constantly invent new purported establishment conspiracies that block the full and true expression of the will of the people in government.

Nonetheless, Urbinati distinguishes between populism and fascism. Not only are populist tactics and narratives present among left-wing and right-wing movements, but more importantly, populism still accepts the rules of the game of representative democracy, while fascism suspends these procedures in order to directly impose its rule by force.[30] Populists often disfigure the constitutional norms that guide democratic decision-making by reforming electoral laws, limiting the freedom of expression or politicizing the judiciary. After all, these institutions are supposed to enforce the will of the people with as little friction as possible. Yet when populism abolishes elections entirely and suspends parliamentary pluralism, it morphs into fascism. Fascism is, in other words, a populism that has entirely cast aside the veneer of liberal-democratic legitimacy to more effectively impose its rule. Yet this project requires a reconstitution of the public sphere along new, non-liberal principles.

## Rekindling the Swindle of Fulfillment

The fascist public sphere responds to the condition of endemic loneliness caused by the neoliberal dismantling of mediating institutions with a mode of publicity that combines three features. It first relies on the public's atomization to secondly target negative affects of loneliness and disenfranchisement with promises of belonging. It, thirdly, unites these atomized resentful individuals again by cultivating liturgical mass rituals in which individuals experience shared submission and fervent allegiance to a fascist leader. Bifo describes fascism as an "identitarian trap" in which neoliberal globalization triggers a reactive need for belonging in a purified imagined community.[31] "Since the working class was defeated by precariousness and the globalization of the labor market, the *Volk* has returned, stupid and bloody as it is, bringing with it the curse of origins, the obsession with belonging."[32] Anger, resentment, fear of falling, and unhomeliness are captured into narratives that direct these negative affects toward various imagined enemies while offering joyful passions of self-esteem and pride in one's ethnic identity as compensatory gratification.[33]

In his critique of late fascism, Alberto Toscano argues that fascism cynically feeds on the negative affects of disgruntled populations with a romantic "swindle of fulfilment."[34] Fascism preys on those out-of-sync with the capitalist present by responding to their utopian desires with images of a fuller and glorious past. While this past used to be an imagined quasi-feudal community of racial purity under traditional Nazism, today's popular nostalgia is recoded as a national or racial Fordism, in which economic growth and the protective state regulations would return specifically for the white male working class.[35] Trump, Farage, or Meloni do not promise a return to the medieval motherland but to an imaginary 1950s. Populations hope to return to the *trentes glorieuses* of the Fordist social compromise. This fascism promises to reinstate the wages of whiteness and turn whiteness again into a foundation for the right to personal private property. As Negri and Hardt summarize, "identity is meant to provide privileged rights and access to property. A primary appeal of populist movements is to restore the (even minimal) economic power and social prestige they imagine to have lost, most often conceived … in terms of racial identity."[36]

In his 1997 essay, *Ur-fascism*, Umberto Eco expands on this nostalgia for identitarian belonging by highlighting how historically Italian fascism created the semblance of community by fostering "popular elitism."[37] Discontented workers and the petty bourgeois were seduced into fascism through Mussolini's promise of belonging to a nationalistically redefined elite. Italians felt oppressed by the imagined elites of financial capital, foreign influence, and left-wing intellectuals, but Mussolini convinced them that *they were the real elites* thanks to their Italian heritage.[38] Through their voluntary submission to the leader, the fascist populace formed an esoteric bond in which they became part of an elite group entitled to dominate others. By swearing allegiance to Mussolini, Italians enacted their ascendance to a political elite bound to dominate others. This esoteric bond acted as an antidote to the masses' atomization and cultural alienation. Whereas Italians in their everyday lives felt subjugated to the abstract rule of invisible conspiratorial forces, Fascist esotericism created a simulation of community that enhanced Italians' sense of collective belonging and self-determination, even if this self-determination was experienced vicariously through the power and agency of the fascist leader.

According to Toscano, late fascism repeats this Ur-fascist trope; it cultivates the performance of an esoteric bond between leader and audience to produce the feeling of collective belonging.[39] He comments, for instance, on right-wing leaders' propensity to talk utter logorrheic nonsense—from the disconnected ramblings of a Trump speech to the post-truth memefied jargon of the online alt-right—but stresses that the impoverished language of right-wing thought-leaders is *not mere nonsense*. It creates a feeling of "being in the know" among the audience. Those who (think they) understand the dog whistles, internet jargon, edgy jokes, or absurdist memes of the alt-right feel a deep bond to an imagined community. In this context, individuals often use the metaphor of "taking the red pill" to explain their conversion to cyberfascism.[40] This image from *The Matrix* signifies the moment in which online media consumers refuse to take the blue pill and continue to be unknowing victims of the global rule of abstractions, and opt for the red pill instead. They subsequently see how deep the rabbit hole goes. By redpilling their audiences, cyberfascist influencers cultivate an esoteric community linked to their personal authority as "revealers of the truth."[41] By performing the role of a right-wing Morphius who shows the audience how the world *really* works, cyberfascist influencers not only fool these audiences into imagining themselves as messianic Neos, saviors of (white) humanity, but also render these audiences dependent on themselves as repositories of esoteric truths. Cyberfascism thereby offers the promise of compensatory social prestige to atomized and isolated individuals, first within the online fascist community itself but later also in society in general. One can acquire "subcultural capital" within far-right communities by being in the know about meme culture and understanding the absurdist humor of spaces like 4Chan,[42] but ultimately membership in the popular elite of cyberfascism itself is imagined as a source of social standing vis-à-vis the sheepishly unknowing masses outside the fascist esoteric circle.

This is also where cyberfascism shows its illusory form of liberation. While right-wing influencers confront their audiences with their social isolation and offer belonging in an esoteric community as compensatory gratification, audiences often remain atomized behind their computer screens or on the streets during disorganized rioting.[43] Cyberfascism keeps its audience in a permanent state of coming back for more without ever offering the empowerment it promises. Audiences consume a steady YouTube diet of self-help advice from Jordan Peterson and cheer along as Ben Shapiro verbally "destroys" allegedly woke college students, but they rarely form sustainable institutions in the offline world or enact genuine self-organization. Their existence as a collective remains bound to shared submission under the charismatic authority of fascist thought-leaders.[44] For Toscano, "fascism promotes a 'repressive egalitarianism' based on an identity of subjection and a fraternity of hatred."[45] It develops a strategy of making the many act without granting them direct collective agency. Because fascist community can only exist at the mercy of its charismatic leadership, the collective never attains independent agency beyond its role as a manipulable crowd doing the bidding of its leaders. The cyberfascist online crowd can share and retweet the narratives of their leaders, but they lack internal institutions to democratically articulate common goals or agendas. This structure of manipulated seriality requires a particular type of leadership, "liturgical or plebiscitary leadership."

## The Liturgical Unity of the People

The formation of cyberfascist collectives that *feel* like powerful communities yet *lack* genuine collective agency requires a specific kind of interaction between political leaders and followers. The liberal public sphere presumes a citizenry of free and equal individuals capable of rationally deliberating on their collective self-government. Individuals must think for themselves, articulate their own opinions and subsequently discuss these opinions within a free and equal conversation.[46] For Immanuel Kant, the unenlightened crowds might still temporarily need leaders to elevate them from their condition of minority, but ideally this is a transitory stage in which modern individuals eventually overcome their submissiveness and become autonomous and rational individuals.[47] By contrast, the fascist public sphere gives people the illusion of self-efficacy and independent thought while simultaneously rendering their agency dependent on submission to the fascist leader. It offers them spectacles of masculine might and violent heroism.[48] Yet ultimately these spectacles are smokescreens that offer the *feeling* of self-determination without *actually* elevating individuals into an enlightened state of majority. Toscano highlights, for instance, how Italian fascism built an impressive "insurrectional machine" that staged massive public gatherings and pompous political displays of power, like the 1922 March on Rome, but was void of any effectiveness in terms of policy change.[49] In its rhetoric, Italian fascism claimed to take back control over key industries and public life in general, yet its actual policies exacerbated the people's subjugation to private capital. The aim was to produce the public feeling of power without giving people actual power.

Eco already noticed this baroque theatricality of fascist propaganda when commenting on the fascists' enthusiasm for military parades and symbolism.[50] Fascism does not form a unified political ideology thanks to doctrinal convergence but through a shared repertoire of public rituals. Even today, the cyberfascist online movement is not unified through strong ideological coherence. Evangelicals support a godless Donald Trump, and online trolls post ironic memes with little to no political conviction. The unity of the movement derives from a shared sense of belonging through participation in the same rites that purportedly embody the will and power of the people. Cyberfascism is a political movement not thanks to a shared belief system but by liking and sharing the same social media posts and by hovering in the same online network around a couple of right-wing influencers like Andrew Tate, Jordan Peterson, or Alex Jones. Just like the Catholic Church can accommodate for a series of very diverse doctrinal orders if everyone obeys the same liturgical rites, online social movements find unity not in doctrine but in shared rites of allegiance.

The etymology of the word "liturgy" already betrays that fascist public spheres conflict with the formation of an autonomous self-governing public. The Greek word "*leitourgia*" derives from the public works that the rich in ancient Greece were expected to perform in service of the rest of the population as a kind of charity.[51] More specifically, it refers to "works" (*erga*) done in the service of the "people" (*laos*). The Greek word "*laos*," however, refers to a very different kind of public than the *dèmos* of political democracy. This is not the people as a self-governing seat of power (*dèmo-kratia*), but a people acquiring unity through its common subjugation to a leader. According to French linguist Emile Benveniste:

The peculiarity of *laos* … is that it expresses the personal relationship of a group of men to a chief. It is an organization peculiar to ancient warrior societies such as those we have established among the Germans and which, in the term *laos*, comes to life in ancient Hellenic society. The *laoi* form part of the retinue of the chief; they are often under his orders; they owe him fidelity and obedience; they would not be *laoi* unless they were attached to him by mutual consent. They may be engaged in his cause in battle, which is the situation most familiar to us, but this is probably due to the epic character of the Iliad. In any case *laos* is the name of the people insofar as they are capable of bearing arms.[52]

The *laos* is a public formed through a shared loyalty to a warlord, a people acquiring a unity and collective will by swearing allegiance to a common flag. Liturgical rites are the rituals and performances that render visible the glory of the leader and the affective unity of the crowd that he mediates.

According to Eco, "the 'people' is conceived of as a quality, a monolithic entity that expresses a 'common will.'"[53] The central claim of fascism is indeed that it represents and incarnates the collective will of "the people" opposed to the imagined elites. However, this "people" as a singular agent does not truly exist. It must be conjured into existence through public rituals that render tangible the presence of "the people" as a uniform subject. The purpose of fascist liturgies is to grant tangible existence to this collective unity. This is where the fascist leader as vox populi enters the stage: the people acquires full presence in and through their invocation via the fascist leader's speech. While the fascist leader *claims* to only voice the independent will of the people, they actually *breathe life into* this common will by embodying it in his own person. As Eco writes, "the people is hence only a theatrical fiction," nurtured into being via virtuosic public performances.[54] In the grand political rituals that stage the leader as vox populi, the followers experience their participation in a collective larger than themselves. They participate in a *laos* that swears allegiance to the leader and becomes their people "insofar as they are capable of bearing arms." However, these *laoi* only exist through their mediation in the mystical body of the fascist leader. Without the leader to incarnate the will of the people, the collective effervescence experienced by the followers of fascism immediately collapses.

While Eco already highlights how TV and the internet offer new opportunities for the theatrical construction of "the people" as a qualitative unity, Giorgio Agamben stresses in *The Kingdom and the Glory* that this variation on the public sphere is much older and only reaches its apex in modern mass media.[55] He links it to the phenomenon of plebiscitary democracy, which has surfaced multiple times throughout Western history in ancient Rome, Christian liturgy, but also twentieth-century totalitarianism, which adapted plebiscitary democracy to new technologies, like radio and television.[56] Liberal democracy establishes the rule of the people by granting each individual citizen a series of political rights and freedoms to subsequently participate in the public sphere and contribute to the formation of public opinion. Plebiscitary democracy, on the other hand, establishes political legitimacy not through rational consensus-formation but with the public representation of hierarchical authority and the public's affectively charged affirmation of this authority in ritualized displays of personal allegiance. It is present in the Roman general parading through the streets of Rome to plebeian acclaim, the Catholic priest representing the glory of God in the Eucharist to which the people respond with a resounding "*amen*," or the totalitarian dictator addressing the crowds to trigger feelings of collective effervescence. Even non-totalitarian states often employ grandiose rituals and symbolism to invoke feelings of national unity and popular consent. Liberal politicians extoll phrases like "God bless America" or "*Vive la France, vive la République*" and expect their audience to shout acclamations in unison, like "U-S-A, U-S-A, U-S-A" and "*Vive le président.*" Such public displays of national allegiance are not mere formalities or decorative veneer, according to Agamben.[57] When the French president ends his speech with "*Vive la France, vive la République*," he invokes "the French Republic" as an imaginary authority to sanction his decisions. He presumably does not act from personal motivations but enacts the will of the French Republic into actual policy on the people's behalf. He thereby renders this elusive reality "the French Republic" present to his audience via a ritualized performance of his mediating role as a functionary of the French people. Through a mysterious quasi-magical trick, the politician brings into existence the entity he is supposed to merely represent. When the French public repeat the phrase with sufficient national pride, they acclaim the president's authority to act in the name of "the French Republic" and thereby performatively affirm that they are indeed the French people, conjured into existence through their common allegiance to the president.

The dialectic of the leader's glory and the rituals of his public glorification comes to full fruition in the plebiscitary rites of fascism. As Agamben writes, "perhaps never has an acclamation, in the technical sense of the word, been expressed with so much force and efficacy as was 'Heil Hitler' in Nazi Germany or 'Duce duce' in fascist Italy."[58] Fascist leaders claim to represent the unitary will of the people, but their success depends on their capacity to incite collective expressions of allegiance in plebiscitary forums. Instead of basing their authority on the procedures of liberal democracy, like elections or parliamentary deliberation, fascism derives its legitimacy from crowded gatherings in which the common people *feel and enact* their participation in a larger mystical body via the performed liturgies of power. The infamous mass gatherings under Hitler or Mussolini rendered in the flesh the will of the people in the common chants of totalitarian allegiance while simultaneously performatively producing the authority of the fascist leaders, whose glorious presence was necessary to make this performance of national unity possible. From the perspective of the fascist leadership, these rituals of acclamation have the advantage of not only fostering a felt sense of collective belonging but also of binding this affective togetherness to a shared submission to the fascist leadership itself. Without their presence as liturgically staged incarnations of the collective will, the people-as-*laos* would not exist.

## How Cyberfascism Masters Social Media

With the theory of plebiscitary democracy, "the entire problem of the contemporary spectacle of media domination over all areas of social life assumes a new guise" for Agamben.[59] Contemporary mass media establish a new stage for the plebiscitary rites of the fascist public sphere. The infrastructure of social media in particular is, according to Mitchell Dean's interpretation of Agamben, more conducive to the plebiscitary formation of liturgical power.[60] It marks a shift from the creation of public opinion through free and rational communication to the formation of public mood through the strategic manipulation of the viral affects that mobilize online audiences. One often imagines social media as the ideal liberal public sphere, where individuals gather and express their opinions freely in order to debate politics. The reality of online communication, however, starkly deviates from this liberal utopia. Social media are more often the venue for vicious culture wars and shouting matches.

According to Dean, this is not a bug but a feature of online media: social media companies are profit-driven enterprises that generate revenue from enticing engagement among their consumers. The more time consumers spend on social media and interact with the platform, the more personal data social media companies acquire to, for instance, sell targeted advertisement space. Dean mentions the case of Donald Trump's 2016 presidential campaign using Facebook data on users' preferences and likes to identify "13.5 million individual voters in sixteen swing states who could be moved to vote for their candidate."[61] The campaign team subsequently targeted these individuals with videos tailored to their personal preferences. Social media do not host a liberal public sphere for rational consensus-formation but establish an attention market in which potential thought-leaders, "influencers," gather a *laos* around themselves through the acclamation of the crowds in the form of likes, retweets, and subscriptions. Audiences subsequently experience a sense of empowerment through their acclamation of particular leaders with whom they cultivate parasocial relationships. Just like the offline plebiscitary leader establishes his authority by staging the "will of the people" in bombastic public rites that trigger a feeling of collective belonging and allegiance, social media provide a stage for plebiscitary leaders to build a *laos*-like follower-base through attention-grabbing stunts and popular online acclaim. With every online post, social media users establish their personal brand that other users can affirm with the attention and positive feedback that they award these posts. Those individuals with the savviest strategy for triggering user engagement become the most powerful voices in the online public sphere. Others are relegated to the margins of the internet. Hence, the latter is not a space of free and equal rational debate but a plebiscite where multiple agents compete for audience attention. Public acclamations in the form of likes and retweets establish the authority of a select elite of thought-leaders who are presumed to speak in the name of the people.

Social media infrastructures establish an interplay of corporate algorithms that promote user engagement, and influencers game this algorithm to maximize their reach across the online public sphere. Social media scholars note that this interplay facilitates the creation of online "affective publics," built not around common opinions or beliefs but shared feelings and affects.[62] When alt-right activists, for example, share YouTube videos of their favorite influencers, like Jordan Peterson or Ben Shapiro, "owning liberal snowflakes" in university campus debates, the goal is not to contribute to the rational formation of public opinion but to trigger affective responses from supporters and adversaries to increase their hold over public mood formation. Whether Peterson's or Shapiro's interventions are true or logically sound matters little as long as they speak to the deep desires and resentments of online affective publics. As Nidesh Lawtoo argues, contemporary fascism counts on the mimetic propensities of online crowds to spread affective contagion like a virus.[63] The better alt-right activists pander to the insecurities and aspirations of the crowds, the likelier social media algorithms will push their messages across the platform and into the political mainstream.[64] The cyberfascist collective is, in that sense, a movement that has mastered the techniques of online virality to maximize social media acclamations and thereby determine public mood. If alt-right activists can mobilize the political affects of social media users, they maximize the attention granted to their framing of political events and thereby push out alternative framings and render their narratives hegemonic. In the age of public mood, hegemony is established not by occupying the institutions of public consensus-formation but by spreading political sentiments until they reach critical mass.

Liberal political philosophers have often criticized this plebiscitary structure of social media as heralding a post-truth era. The truth allegedly no longer matters, since cyberfascist movements target the masses' base instincts. In *The Game,* Italian novelist Alessandro Baricco pushes back against this narrative because it falsely reassures liberals that liberal and fascist public speech are qualitatively distinct.[65] Baricco notes that mainstream liberal politics has had a complicated relationship to the truth since its very conception, especially in Italy, where corruption and deceit have been standard even among centrist political leaders. Social media did not cause politicians to suddenly become bullshit artists. Moreover, constant insistence on "the facts" is a defense tactic of intellectual elites who hold power over the determination of what counts as "a fact" and how these facts can be deployed in rational public deliberation. Baricco here points to a weak spot in the liberal defense of public opinion and the public sphere of free and open discussion: it often presumes the dominance of those with sufficient educational credentials and symbolic capital to play the game of rational political deliberation. For Baricco, social media have granted the masses genuine access to political participation that the highly educated and well-connected intellectual aristocracy would have otherwise denied them.

But mass access to the public sphere has also facilitated the spreading of so-called fast-truths as its unintended side effect. These are statements stripped of context and nuance in order to maximize their potential for quick and easy consumption. Social media favor immediate click-based engagement, so online statements must be reformatted to fit the requirement of viral engagement-based diffusion. Just like fast-food constitutes food that has been meticulously designed to support quick consumption yet lacks any nutritional value, fast-truth is news that has been designed to maximize affective engagement with minimal amounts of information. Baricco illustrates this phenomenon with the popular news headline "Sales of vinyl in 2016 exceed those of digital music."[66] With added context, it turns out that the sales of vinyl music records beat digital downloads … for one week … only in the UK … not considering illegal downloads. The headline is not, strictly speaking, false but it has gotten rid of context and precision to maximize the speed at which it can travel on social media. This headline is bound to trigger a sense of pride among old-school music fans and anger among those who dislike music snobs, the ideal mixture for a Twitterstorm. Social media users will either acclaim the message with likes and shares or bombard it with online outrage, but both accelerate the headline's online diffusion. The message can briefly dominate the mainstream news cycle because, as a fast-truth, it is stripped of all background information that would require intimate knowledge of the music scene before forming an opinion. Fast-truths offer online audiences the luxury of formulating what seems like an opinion, purely on the basis of gut reactionary feeling. The message has been redesigned for aerodynamic purposes to influence the public mood.

Baricco praises right-wing populists' strategic skill to use social media's affordances for spreading fast-truths.[67] Cyberfascists continuously concoct fast-truths about "woke gone mad" not because they genuinely wish to uncover the deep truth about "woke ideology." These news stories are rather tactical maneuvers for dominating the public mood online. They specifically leave out contextual information so that affects of anger and hatred are easily triggered. The subsequent social media storm quickly becomes the talk of the town and thereby pushes any other political debate to the sideline. As social media users' attention is a finite resource, any space devoted on their newsfeed to the relentless cycle of culture war stories is space that cannot be taken by other, more genuine concerns. Politicians like Trump, Salvini, or Meloni know exactly how to play the online attention game to make the news coverage about themselves and how dangerously insane their "woke" adversaries are. By designing online communication specifically to the requirements of plebiscitary dynamics of social media, these politicians translate online hegemony into offline political power. By dominating the public mood of social media, right-wing populists have won elections and seats in governments.

The left, on the other hand, has struggled to adapt to the era of fast-truths, according to Baricco. The policy agenda of the left is often too nuanced and complex to grab and retain attention or trigger acclamations in the online public sphere. Lazzarato similarly argues that the left lacks a war machine that properly instrumentalizes the affordances of a public sphere dominated by social media platforms.[68] In the industrial age, the Leninist vanguard party masterfully channeled the potential of factory workers' collective power into a communist takeover of the state apparatus. Workers were already drilled into obedience due to factory discipline, so Leninist political parties relied on the same centralized top-down power-structure to organize the masses in favor of left-wing political action. The online public sphere, however, has dismantled this uniform and standardized audience, and the left has struggled ever since to articulate new institutional formats to mobilize public power against capitalist domination. Today, cyberfascism proves more adapted to fast-truth discourse. It successfully leverages the affective dynamics of social media to hegemonize mainstream politics. It has transformed disconnected individuals into "informational partisans,"[69] who express their allegiance to cyberfascist thought-leaders by acclaiming and spreading the latter's online speech.

In her critical work on the success of conspiracy theories during the Covid-19 Pandemic, Donatella Di Cesare adds a crucial caveat to Baricco's and Lazzarato's admiration of fast-truth politics. She notes that, like cyberfascist public communication, online conspiracy theories also speak to people's deeply held anxieties to garner acclamation and informational partisanship to odd and far-fetched worldviews. Conspiracy theories similarly repackage decontextualized facts and people's (often justified) suspicion of governmental elites into fast-truths in order to trigger social media algorithms' preference for affectively charged messaging. According to Di Cesare, "the efficacy of the myth [of the conspiracy] lies not in its claim to truth, but in the demands to which it responds, in the emotions it incites, in the suggestiveness it displays."[70] Conspiracies offer cognitive shortcuts to avoid the complexities of actual reality in favor of simple narratives that pander to people's frustrations of powerlessness and their sense of disillusionment with traditional politics.[71] They cater to people's "nostalgia for legibility" and establish online tribes held together through a shared pathos of resentment.[72] In contrast to Baricco and Lazzarato, however, Di Cesare analyzes the easily digestible fast-truths of online conspiracism not as a political tactic the left ought to imitate, but as a dangerous force of depoliticization.

> Precisely because conspiracism is a weapon of mass depoliticization, a political reflection is needed that makes it easier to step away from this all-embracing explanatory scheme. … We cannot fail to recognize that conspiracism stems from the fear and isolation of the citizen who feels excluded from the public space. Where the *polis* has become inaccessible, where the interpretative community is shattered the common truth is also shattered. There, the specter of the plot lurks.[73]

The plebiscitary dynamics of social media and their integration into cyberfascist politics feeds off the mass atomization implemented under neoliberalism and exacerbates this atomization by offering individuals the illusion of common belonging through the theatrics of fascist displays of power and glory. Plebiscitary democracy and the fast-truth discourse it facilitates do not foster self-governing *demoi* but fanatic *laoi* dependent on leader figures performing the illusion of common belonging and unity. Genuine democracy requires, on the other hand, an effort to emancipate the people from a state of dependence and the representation of their will by hierarchical authorities. If the left strives for genuine political enlightenment, toward "humanity squared, enriched by the collective intelligence and love of the community,"[74] then imitating the tactics of cyberfascism will have counterproductive results.

## The Rise of the Digital Party

Paolo Gerbaudo's *The Digital Party* elaborates on the counterproductivity of imitating the viral politics of cyberfascism for "social media"-based parties like Podemos, the Five Star Movement, and La France Insoumise. He describes how the democratizing promises of social media fostered the emergence of a new political ideology, called "participationism," which claims that digital technologies can be leveraged to stimulate direct democratic participation from the crowds and thereby abolish the oligarchic power of professional party politicians.[75] Political parties like the Five Star Movement pride themselves on giving their members a direct voice in the decision-making process via online tools, like the deliberative platform Rousseau.[76] The latter was an online discussion and voting tool in the party's early days that enabled members of the movement to formulate their own legislative proposals, discuss them with peers, and vote on them via online referenda. It seemed like the ideal liberal public sphere in which individuals would finally deliberate as equals on the laws that govern their lives.

However, Gerbaudo observes that, rather than establishing genuine direct self-government, participationist politics mimics the characteristics of plebiscitary democracy we have identified in cyberfascism.[77] Rather than empowering individuals to become autonomous citizens who collectively master their own fate through rational and free deliberation, digital parties install a hierarchy between "hyperleaders" and a mostly passive membership base. Gerbaudo relies on Antonio Gramsci's analysis of political parties being traditionally composed of: (1) a "principal cohesive element," i.e., the party leadership; (2) a "mass element," or its popular support base; and (3) an "intermediate element" of party cadre bureaucrats.[78] According to Gramsci, the mass element is unable to spontaneously organize itself, yet the party leadership is too small directly coordinate the masses effectively. Traditional political parties hence require a large cadre of local officials, administrators, journalists, etc., to mediate between the leadership and the base. These cadres not only translate the party's ideological mission to the level of the base but also offer the central leadership feedback from the base and constitute a training ground for potential political talent to move from the base to leadership positions. Participationism and digital media, however, put leaders into direct contact with the base without the need for cadre intermediation. Similar to neoliberal ideology, participationism offers the promise of personal freedom of expression yet simultaneously dismantles the institutions that gather and represent ordinary citizens' interests to central authorities. This policy limits the danger of backroom politicking and self-serving bureaucracies, but that does not necessarily stimulate genuine active participation from parties' support base. Instead, political party members are disaggregated into a mass of atomized individuals without the institutional support to collectively coordinate their agency.

According to Gerbaudo:

> The hyperleader diffuses his image and words instantaneously through all sorts of communication networks and personal communication devices—computer, mobile phones, tablets—to an online crowd of internet supporters and sympathizers who, despite their physical dispersion, become united in following a single leader. The hyperleader becomes the symbolic center of the movement.[79]

Like cyberfascism's tendency to establish a *laos* around a leader who symbolically stages the unified will of the people in their own persona, charismatic leaders of digital parties (Jean-Luc Mélenchon, Pablo Iglesias, Beppe Grillo, Bernie Sanders) project a common political project by fostering affective attachment to their own persona. Traditional political parties foster unity among their members through a network of middle managers with deep roots in civil society, but digital parties make up for this loss through social media communication from the leadership. The latter become online celebrities with whom sympathizers foster parasocial relationships. Left-wing populists establish their authority through their presence in mass media and, most particularly, through their social media communication. They master the technological affordances of these platforms to grab people's attention, manipulate public mood, and build a loyal support base of followers who like, share, and retweet their statements. Digital parties repeat the plebiscitary dialectic of leaders' spectacular display of authority and the crowd's acclamation of this authority through their online engagement with the leader's messages. As a side-effect, the movement becomes highly dependent on the leader and their reputation, as collective unity only exists insofar as it is bound to the charismatic persona of this leader.[80] Once the latter suffers a blow in their reputation—as happened with Jeremy Corbyn after, among other things, allegations of antisemitism—the movement itself quickly collapses.

On the side of the masses, digital parties rarely foster the direct democratic participation that they promise. Digital party sympathizers rather act like Lazzarato's informational partisans who outwardly militate for the leader's project and spread the movement's message, but they hold little genuine control over the internal agenda.[81] When studying the outcomes of, for instance, Podemos's internal referenda, Gerbaudo observes that these referenda almost always lead to landslide victories for the party leadership.[82] Local militants rarely oppose the central leadership's decisions, because their collective identity as a political movement is built on their affective attachment to the leadership itself. If sympathizers disagree, they are far more likely to exit the movement rather than internally voice their concerns. The party's success depends not on the rational force of persuasion and deliberative democracy but on the mobilizing potential of affectively charged online communication. Given the lack of a party cadre with strong roots in civil society, digital parties' main challenge is to sustain popular enthusiasm and online engagement with their message.[83] If they fail to retain audience attention, the movement peters out.

## A New War Machine for the Left?

If mimicking the far right's move toward cyberfascism is counter-productive for the left, Lazzarato's accusation remains that the left has failed to invent a new institutional form, after the Leninist vanguard party or the Fordist social compromise, to respond to the challenges of contemporary politics. Changes in the internal composition of capital have led to mass atomization and the decline of mediating institutions, like traditional political parties and trade unions. Social media promised to construct a direct-democratic public sphere, in which everyone could participate in political deliberation as free and equal individuals, but they actually facilitate a plebiscitary public sphere, in which aspiring influencers gather acclaim by playing into the algorithms that favor user engagement and affectively charged messaging. Social media users acquire strong online reputations by maximizing clicks, likes, and shares, which cyberfascist movements leverage to dominate the online public sphere. They pander to people's negative affects of insecurity, hatred, and resentment in order to maximize their online presence and thereby push dissenting voices out of the picture. Cyberfascism offers the "swindle of fulfilment" by linking these negative affects to a sense of collective belonging, but the latter rather keeps individuals subjugated than nurturing genuine emancipation. As Toscano writes, quoting Leo Löwenthal, fascism enacts:

> a form of psychoanalysis in reverse; in other words, the assemblage of "more or less constantly manipulated devices to keep people in

permanent psychic bondage, to increase and reinforce neurotic and even psychotic behavior culminating in perpetual dependency on a 'leader' or on institutions or products".[84]

Rather than establishing the popular empowerment that it promises, cyberfascism perpetuates the social atomization and powerlessness of the masses with the compensatory gratification of belonging to a "popular elite" of an ethnically pure *Gemeinschaft*. There is an elective affinity here between cyberfascism and the technological affordances of social media insofar as both favor a plebiscitary public sphere, where a select group of charismatic leaders cultivate emotional attachment of the crowds to their persona via a dialectic of the pompous display of power and acclamations emanating from the crowd. Rather than fostering a *dèmos* capable of collective self-government, this produces a *laos* of dependent but loyal followers who unthinkingly repeat and spread the gospel of their leaders.

While mimicking this strategy for a left-wing project of popular emancipation is hopeless, alternative forms of institutionalized resistance to the hegemonic order are not clearly available, which explains the allure of digital party tactics on the left. It would be hubris to "solve" the problems of the left in a few paragraphs. Lazzarato is correct that the left has not yet been able to formulate a clear institutional answer to the new structural transformation of the public sphere. But there are also promising ventures, like the reappropriation of platform technology by cooperatives and worker organizations like Coworker.org (see Chapter 3) or the revival of unionism across the globe.[85] However, these initiatives have not yet coalesced into a firm war machine for the left. The question of an emancipatory war machine to overcome its cyberfascist counterpart constitutes a challenge for future activist institutional experiments.

# 5 IDENTITY, MIGRATION, POSTCOLONIALITY

## Chapter Summary

In the final chapter, we consider the question of national and cultural identity as touched upon in Chapter 4 from a different angle. The alleged disappearance of Italian and European popular identity plays a key but ambiguous role in much of contemporary Italian thought. Pier Paolo Pasolini offered a somber diagnosis of the "disappearance of the fireflies" in Italy's post-1960s hedonist capitalism, for example. The rapid decline of the natural and cultural ecosystem of traditional Italy led to the disappearance not just of animals linked to popular culture, like fireflies, but also to the demise of "the people" itself as a carrier of its own distinct form-of-life. The disappearance of the natural lifeworld also entails the disappearance of popular, historically and locally rooted forms of collective life. The double-bind of Pasolini's analyses continues to haunt contemporary Italian thought, in particular the recent work of Giorgio Agamben, rivaling Pasolini's pessimism. Agamben's radical anarchist pleas for a fundamentally porous "coming community," or his conceptualization of "the refugee" as the new paradigm for political subjectivity, are, paradoxically, shot through with cultural nostalgia, and political binaries (the lifeless technocratic State versus the living potential of the people). They sometimes uncomfortably echo culturally conservative or right-wing populist tropes. In contrast, we set forth the renewed significance of Gianni Vattimo's weak thought for a radical critique of such residual Pasolinian nostalgia in our context of resurgent nativist ontologies. Moreover, we will look closely at the work of Sandro Mezzadra as an antidote to the latent Eurocentrism in many of the leading theorists in Italian thought. Mezzadra reformulates key notions in Italian thought in a resolutely post-colonial perspective, resituating Italian thought beyond its geographical and historical borders. Moreover, taking our cues from Mezzadra's call to provincialize Italian thought, we examine how post-workerist and post-autonomist concepts and political strategies may connect to non-Western, indigenous and decolonial ideas and concerns.

In a speech for the "Italian Pride" [*Orgoglio italiano*] in Rome, late 2019, the future prime minister of Italy Giorgia Meloni declares: "I am Giorgia! I am a woman! I am a mother! I am Italian! I am a Christian!" [*Io sono Giorgia! Sono una donna! Sono una madre! Sono Italiana! Sono Cristiana!*].[1] And she adds: "*You will not take this away from me!*" [*Non me lo toglierete!*]. Meloni will enter office in 2022 as the first female prime minister of Italy after being the leader of the far-right party Fratelli d'Italia [Brothers of Italy] since 2014, a movement she co-founded, after having moved through the ranks of the openly neo-fascist movements *Movimento Sociale Italiano* (MSI) and *Alleanza Nazionale*. Meloni's speech at the Italian Pride perfectly captures the identitarian ideology that governs Western fascist politics today. It is both rhetorically captivating and politically disconcerting: what Meloni proposes here is nothing short of a *political ontology*. Her speech is primarily concerned with questions and assumptions regarding *being*. Identity is defined not as something that is historically contingent or related to social status, or as something we are able to construct for ourselves, but, on the contrary, as rooted in a variety of ontological truths we are supposedly born into and which continue to define us for the remainder of our lives: biological sex, nationality, faith.

As we noted in Chapter 2, various contemporary Italian theorists are proposing new political ecologies and ontologies, new ways of understanding ourselves as living matter (Braidotti), as existing in unison with earth-beings and non-human forces (Luisetti), or as made of stardust (Coccia). These posthuman approaches discussed in Chapter 2 also constitute political ontologies, but in forms that move beyond all too human identities and modes of being. The occasion for which Meloni delivered her homily is telling. The Italian Pride was primarily organized as a denunciation of contemporary progressive debates regarding gender, sexual identity and non-traditional families. Meloni denounces these issues—which by no means are universally accepted in Italy or Europe—as the new *pensiero unico* [*uniform thought*] against which the conservative right is waging a heroic battle. For this *pensiero unico,* "everything that defines us is the enemy," Meloni says. The family is allegedly the enemy, and so is identity at large: "we" are purportedly no longer allowed to accept any identity (unless we "identify as" …), no longer allowed to have roots [*radici*]. Bureaucratic jargon pushes out the lived reality of, among others, biological sex or national culture. In her speech, Meloni claims that the age-old terms "mother and father" are on the verge of being replaced by "parent one and two." We are reduced to being mere *codes* [*codici*], Meloni claims, deprived of personhood, deprived of humanity and identity. "But I am a person, and I will defend our identity," she adds (before enumerating all the things she emphatically *is*: woman, mother, Italian, Christian).[2]

What makes Meloni's speech relevant for critical analysis is that it touches upon numerous issues addressed in contemporary Italian thought: what constitutes a community? How to immunize one's identity against alien bodies? How to *belong* without this belonging becoming an instrument of exclusion and dehumanization, or an excuse for installing the state of exception? In this chapter, we will see how questions as well as critiques of identity, and the political ontologies that accompany these, play a leading role in contemporary Italian thought. We will see how such questions are related to the issue of migration—as Italy finds itself at the forefront of the European migrant crisis—and post- and decoloniality. Moreover, intriguingly, Meloni's speech also points to a tension in Italian thought itself—or at least in certain Italian thinkers like Agamben—between the urgency to deconstruct identitarian categories and uncover the *anarchè* [absence of a foundation] of all that is, and a certain melancholy, a feeling of loss of Italian and by extension European identity.

## Pasolini: The Disappearance of the Fireflies

To better grasp this tension, we need to travel back to November 2, 1975. The body of a man, savagely beaten and mutilated, is found on the beach at Ostia, just outside Rome. This man is Pier Paolo Pasolini, at the time arguably Italy's most prominent public intellectual and artist, a writer and filmmaker. The exact circumstances of Pasolini's gruesome death remain clouded in mystery, but it is highly likely that this was a political killing ordered by a new, fundamentally secretive form of power that is defiant of traditional ideologies. It is precisely the form of power that Pasolini decried in his final works as the "new fascism." As we argued in the introduction to this book, Pasolini's death can be considered a turning point in Italian intellectual and political history. It marks the demise of the ideological binaries that governed twentieth-century Western politics (socialism versus capitalism, revolution versus conservatism, universalism versus nationalism, secularization versus Christianity), which now dissolve in what Pasolini calls "the anthropological mutation" of citizens into consumers and mere "human capital," of environment and traditions into resources, and of government into technocracy.[3] Much of contemporary Italian theory can be read as attempts to come to terms with this mutation.

A few months before his violent death at Ostia, Pasolini writes his so-called "Article of the fireflies" [*l'articulo delle lucciole*], which uses the disappearance of Rome's fireflies due to environmental pollution as a metonymy for the collapse of an ecology that not only consists of natural beings but also crucially includes Italian *cultural identity*. Pasolini refers to the disappearance of the fireflies as an event, a point of no return, an irreversible mutation:

> At the beginning of the sixties, the fireflies began to disappear in our nation, due to pollution of the air, and the azure rivers and limpid canals, above all in the countryside. This was a stunning and searing phenomenon. There were no fireflies left after a few years. Today this is a somewhat poignant recollection of the past—a man of that time with such a souvenir cannot be young among the young of today and can therefore not have the wonderful regrets of those times. The event that occurred some ten years ago we shall now call the "disappearance of the fireflies."[4]

This event has purportedly opened a chasm between generations—the young are now of a different species—but also a chasm within individual subjects like Pasolini himself. In the texts published shortly before his murder, Pasolini describes how his own body and desires are prone to the "decay" he sees proliferating across Italian society.[5] In his life and career as a writer and filmmaker, Pasolini has strongly identified and worked in solidarity with "the people." For Pasolini, the Roman proletariat embodied an anti-capitalist, anti-modern, and authentic form-of-life.

However, "the people" have now disappeared, along with the fireflies. As Pasolini writes, "anthropologically speaking, the people are long gone."[6] He uses the harshest of terms to renounce his films of the early 1970s, in which he was dreaming up a sensuous ecology of young proletarian bodies set in a resolutely pre-modern world inspired by the literary canon (*Decameron, Canterbury Tales*). His film-cycle *The Trilogy of Life* is the acme of Pasolinian political aesthetics: a vitalist ecology of innocent bodies and authentic traditions, dialects, and cultural idiosyncrasies. Agamben would have typified Pasolini's bodies as forms-of-life; a life, individual as well as collective, which cannot be separated from its cultural manifestations—which acts as a counterweight to the death drive of postwar consumer capitalism.[7] This political as well as aesthetic fantasy is now denounced by Pasolini himself. The death drive of late capitalism can no longer be warded off, as he writes that "the collapse of the present implies the collapse of the past. Life is a pile of insignificant, ironic ruins."[8] In the article on the fireflies, Pasolini refers to this "devastation of the present" as the "new fascism."[9] Mussolini's "old fascism" was merely pomp and circumstance, which, according to Pasolini, ultimately failed to enduringly alter popular consciousness and popular forms of life. The immense diversity of Italian local idiolects emerged unscathed from the material devastation of the Second World War. The new fascism, however, is far more authoritarian and effective, because it lacks any *positive* content. For Pasolini, consumer capitalism and technocratic governance devour the ecology of customs, bodies, sensuous experiences, dialects, and their local natural surroundings. It replaces them not with anything substantial (a new ideal, a new identity, a new sense of the future) but with infinitely malleable and replaceable subjects. People are turned into mere *codes*, so to speak. The new power remains "fascist" in so far as it ensures "the brutal, totalitarian reorganization and homogenization of the world"; as Pasolini claims, the "anthropological mutation of the Italians is this complete homogenization into a single model."[10] Consumerist hedonism and its political twin, technocracy, have left nothing but ruins: environmental ruins, cultural ruins, bodies and identities in ruins.

Pasolini's peculiar brand of a populist Marxism that romanticizes authentic, living Italian popular culture, in its countless regional accents, against dehumanizing, bureaucratic and machinic technocracy at times uncomfortably resonates with contemporary populisms. Both are political ontologies that hinge on a sense of shared and rooted identity, a lived identity versus the inert, bureaucratic coding and subsequent denial of personhood. Real neo-fascism disguises itself as resistance against what Pasolini sees as the new fascism of global consumerism. Obviously, Pasolini would reject what comes further down the line of Meloni's political project: another "totalitarian reorganization and homogenization of the world," perversely presented as resistance against an alleged *pensiero unico*. As a homosexual leftist intellectual and artist, he would no doubt be in Meloni's firing line. While remaining cautious not to draw false equivalences, we argue that, nonetheless, the tension palpable in Pasolini's final works—emancipation now takes the form of resistance *against* modernization and universalist technocracy; a resistance that mobilizes cultural identities and traditions—today casts its shadow on Italian thought, particularly on Agamben's work.

## Agamben: The Disappearance of the People

In his book *When the House Burns Down,* originally published during the Covid-19 pandemic, Agamben presents us with a grim image of the Western world. His vision has clear Pasolinian echoes: "We live in houses, in cities burned to the ground, as if they were still standing," Agamben writes, "the people pretend to live there and go out into the streets masked amid ruins as if these were the familiar neighborhoods of times past."[11] Both *oikos* and *polis* have effectively disappeared; we now live in a planetary Potemkin village. Whatever was familiar to us—identities, cultures, shared histories, ways of life, freedoms, worldviews—has been reduced to ashes in "a single immense blaze we pretended not to see,"[12] but we remain in denial of the disappearance of our world and pretend not to notice the ruins. For Agamben, we are going through a veritable civilizational transformation "that goes to its ruin."[13] Just as Pasolini denounced the loss of vitality of youth and traditional popular forms-of-life in consumer society, Agamben diagnoses the dire state of our culture as it feels "itself to be at the end, with no life left."[14] Sovereign biopolitics—the permanent state of exception and total mobilization of the population, which became painfully clear to Agamben during the pandemic (see Chapter 1)—is a symptom of a culture that has no shared identity left and that does not attempt to salvage or reconstruct one either. The pandemic shows that the people are now effectively reduced to their bare biological existence, as they are governed by the impersonal "number, figure and lies," "digital invisible and cold"[15] of all-pervasive technocracy. These remarks come eerily close to Meloni's laments about the rooted, embodied individual being replaced with mere codes.

Agamben's apocalyptic visions are sometimes ideologically hard to read. They echo left-wing critiques of the anthropological mutation that took place in postwar society, like Pasolini's, as well as Guy Debord's analyses of the society of the spectacle,[16] but they are also reminiscent of right-wing analyses of the decline of the West and the total mobilization if not enslavement of humanity by technological reason. "How long has the house been burning?," Agamben asks.[17] At least since World War I, when "something happened in Europe that threw everything that still seemed whole and alive into the flames."[18] But perhaps, Agamben adds in a turn of phrase that is reminiscent of Heidegger's *Seinsvergessenheit* [the "forgetting of being"], "the fire began long before that, with humanity's blind drive towards salvation and progress."[19] Agamben here joins the ranks of Western critics of technological progress, which consists not only of left-wing critics, such as Ivan Illich or Günther Anders, but also of staunch conservatives, like Heidegger, Ernst Jünger, and Carl Schmitt. For these thinkers, if not since Plato then at least since Descartes, Western thought has allegedly favored abstraction over embodiment, reason over experience, the dissection and classification of the world over its wholeness. Western thinking has gradually veered into a nihilism that has come to dominate not just philosophy but also politics, governance, society, economy, and even our self-understanding as human beings. We can see how this type of critique risks lapsing into not only legitimate anti-technocratic thinking or a critique of the dehumanizing consequences of biopolitics but also into a less sophisticated form of anti-modern, anti-technological, and anti-scientific thinking. In politics, we end up with a description of political development not as an emancipatory or egalitarian process but as a slide toward totalitarianism. Society is allegedly entirely governed by technocratic and bureaucratic reason, itself modeled upon modern science. Modern societies reflect a politics in which an *inanimate*, impersonal governing apparatus captures, molds, and depersonalizes *living* human subjects into data, into infinitely malleable and fungible cogs in the machine.

In a short but emblematic text, entitled "Leviathan's Riddle," Agamben presents us with an image of the modern State as an *automaton*, "an engine that moves itself by springs and wheels as a watch does";[20] as the personification of modern government, the Leviathan (see Chapter 2) "is not something real"[21] but rather a device, a kind of gigantic mechanical Turk, which provides the illusion of being alive. What this machine does—not unlike the anthropological machine we discussed in our chapter on Italian thought and posthumanism—is to include the people by, paradoxically, purging them of all the characteristics that constitute "the people." Pieced together from the *multitude* of bodies, each with their own peculiar idiolects, customs, histories, and gestures, the Leviathan turns this multitude of lived experiences into a bureaucratic, legal, and political abstraction that is "the people." Again, for Agamben, Hobbes' *Leviathan* is representative for modern Western political thought and governance. In Hobbes, Agamben claims, "the multitude has no political meaning and must disappear so that the State can exist," "[the multitude] is the unpolitical element on whose exclusion the city is grounded."[22] According to Agamben, Hobbes demarcates a pivotal moment in Western political thought: the separation of the people into two contradictory meanings. On the one hand, "people" refers to the unified political or administrative body of citizens that constitute the Leviathan; on the other hand, it refers to the multitude, the demographic population in all its differences that constantly evades counting within the strict administrative apparatuses of the body politic. "The people" in modern Western politics have consequently become a kind of Schrödinger's cat, both present and absent, dead and alive at the same time. It is by means of their inclusive exclusion into the body of the Leviathan that the State exists and governs on their behalf as citizens, while the plebeian "popular classes," as unassimilable multitude, perpetually contests the homogenizing power of the state.[23] Especially in modern democracies, in so far as they coincide with capitalist technocratic governance, the *dèmos* [people], as the multitude of cultural or linguistic identities, remain structurally absent. In "Leviathan's Riddle" and *Stasis: Civil War as a Political Paradigm*, Agamben stresses that the *oikos,* the family home in which the people dwell and from which they derive their identity and sense of belonging, always already complicates and subverts the universalist pretensions of the State that rules the *polis*, the city or public life generally speaking.[24] Once again, we sense an apparently irresolvable tension in Agamben's analyses. His conceptualization of "the people" as a multitude of cultural and linguistic differences and situated bodies can be read as a confirmation of the fundamental *anarchè* [absence of ground] of modern politics despite its totalizing and homogenizing ambitions.[25]

*However,* in order to fulfil this role of a kind of anarchic and destituent potential, "the people" have to remain defined by their local idioms, accents, and customs. Their geographical and cultural identities form the basis for any friction against the administrative apparatuses of sovereign biopolitics. In Agamben, Pasolini shakes hands with Heidegger.

At times, this brings Agamben to adopt contrarian and somewhat contradictory political views. In an opinion piece from 2013, written at the tail end of the economic Eurocrisis, Agamben delivers a radical critique of the European Union with which Meloni would likely not disagree. Agamben argues that "the European Union has been formed by ignoring the concrete cultural links that exist between nations."[26] This Europe purportedly "strives to exist on a strictly economic basis, abandoning all true affinities between lifestyles, culture and religion." In its current form, the European Union, as a modern-day Leviathan, turns the multitude of historical nations and cultural spheres into abstract units or codes of bureaucratic governmentality. For Agamben, given the patchwork of cultural and linguistic identities and affinities that is Europe, "not only is there no sense in asking a Greek or an Italian to live like a German but even if this were possible, it would lead to the destruction of *a cultural heritage that exists as a way of life.*"[27] The homogenization of Europe's manifold local identities into what Agamben imagines as a kind of Protestant over-organized, stingy, and technophilic subject will only lead Europe into ultimately untenable antagonisms. "A political unit that prefers to ignore lifestyles is not only condemned not to last, but, as Europe has eloquently shown, it cannot even establish itself as such." Agamben then proposes to consider reconfiguring the European Union into different transnational political units, or empires, that would be based on cultural and linguistic affinities, shared legacies and kindred forms-of-life, i.e. a Latin empire versus a Germanic or Anglo-Saxon empire.

However, Agamben is no nativist trying to reduce European cultures to their traditional communitarian customs. In stark contrast to his musings on the constitution of a Mediterranean political union based on alleged culinary and aesthetic penchants, Agamben is extremely sensible to the plight of refugees and sees in them a new political figure capable of capturing the "by now unstoppable decline of the nation-state and the general corrosion of traditional political-juridical categories."[28] The refugee, in Agamben, becomes an emblematic figure for a politics which resists the Leviathan without regressing into nativism: "the refugee is perhaps *the only thinkable figure for the people of our time* and the only category in which one may see today—at least until the process of dissolution of the nation-state and of its sovereignty has achieved full completion—the forms and limits of a coming political community."[29] Rather than being pitted against "the people" in the ethic sense of natives, those who may claim their birthright, as is clearly the case in Meloni's neoconservative politics, in Agamben, the refugee becomes the only figure left to embody anarchic, subversive, and destituent potential against the homogenizing and increasingly defensive State. The refugee replaces older political subjects such as the citizen, the worker and even "the people."[30] The refugee is as close as we can get to a name for "the human" itself in our contemporary geo-political order that remains ingrained in the nation-state.[31] As the nation-state turns nativity and birthright "into the foundation of its own sovereignty" and, as a consequence, of the citizenship and assorted rights it grants to those born on its territory, it immediately absorbs the purest of bare life, newborn human life, into the bureaucratic and technocratic Leviathan it fundamentally is. The human being is thus "the immediately vanishing presupposition (and, in fact, the presupposition that must never come to light as such) of the citizen."[32] By appealing to the right to life and shelter by the sole virtue of being human (and not by being a citizen), the refugee "brings a radical crisis to the principles of the nation-state and clears the way for a renewal of categories that can no longer be delayed."[33] The figure of the refugee touches at the heart of political modernity as it undoes "the very principle of the inscription of nativity as well as the trinity of state-nation-territory that is founded on that principle"[34] and that is absolutely central to modern (geo)politics. In this new geopolitical configuration in which nativity, the fact of being born into a territory and the cultural and linguistic communities that dwell there, is resolutely cut loose, or "destituted" in Agamben's terminology, from nation- and statehood. "The people" of Europe, understood as living human bodies, would now find themselves in "a position of exodus or refuge; the status of European would then mean the being-in-exodus of the citizen."[35] Instead of being cut up into "empires" based on shared ways of life, Europe would be "an aterritorial or extraterritorial space" for "the people" recast as radically unbound naked life, for a "coming community" that is not rooted in a prior shared identity but in the anarchic potentiality to destitute any biopolitically constituted identity.[36]

# "Moving Backwards Towards the Present": Agamben and Eurocentrism

In both his apocalyptic visions of our post-Covid-19 world and his debunking of the European Union, Agamben's thinking remains clearly Eurocentric. The slow-burning Apocalypse Agamben describes is that of European civilization and culture. Yet he claims that with the decline of the West "*humankind* today is disappearing, like a face in the sand erased on the shore."[37] This sentence is a reference to Michel Foucault's *The Order of Things* in which the latter claims that the *idea* of humankind ("man" as a concept in the history of epistemology) may very well disappear from our current scientific thinking. But in Agamben the *epistemological* concept of humankind is substituted for a *historical-political* conception of humankind manifest in contemporary governmentality, and particularly the biopolitical response to the Covid-19 pandemic. Agamben inscribes actual humankind—or perhaps better still, the multitude of existing human bodies and communities—into the history of the decline of Western thought and culture.

Is the house burning down, or are other homes being put up next to ours? Is Western culture on its way out or merely transforming through the increasing infusion with the cultures of refugees and migrants? Obviously, Agamben is clear about the fact that his archaeological project always entailed an archaeology of European thought, an excavation of its theological–political roots. Yet, despite its emphasis on history, there is something oddly static about Agamben's conception of European or Italian culture. Its origins not only continue to haunt the present but firmly keep the present in its grasp to the point of destroying it in an ever-increasing intensification of the logic of bio- and technopower. This rigid narrative of European cultural and intellectual-historical decline cannot but invoke mourning over a loss of identity. Society and politics were already corrupted with the ancient Greeks … and things only went further downhill from thereon. Agamben can only admit phenomena such as globalization or mass culture as steps toward the abyss of a homogenized technocratic *pensiero unico* adverse to any singular, situated identity, and never as positive transformations. For Agamben, we can only "move backwards towards the present"[38] and find resistance in the depths of the cultural archive.

Like Pasolini before him, Agamben cannot find potential in the present of an increasingly multicultural Europe or Italy, in the emerging global mass culture or new technologies. The truly global challenge of the Anthropocene also fails to offer any potentialities for emancipation. Tellingly, the only glimmer of hope Agamben allows for are the "now-dead languages"[39] of philosophy and poetry. What remains after the house has burned down is no longer anything tangible but the immaterial language of ideas and poetry. In other words, the intellectual and aesthetic tradition handed down to us constitutes the way out of the burning house of Western culture. Both philosophy and poetry dwell in language, and as such may reconnect us with the potential that dwells in language to imagine a new humankind, a new culture and a new world. Not everyone will be able to speak or understand this language, Agamben writes, as "even in their burning language people continue to talk nonsense,"[40] but the key, once again, is *logos* that has always been so central to the European tradition.

## Weak Thought versus Identitarianism

As we mentioned in the introduction to this chapter, conservative politicians such as Meloni offer a *political ontology* that appeals to many. As ontology, it claims to *identify* beings and their place in a global order of being in which a Great Chain of man-versus-woman, Italian-versus-migrant or traditional-versus-woke determines who counts as human versus the rest. Yet, in opposition to identitarian ideologies, dissident and critical political ontologies take shape. The refugee as the key political figure of our times in Agamben (instead of being a mere transit figure), or Pasolini's pessimistic diagnosis of an anthropological mutation for the worst in the 1970s, and in our chapter on posthumanism and environmentalism we delineated new ontologies that posit our living, earthly, or even cosmic matter as a new *archè* for political consciousness and engagement. All of these assume that we can step from a state of *being*, an alleged identity, into a political *praxis*. In his conception of *pensiero debole* [weak thought], Gianni Vattimo is skeptical of such need for ontological grounds. For Vattimo, even the most well-intended and progressive ontologies are anachronistic, if not outright reactionary. They are nostalgic for a *natural* state of all things, even if this state is one of flux and impatient desire. However, such attempts at grounding praxis in ontology are ill-fitted for today's social and technological reality, Vattimo claims:

> The strong frameworks of metaphysics (*archai*, *Gründe*, primary evidences, and ultimate destinies) are only forms of self-assurance for epochs in which technology and social organization failed to render us capable of living in a more open horizon (as is the case in our day and age), in a horizon less "magically" guaranteed. The ruling concepts of metaphysics … turn out to be means of discipline and reassurance that are no longer necessary.[41]

The very notion of "being," the very possibility of thinking in terms of being and identities, is in itself historically, socially, or technologically mediated and therefore subject to significant changes over time. Meloni's weaponization of her identity as an Italian woman, mother, and Christian, but also the discovery of our being as living matter, only make sense in the here-and-now of populism and the Anthropocene instead of referring to transhistorical categories such as "woman" or "life." They reflect no universally valid ontological ground but historically contingent discursive and political shifts. The need for an ontology, political or otherwise, in fact affirms the transience of being, as being is used as a shelter against historicity, against the passing of time. According to Vattimo, we should "liberate being from the idea of stable presence" and understand it in its temporal essence. This entails the "enfeeblement" of being and the creation of a "weak thought" that "prepares a new ontology."[42]

Weak thought does not so just abandon the alleged identity of beings in favor of a pure and finally unshackled difference, as this would result in yet another form of a-historicism. It would reduce being to pure and incomprehensible contingency. Vattimo accepts that we cannot but think and act politically from the categories historically handed down to us, like "humanity," "(wo)manhood," or "national identity." But he urges us to simultaneously reconsider beings and identities from a post-metaphysical perspective, as a heritage, as "traces of what has lived"[43] and not as inalterable givens. Vattimo proposes a weak ontology that, on the one hand, acknowledges the inevitability of a historically constituted thinking in terms of identity and being, but that, on the other hand, sets to "perverting them through the exposition of their constitutive mortality and transience."[44] Vattimo speaks of a "degrounding of thought": any claim to being and identity within the world as the ground for our understanding of and agency in that world can only be an interpretation which, in turn, is simply an intervention in a historically specific socio-cultural or political situation and is thus constitutively limited by the latter.[45] Tradition, and the identities we presume are forever rooted in it, are in reality nothing more than "a closely netted interplay of interferences."[46]

Thus, the avowed "weakness" of weak thought is by no means a "lack" nor is it otherwise negatively coded. Vattimo proudly claims weakness of thought as well as weakness of being. Today, "being experiences the fullness of its decline … fully living its weakness."[47] We should not attempt to hold off this decline, compensate for this weakness, even less try to restore alleged prior and original identities, or seek new ontological grounds in previously ignored bodies or local ways of living and thinking. *Pensiero debole* rejects Meloni's *Io sono*, as if the categories she proudly claims had not been corroded in recent decades. Rejecting revivals of Catholic fundamentalism among American and European conservatives, Vattimo proposes, among other things, a "weak Christianity."[48] But he also argues against the materialist or nostalgic desire to experience true being "as occurring somewhere else, in an originary ground and thence yet again as an entity."[49] The task would be neither to vociferate *Io sono!* and *Noi siamo!* nor to replace the former by a nonhuman or decolonial *Voi siete!,* but "accompanying being along on its twilight journey and preparing for a post-metaphysical world."[50] Vattimo's incitement raises a key question: what will be left of Italian thought in this post-metaphysical world? If *italianità* is indeed not a metaphysical ground but a contingent and malleable object of interpretation and reinterpretation, what are then the bounds of Italian thought? Sandro Mezzadra's work may allow us to answer this question.

## Mezzadra: Italian Thought beyond Europe

In the introduction to this book, we mentioned how, for Sandro Mezzadra, the phenomenon of migration offers a point of entrance into all sorts of political, philosophical, and geographical questions radically different from the predominantly Eurocentric vocabulary of much of Italian thought. The latter stresses Eurocentric notions, such as class struggle, autonomy, and even biopolitics, as well as its insisting on various genealogies of European thought as sources of inspiration. Italian thought often focuses on the European cultural archive as a primary site of struggle. This is not to say that (post-)workerist critiques of precarity or immaterial labor or philosophical archaeologies of immunity are no longer legitimate, or that Mezzadra dismisses them as "merely" European or Eurocentric. That would be just as unproductive as older dismissals of non-European culture. But crucially, these concepts are situated in a global geo-political context that is rapidly changing, and which inevitably affects European and Italian societies. The precarious workers of Rome and Milan—from delivery riders and call center operators to cultural workers—now find themselves in the same boat as recently arrived migrant workers from Bangladesh and Albania. Moreover, Italy finds itself at the forefront of the European refugee crisis, which is by now permanent, to the point of defying the very notion of "crisis" (see the conclusion of this book). Daily waves of refugees arrive at the Italian island of Lampedusa from across the Mediterranean, risking their lives for a future in Europe. Yet they encounter a "fortress Europe" of which Italy now finds itself to be a first defender. Migrants and refugees are indicators of changing global hierarchies. The conservative rhetoric of Giorgia Meloni and others thereby constitutes a vehement rejection of these changes, which risk provincializing Europe to such an extent that it becomes one mere region among others in a multipolar world order.[51]

Unlike Agamben's ultimately cerebral take on the refugee as a limit-concept rather than a sociological reality, Mezzadra takes this new geopolitical development as a starting point for his analyses. In *Border as Method, or The Multiplication of Labor*, co-authored with Brett Neilson, we read how "in the current global transition, under the pressure of capital's financialization, there is a need to test some of the most cherished notions and theoretical paradigms produced by political economy and social sciences ... from the international division of labor to center and periphery."[52] Globalization has led to the expansion of capitalist frontiers to new markets, new forms of labor, new economic and political alliances, but also to the blurring of traditional boundaries between formal and informal economies, between work and non-work, between citizen and denizen. These socio-political changes necessitate a fundamental rethinking of the categories we use to comprehend these transformations, like "labor," "class," or "nation." Mezzadra and Neilson argue that we see a multiplication of labor today, not just in the sense that new types of labor are added (such as immaterial, cognitive or affective labor), but more importantly that labor practices become heterogeneous due to migration flows. In the migrant experience, labor is no longer the medium for social emancipation vis-à-vis capital and the State that it once was for native working classes in the Global North. The precarity of their working conditions are deeply entangled with the issue of precarious citizenship. Despite Marxist theory's avowed internationalism, the worker is mostly conceived of as a citizen-worker, even when confronting a hostile capitalist State. Citizenship rights provide the primary toolbox for expanding labor rights and protections. The migrant worker, however, does not have access to the forms of political subjecthood and agency that come with citizenship. In this sense, "liberating political imagination from the burden of the citizen-worker and the state is particularly urgent to open up spaces within which the organization of new forms of political subjectivity becomes possible," Mezzadra and Neilson write.[53]

Paradoxically, for Mezzadra and Neilson, globalization does not signify a smooth borderless world but a *proliferation of borders*, some visible (walls, border patrols), some invisible (legislation, surveillance). Borders become harder to localize as detention centers for migrants are built in urban centers or on remote islands. European and American border security is outsourced to countries in North Africa and Mesoamerica, becomes militarized and ends up in legal and political grey zones. The European Union, for instance, condones so-called push backs in the Mediterranean whereby migrant boats are forced back into open sea, against European regulations. Despite claims made by far-right politicians, borders are no longer a matter for the nation-state alone. On the one hand, global capital does not care about borders: labor markets and national economies need the same migrants that states desperately try to regulate or keep out. On the other hand, borders are more and more externalized, as Northern member states of the European Union are dependent on Italian and Greek border security. At the same time, special economic zones proliferate, blurring the boundaries between states and corporations and merging their interests. Rather than freely moving about in a borderless world, more and more human subjects are "in transit," as they move from one geographical or legal border to another.[54] For Mezzadra and Neilson, this means that subjects, in particular migrant workers, need to negotiate their identity at each passage. Their legal identity ("Do I have a right to enter, to work?"), but also their cultural

("Where is my community?") and political identities ("What can I do? How can we organize?") are constantly in flux and exposed to political tensions. In stark contrast to the nationalist imagination, according to Mezzadra and Neilson, borders are "far from serving merely to block or obstruct global passages of people, money, or objects."[55] In fact, borders assemble and *articulate* all these crossings and subsequently produce new subjects as well as new configurations of daily life in now global societies. "Borders play a key role in the production of the heterogeneous time and space of contemporary global and postcolonial capitalism,"[56] Mezzadra and Neilson argue.

To understand these fundamental global changes, the concept of "border" becomes a heuristic device, a specific angle from which to analyze contemporary phenomena such as transformations in labor, migration, techniques of securitization and surveillance, or cultural hybridization. It is this change of perspective that allows Mezzadra and Neilson to question some of the fundamental assumptions of Italian biopolitical theories of biopolitics, which they deem too rigid and absolutist. As we noted in our previous chapters on biopolitics, the fundamental structure of Western biopolitics, according to Agamben, is that of a paradoxical simultaneous inclusion-exclusion. To affirm, protect, or immunize the vital identity of the people, the body politic or the individual, something else—and usually someone else—needs to be excluded, warded off, and repressed. This liminal bare life becomes the vanishing mediator for any kind of positive identity, a gesture that needs to be infinitely repeated. Those who are excluded find themselves in a state of exception, in-between the law and absolute lawlessness, reduced to bare life. For Agamben, the modern paradigm of this state of exception is the *camp*, most terrifyingly the concentration camps and gulags of twentieth-century totalitarian regimes, but also the refugee camp.[57] In the camp, the state of exception finds its material localization. However, Mezzadra and Neilson criticize Agamben's conflation of the state of exception with exceptional spaces like the camps. They agree that limit-cases, such as camps for "illegal migrants" in Lampedusa or the Jungle of Calais, evoke Agamben's idea that "the camp catches its inhabitants in a legal order for the purposes of excluding them from this very same order."[58] However, Agamben turns the exception into the rule, which ultimately leads to excessively despairing assessments of global political phenomena, such as attempts to regulate labor migration, or refugee detention centers. By reducing the sociology of migration to its worst outcomes in camps of abandonment and despair, Agamben obscures migrants' real political agency and emancipatory potential. Migrants are monolithically and prematurely identified with the image of the universal victim.

For Mezzadra and Neilson, the "border between inclusion and exclusion is stretched and reworked by the spatial and temporal dynamics of contemporary capitalism."[59] Agamben's assessments remain anchored in European history, culminating in the immense trauma of the extermination camps of the Holocaust. Agamben cannot escape the lure of taking on an apocalyptic tone. Not all refugees find themselves in a camp, not all migrants are ruthlessly reduced to bare life. As we mentioned earlier, in Mezzadra and Neilson's eyes, the biopolitical apparatus, of which the border is perhaps the most condensed form, consists of a complex articulation of legal, political, technological, and cultural factors that do not so much dehumanize or incapacitate migrants and refugees inescapably. Though tragedies certainly occur, borders also produce heterogeneous subjects who constantly renegotiate and at times contest the assemblages of power through which they are pushed. In this sense, there is a continuity of such negotiations and struggles between the experience of refugees and migrants, and, for example, their offspring in the French *banlieues*.[60] The *banlieues* are spatially, legally, culturally, and politically segregated suburbs at the border of French society. Rather than being a camp of sorts where subjects are suppressed by the allegedly sovereign power of the French Republic, the *banlieues* constitute a space where new socio-cultural identities and political networks are constantly created, which often spread out into wider French society. The *banlieues* act as a kind of laboratory for music, fashion, and a renewed sense of French multi-ethnic identity. At the same time, the *banlieues* are also the scene where French colonial history comes back to haunt practices of policing, as well as France's alleged republican universalism. The scapegoating of the *banlieues* as a hotbed of crime and other social woes leads to "a resurrection of the colonial distinction between citizen and subject."[61] "Agamben's approach [on the other hand] centers on transhistorical and even ontological arguments that have little to do with capitalist developments,"[62] Mezzadra and Neilson clarify that, in a world characterized by global flows of capital and people, Agamben's static model of inescapable concentration camps fails to capture the fact that migrants and refugees experience a range of temporalities, provisional identities, and, albeit limited, types of agency. Both migrants and refugees are in transit and dwell in transit spaces; they pass through different and often conflicting legal and political contexts. In this light, Agamben's insistence on the sovereign, boundless character of biopower exercised in the state of exception "risks wiping out the movements and struggles through which migrants challenge the border on an everyday basis."[63] Agamben's exceptionalist approach is, according to Mezzadra and Neilson, "in many ways the flip side to the human rights perspective in migration politics, since Agamben's schema presupposes either a wholesale stripping of migrants and refugees (as exception) or the existence of a full legal plenitude (as norm)."[64]

## Workerism without Borders?

The concept of "border" offers Mezzadra and Neilson a different, more heterogeneous perspective than that of European Marxism. On the one hand, Mezzadra and Neilson are inspired by Italian *operaismo*, particularly the workerist notion of "class composition" (see Chapter 3), "which suggests a complex play of social forces, experiences, and behaviors in the making of class."[65] For the workerists, class was always much more than one's objective position in the social structure of capitalism and its antagonisms; workerist "class composition" is resolutely anti-deterministic: there is a subjective element to class, as class composition takes place in practice. Class emerges "in practices of struggle and experiences of labor organization,"[66] which extend beyond the factory floor into daily life, and which mobilize and articulate social, cultural, and gendered lived experiences. Workerist analyses of class composition thus constitute a first and crucial step in understanding "the emergence of new constellations of labor beyond the exclusive reference to the industrial worker that has dominated Western Marxism."[67] On the other hand, for Mezzadra and Neilson, the workerist picture remains incomplete, as it ignores "the deeper questioning of this emphasis on the industrial worker by anticolonial thinkers and practitioners."[68] This line of questioning has become essential in a world determined by globalization and the *condizione postcoloniale* [postcolonial condition].[69] Contemporary politics continues to struggle with the heritage of colonialism, in particular when it comes to issues of migration from the Global South to the Global North. Especially, labor migration provides a key source of political tension in an increasingly unstable and multipolar world order. Moreover, Mezzadra and Neilson stress the urgency to include feminist arguments, like those pioneered by Federici (see Chapter 1), which point out how another boundary, that between productive and reproductive labor, between "housework," or "care work," and "real work," has always been misleading. Today these lines are becoming increasingly porous in global and heterogenous labor markets. Many migrants, especially women, perform types of labor that can be called "reproductive" (childcare, housekeeping, feeding families and other care work, but also sex work) and find themselves in the globally expanding grey area between private and professional life.

> The combined implications of these historical, anticolonial, and feminist reflections are important ... because forms and experiences of labor mobility, both historically and in the present day, are repeatedly linked with processes of heterogenization of the workforce. A crucial contribution of these theoretical and political elaborations has been to show how such a differentiation of labor is the historical and geographical norm, rather than the exception of capital writ large.[70]

By reading Italian workerist concepts such as "class composition" through the wide-angle lens of globalization and our postcolonial condition, Mezzadra and Neilson integrate Italian theoretical legacies into global debates, which invite Italian thought to shed its Eurocentrist feathers. The same goes for the central post-workerist concept of "immaterial labor." Mezzadra and Neilson recognize that "immaterial labor" as developed by Italian exiles in Paris in the 1990s was a first attempt to rethink "the political conditions of antagonism and subversion under post-Fordist conditions."[71] But the concept had struggled from its inception with the implied claim "about the hegemony of these kinds of laboring activity and the way they were supposed to drive capitalism's development in its global phase."[72] Lazzarato, Negri, and others were perhaps too concerned with the renewal of Marxist theory through the experiences of Western-European metropolitan workers to see that "immaterial labor" is perhaps better understood as one symptom among many of the global heterogenization of labor.[73] Under globalization and the prevalence of labor migration, "laboring figures are constantly shuffled and recombined," as with the example of female migrant care work.[74] "Rather than assuming that the concept of immaterial labor can hold together experiences as different as those of carers and traders,"

Mezzadra and Neilson argue, "it is necessary to piece together fragments and follow leads to discern the processes of societization that generate both divisions and linkages between and beyond them."[75] Now that processes of globalization and the intensification of labor migration have profoundly altered post-Schengen Europe, it is perhaps best to approach "immaterial labor" not as an analytical tool but as "a historical concept that opened a new field of research and debate on labor after the crisis of Fordism but has been superseded more by material circumstances than theoretical criticisms."[76]

# Provincializing Italian Thought? From Mezzadra to Negri and Hardt

In his book *La condizione postcoloniale*, Mezzadra argues that post- and decolonial theory allows to provincialize Italian thought.[77] The post- or decolonial perspective de-centers Western thought and includes a multitude of historical narratives and epistemological viewpoints from other parts of the globe. It proposes, for example, a different story of capitalism, in which the key scenes are located far away from the industrial centers of metropolitan Europe, in plantations and extractivist infrastructures that act as labor resource pools, laboratories for capitalist governance, and fuel centers that sustain infinite flows of commodities. Post- and decolonial theory propose a different history of the world: not another world history, another unifying narrative, but a complex, rhizomatic narrative that does justice to the pluriverse we inhabit and in which "Europe" is but one of many nodes. For Mezzadra, postcolonial thought privileges *difference* and the potential politics of differences that may emerge from it.[78] For Mezzadra, colonialism finds itself caught in a feedback loop in which it is driven by capitalist expansionism while constantly fueling it by tapping into new resources, labor forces, and markets. Capitalist accumulation dynamics impose a single history on the world as capital reduces all its outsides into vehicles for further self-accumulation. It forces both a Eurocentric narrative of progress onto the world, in which "Europe" represents the most advanced stage of human development, *and* a capitalist temporality of growth, short-term interest, the compartmentalization of our calendar according to capitalist utilitarian principles. Mezzadra speaks of the "violent synchronization" of modern colonial/capitalist time.[79] In contrast, the temporality of the "post-" in "postcolonial," Mezzadra claims,

> is a time in which domination and exploitation have certainly not ceased, but in which rather the possibility of identifying privileged places to act out transformation appears suspended (this is the ultimate sense, it seems to us, of the postcolonial insistence on *decentralization*): a time in which, on the other hand, any judgement on the "backwardness" or "advancement" of a given situation becomes *provincialized*, in the sense that it can only find its operational criterion in the present—and not in a model of "development" assumed as normative.[80]

The prefix "post-" does not herald the end of colonial structures of exploitation—neither is the prefix "de-" in "decolonial" purely negative—but it opens a space and time for introducing a plurality of different voices, histories, and epistemologies. At the same time, postcolonialism's politics of difference puts a definitive end to the idea of a privileged political subject or location, whether it is the industrial worker on the factory floor or the immaterial cognitive worker behind her laptop in Starbucks, and its tacit Eurocentric, gendered, and racializing assumptions. Even in the workerist imagination, "the worker" tended to remain European, metropolitan, and male. As we noted earlier, for Mezzadra, this entails, most importantly, a fundamental reevaluation of the theoretical legacy of Italian Marxism: what does "real subsumption" mean in the pluriverse?[81] Are we all co-opted by global capitalism in the same way? Are the relations between the members of the "multitude" really all that horizontal, or do old hierarchies remain? Is the immaterialization of labor in the Global North really a breeding ground for a new global political subject for whom "labor" supposedly means the same thing in every corner of the world?

Perhaps there is something ironic about the necessity for provincializing Italian thought. Italian philosophy has long struggled to free itself from a certain provincialism vis-à-vis the philosophical superpowers Germany and France, and now it finds itself faced with a series of transformations and crises on a global scale, like the European refugee crisis, which challenges its concepts and viewpoints. These viewpoints force Italian thought to question the identity it so carefully and precariously discovered for itself, particularly in its emphasis on the admixture of workerist and biopolitical theories (see the introduction to this book).

In their work *Commonwealth*, Negri and Hardt attempt to include non-Western perspectives in their conceptualization of the multitude and the latter's politics of difference. Moreover, they point out the epistemological groundwork that needs to be done for this inclusive multitude to emerge. Among other things, they analyze the pivotal role played by *representation* in Western political thought. For modern political power, representation is doubly effective. On the one hand, the multitude of "concrete identities [is] transformed into abstract representations from which the structures of political mediation can produce (schematically) a formal unity."[82] Once more we recognize the towering figure of the Leviathan. The infinite multiplicity of living bodies is abstracted into supposedly general categories like "the people," "Italians," "women and men," and so on. The definition of these collective identities decisively constitutes the prerogative of the State. On the other hand, as a tool for governance, representation first and foremost "requires that identities remain static and separate: we are forced continually to perform our identities and punished for any deviation from them."[83] Even if the modern emphasis on representation also allows for mediated identities to make emancipatory claims *as a category* (as women or as workers), this requires that they "faithfully perform their separation and unchanging character."[84] In contrast, a truly emancipatory movement for our times would entail a process of articulation of seemingly unbridgeable differences. Truly emancipatory politics refuses the identities on offer under the State's representative politics. "Making the multitude," Negri and Hardt write, "and thus the event of insurrection … is not a process of fusion or unification … but rather sets in motion a proliferation of singularities that are composed by the lasting encounters in the common."[85] Negri and Hardt are well aware that *this* "making of the multitude," which keeps it suspended in its radical plurality, parts way with modern, twentieth-century Marxist theory. "Today we are a long way from the construction of *a political figure* adequate to the revolutionary process … however it emerges it will have to take a path radically different from that [communist] tradition."[86]

In *Commonwealth*, pertinently, Negri and Hardt stress that the multitude should avoid the decidedly modern and Western *temporality* of the political subject that Marxism attempted to construct: an objective working-class subject steeped in the dialectical progress of history, catapulted into the latter by capitalism's ruthless subsumption of our living time, eagerly anticipating a brighter and liberated future. As Negri and Hardt explain, the Marxist thinkers of the twentieth century often remain stuck in the binary opposition between the *modern* and the *antimodern*. Marx and Lenin ridiculed the puerile or the romantic reveries of anarchism, but also Theodor Adorno and Walter Benjamin denounced the resurgent archaic barbarism within modern times,[87] of which the latter supposedly is capable only of breeding monsters, i.e., the monsters of nativism, racism, and antisemitism.[88] According to Negri and Hardt, modern Western Marxism thus remains blind for the many ways in which non-Western, colonial subjects, embodied in Shakespeare's character of Caliban,[89] the half-man half-monster living on the magician Prospero's distant island, raise awareness of the necessity to break out of this binary:

> From the perspective of the European colonizers the monster is contained in the dialectical struggle between reason and madness, progress and barbarism, modernity and antimodernity. From the perspective of the colonized, though, in their struggle for liberation, Caliban, who is endowed with as much or more reason and civilization as the colonizers, is monstrous only to the extent that his desire for freedom exceeds the bounds of the colonial relationship of biopower, blowing apart the chains of the dialectic.[90]

The figure of Caliban does not so much represent yet another privileged political subject, this time for our postcolonial age, but rather a third position, in-between modernity and antimodernity, which remains structurally open-ended and inclusive. For Negri and Hardt, Caliban captures what they call "*altermodernity*."[91] Altermodernity may partly overlap with antimodernity, as it may emerge from anti-colonial or indigenous struggles that appeal to identity and tradition, but it significantly "shifts the emphasis from resistance to alternative."[92] Rather than confining non-Western identities into static cultural, religious, and political essences that can easily be exploited by new forms of (bio)power that turn tradition into a justification for oppression, altermodernity incorporates these identities into new fields of struggle, which are, "at least potentially, newly aligned, not in the sense that they are unified or that one holds hegemony over others, but in that they autonomously forward on parallel paths."[93]

Negri and Hardt provide the example of social struggles in Latin America, like the Zapatista movement, where indigenous groups, peasants, and workers joined forces over labor struggles. These social movements are multi-coded along racial and cultural axes *and* along "the axis of the various sectors of labor engaged in common struggle."[94] As such, these struggles throw traditional relations of hegemony and representation in modern social conflicts (workers above indigenous subjects, labor above culture, emancipation above tradition, economic autonomy above cultural autonomy) into question. "In altermodernity the obstacles and divisions of antimodernity—particularly those between civilizational and labor struggles—have been displaced by a new physiognomy of struggles that poses multiplicity as a primary element of the political project,"[95] Negri and Hardt affirm. In altermodernity not a single subject emerges that marches along the drumbeat of history and revolution, but "a multiplicity of social singularities defined more or less by their culture or ethnicity or labor position."[96] It constitutes a global, cross-cultural and multiethnic *multitude* that designates a kind of "applied parallelism" in which appeals to cultural, linguistic, or indigenous autonomy go hand in hand with equality and interdependence "among vast multiplicities of singularities."[97]

What brings these multiplicities together, according to Negri and Hardt, is their claim to *the commons,* the natural and cultural resources available to and shared by all those who live together. The common denominator within the multitude is its opposition to global processes of privatization, like the corporate expropriation of water and natural resources, for example, and the struggle for their restitution to common use. It is in the struggle over the commons that the multitude is engaged in a process of metamorphosis, as resistance and collaboration are transformative experiences. Altermodern struggles neither assume the forwardly propelled subject of modernity nor the static subjects of cultural traditions, but their joint articulation and transformations as they mutually engage challenge and inform one another in terms of knowledge sharing, organizational strategies, or modes of democratic decision-making.

Despite criticisms leveled against their conceptualization of the multitude and strategies to include indigenous struggles into the multitude—in *Commonwealth* the latter remains predominantly engaged in labor struggles and not, for example, struggles over land—Negri and Hardt do make a crucial proposition: to embed workerist ideas in the push towards altermodernity.[98] In a sense, Negri and Hardt offer a glimpse of what *demodernizing Italian thought* may look like. Just like *alter*modernity does not mean *anti*modernity, *de*modernizing does not entail the wholesale rejection of modernity. Demodernizing Italian thought means, in a post- or decolonial perspective, to untie key elements in Italian thought, like biopolitical theory or the critique of capitalism, from Eurocentric, modern(ist) premises. It questions ideas like the notion of a privileged political subject like the working class, a teleological sense of history, the claim that exclusively labor is pivotal to modern political conflict or the assumption that biopolitics is ultimately to be understood in light of European totalitarianism and not colonial imperialism. Negri and Hardt briefly note that "it would be a mistake … to identify Marxism as a whole with a progressivist notion of modernity."[99] Proletarian revolts from the Luddites to the Chinese Revolution are often the expression of a desire for a non-capitalist way of life that preceded primitive accumulation and the privatization of the commons (or at least looks remarkably like it).[100] Even the later Marx himself, Negri and Hardt claim, inspired by anthropological research, becomes more and more convinced that pre-capitalist and non-Western forms of collective living and sharing common property could serve as a model for a communist society—the germ of demodernizing Marx is already present … in Marx.[101]

## Demodernizing Italian Thought?

The work of Franco "Bifo" Berardi offers a potential starting point for demodernizing Italian thought and in particular autonomist ideas, albeit differently from Negri and Hardt's attempts. In works such as *After the Future*, *Futurability* and *Precarious Rhapsody*, Berardi claims that today's progressive social and political movements must organize themselves *in the absence of a future*. For Berardi, who was one of the key figures in the *Autonomia* movement of the mid- and late 1970s, also known as the "Movement of 1977," that particular year marked *the end of the future*.[102] Two decades before Francis Fukuyama declared the end of history,[103] implying that the Marxist dream of a history determined by a dialectical march toward new and shining horizons had in fact been replaced by hegemonic global capitalism and its teleology of infinite economic growth, the Movement of 1977 heralds another end of history, not as something to be held *against* emancipatory movements but as something to be welcomed *within* those movements. "*La rivoluzione è finita, abbiamo vinto!,*" declares the autonomist journal *A/Traverso* proudly in the summer of 1977: "the revolution is over, we have won!"[104] Not that a classless society had finally arrived in Bologna or Turin, but the aim of this speech act was to ironically perform and anticipate older progressivist tropes in order to escape them. In left-wing discourse, "Revolution" and "History" had always been coupled and written in singular with capital letters. But for *Autonomia,* it is in their separation, in crossing them out—hence the slash in *A/Traverso*—that true liberation lies. "*Dopo il '77 non c'è più la Storia. Ci sono le storie*"[105] ["After '77 there is no more History. There are stories."], Berardi writes in his memoir *Dell'innocenza. 1977: l'anno della premonizione.*

The *Autonomia* movement of the 1970s, which to an extent is the successor to workerism, abandoned the idea that a socially progressive movement necessarily implies a unified, homogeneous subject like the proletariat, which shared supposedly objective interests (foremost *economic* interests) and a common objective (a revolution that would give birth to a classless society). The *Autonomia* movement consisted of an assemblage or multitude of different groups and movements that refused to huddle together under the umbrella of a uniform communist revolution. Feminists, gay rights movements, students, the counterculture that had emerged from the sixties, anarchists and other "spontaneous" far-left groups, and the embryonic green movement constituted the *Indiani metropolitani* or "Metropolitan Indians." Moreover, *Autonomia* did not just strive for the autonomy of workers from capital but the emancipation from capital *per se* in a wholesale rejection of "productivism." Fueled, among other things, by the countercultural imagination of the "drop out" (and later, tragically, the junkie) and feminist critiques of the false opposition between production and reproduction, the Movement of 1977 did not only practice work refusal [*rifiuto di lavoro*] as a tactic for emancipating workers from capitalist social relations, as the workerists intended,[106] but questioned more radically the liberating potential of labor itself. It sought to rid individuals from the fetishization of work and the pressures of being a productive member of society. Far from being reactionary, *Autonomia* thus rejected the idea of a horizon or objective *telos*, that is to say, the aspiration for a homogenous better future as the alpha and omega of political engagement. On the contrary, it is the absence of any fixed idea of the future that opens up the potential for the invention of new forms of horizontal and rhizomatic political organization, a multiplicity of politically relevant subjects and new strategies for direct action. Among such strategies used by *Autonomia* are the creation of *centri sociali* [self-managed socio-cultural centers in Italy's major cities] and, most famously, the creation of "free radios" and later TV stations. More so than the workerists, *Autonomia* was aware of the role of mass media and pop culture in the formation of contemporary identities—identities that, in a sense, are "pre-historical," savage identities, cut loose from the *telos* of history and modernity.

However, Berardi also stresses the *ambiguity* of "the end of future" that arrived in Italy's student cities in 1977. On the one hand, for Berardi, the year 1977 heralds the "passage beyond modernity."[107] The acme of autonomist thought and action in Italy witnesses the closure of the modern horizon as *Autonomia* decisively breaks away from the epistemology of modernity. In this sense, the Movement of 1977 *positively* accomplishes an anthropological mutation of sorts, opposite to the one decried by Pasolini. The subject that emerged in Italian postwar society was not simply the hedonistic, consumerist, and Americanized individual but, on the contrary, a kind of "pre-modern," liberated, multiple, and sensuous subject. The Movement of 1977 constructed a humankind that was perhaps much more akin to Pasolini's nostalgic yearning for an authentic popular subject than the artist infamously critical of the student movement would have cared to admit. The year 1977 therefore marks the "premonition of an anthropological mutation and the emergence of a new transformative subject,"[108] Berardi affirms. On the other hand, the decade of what Berardi describes as "the implosion of the future" as the horizon of emancipatory thought *also facilitates* the emergence of Pasolini's "new fascism" and the assorted new planetary petty bourgeoisie of early neoliberalism.[109] *This* anthropological figure constitutes the subject of a post-historical humanity that fulfills the project of modernity by universalizing the subject of Western capitalism, the Vitruvian man of economic globalization. "Not merely advancing a set of political demands, the movement of '77 [derived] its power from the new forms of social cooperation and technical capacities that would become the foundation of the post-Fordist economy … In that regard, it prefigured the counterrevolutionary response that followed," Sara Nelson and Bruce Braun observe.[110]

In his works reflecting on the botched transformations of the late seventies, Berardi recalls that "*No future!*" also became the defining slogan of the punk years that immediately followed the movement of '77 in all their depressed rage and political impotence. The experimental joy of the *Autonomia* era was gone and punk despair seemed to confirm the rising hegemony of capitalism and Western-style democracy across the globe, culminating in "the end of history," ultimately another way of claiming there is no longer a future. Berardi therefore insists on the need "to resume the thread of analysis of social composition and decomposition if we want to distinguish possible lines of processes of recomposition to come."[111] Perhaps such a process of recomposition first and foremost must connect the lines that connect autonomist unruly identities and *modi operandi* to non-Western, decolonial, and indigenous subjectivities and modes of thinking. As Marcello Tari emphasizes in his incisive study of the autonomist movement, *Autonomia* explicitly claims a kind of altermodernism in its recombinations of Western and indigenous cultural references, most notably in the figure of the Metropolitan Indian who embodies the refusal of "the phantasm of civil society."[112] Against civil society as a separate sphere constituted under the aegis of the state, *Autonomia* pushed for radical multiplicity, an "assemblage of assemblages" of "offensive ways of living," which clearly resonates with the inclusive, global, and indigenized multitude proposed by Negri and Hardt.[113] In particular, as Nelson and Braun suggest, in the Anthropocene autonomist thinking and tactics may help us to "stage a different encounter between *anthropos* and the planetary forces [of] Gaia."[114] Nelson and Braun argue that we need to recognize that the heyday of workerism and autonomism generally coincides with what in environmental theory is known as "The Great Acceleration," the postwar industrial boom and the subsequent explosive growth in fossil fuel consumption.[115] Only then can we unlock autonomism's radical potential for producing new political identities and new types of being-in-common beyond any residual modernism, Euro- and anthropocentrism, perhaps shifting the emphasis away from the workerist conceptualization of "autonomy" to that more inclusive and experimental version of the *Autonomia* movement.

In this chapter, we observed how questions of identity and its political significance haunt contemporary Italian politics as well as Italian thought. We detected an essential tension in the work of Agamben, echoing

Pasolini: the resistance against the alleged homogenization of our world must entail a return to the potentialities of culturally and geographically rooted forms-of-life to find a future in what has been, perhaps a form of "demodernizing" in its own right. At the same time, among others in his conceptualization of the figure of the refugee, Agamben advocates a radical non-identitarian and non-nativist political subjectivity. Against the paradox of a future-oriented nostalgia, we noted how Vattimo categorically rejects all "primary evidences and ultimate destinies." In the work of Mezzadra, Negri and Hardt, and Berardi, we recognized how they open up Italian thought to now global questions of migration, political organization and political subjectivity, recombining biopolitical and autonomist ideas with decolonial and indigenous thought. Our current (geo)political predicament, from the surge of populism to the rapid decline of Western hegemony, demands that Italian thought seeks out new alliances and constellations. The fundamental porosity of Italian thought, as identified by Esposito and others, may once more prove to be the surprising foundation for its continued relevance: it is because of its contradictions and lack of a fully fledged identity that Italian thought is instrumental for understanding the present.

# CONCLUSION: TOWARD A POLITICS OF INVISIBLE CITIES

## Chapter Summary

Today's political predicament is marked by a deep sense of crisis. The world seems threatened from multiple sides at once with the rise of far-right politics, climate catastrophe, institutional decay, pandemics, and so on. In the conclusion, we present Italian thought as a conceptual resource for coming to terms with the contemporary polycrisis. The book has shown how historically Italian thought has often explicitly related itself to political crises and continues to do so today for a new generation of critical theorists. We present Italo Calvino's novel *Invisible Cities* as a paradigm for a politics of potentiality that reveals hidden emancipatory potentialities in critical junctures of our political condition. Just like Marco Polo in Calvino's novel looks beyond the visible cities of the global Mongol Empire to discover invisible, potential cities that promise an escape from the dying Empire, Italian thought today has created concepts like "affirmative biopolitics," "cyberfascism" or "general intellect" that evaluate our contemporary era and articulate potential alternatives.

Italo Calvino's novel *Invisible Cities* commences deep in the palace of Kublai Khan. The leader has amassed an enormous empire, the globe unified under a single political order. The Khan's rule seemingly signifies the end of history, as there are no more worlds to conquer. Calvino's novel appeared in 1972, the year that Apollo 17 returned to Earth, concluding the Americans' explorations of the Moon. It was also the year of Richard Nixon's visit to China, which heralded a slow end to the international standoff between capitalism and communism, and the first repercussions of the collapse of the Bretton Woods global monetary system were being felt, which would eventually birth the rise of global neoliberalism. Indeed, history seemed on a one-way track toward global unity under capitalist globalization and American liberalism. However, in 1972 the Watergate Scandal also emerged, Palestinian militants kidnapped and killed members of the Israeli Olympic team in Munich, and Ferdinand Marcos announced a state of exception in the Philippines that would last until his ousting in 1986. The cracks in the global empire were already starting to show. In Calvino's novel, the Khan's empire is also on the verge of collapsing under its own weight. Held up inside his palace, the Khan knows his territory barely through the illegible signs his servants present on the country's many maps. These cartographic representations show the names of many far-off places that the Khan cannot even imagine. All the while, the fabric that keeps the empire together is gradually loosening. That is why he invites Marco Polo to his court. The Italian explorer will testify of the many places he has visited on his route between Venice and the Orient.

Today, we are similarly breathing the air of impending collapse as wars rage in Ukraine and Gaza, and Donald Trump has his second presidency in a chaotic stampede moving toward dictatorship. In the 1990s and 2000s, it seemed like the world had reached the end of history and that the global empire had achieved uncontested hegemony. Capitalist globalization and liberal democracy seemingly had formed a tandem that would soon envelop the Earth. But a few Italian philosophers noticed the cracks in the system, which gave rise to a wave of Italian thought. Agamben highlighted in *Homo Sacer* how governments were using the state of emergency to suspend the Rule of Law and expose populations to the sovereign decision over life and death, as we saw in the US War on Terror and the abusive treatment of refugees and migrants across the globe. Lazzarato emphasized in *The Making of the Indebted Man* how economic debt was increasingly a tool to curtail democratic self-determination in service of financial capital, as attested in the 2008 global financial crisis. Negri and Hardt noted in *Empire* how the transformation of work under post-Fordism was generating a resistant multitude of new subjectivities trying to wrest itself from the grip of capital, as we witnessed with Occupy Wall Street or the Arab Spring. The cracks that started to appear in the 2000s and 2010s have today only grown larger and have changed shape. To gauge the multifarious challenges of a Global Empire collapsing under its own weight, we have invited several generations of Italian conceptual explorers to show us the way. Their work helps us make sense of the major fault lines of today's political conjuncture. In this book, we have discussed five features of this political polycrisis.

We first discussed the contradictions of contemporary biopolitics in and after the Covid-19 pandemic. Agamben indiscriminately rejected all biopolitical measures enacted to stem the tide of the pandemic. In his view, lockdowns, social distancing, and facemasks were ploys for enforcing a global state of emergency that reduced everyone to bare life. However, we noted that any government policy, in fact, enacts a differential exposure to the risk of death. Imposing a lockdown protects some parts of the population who can work from home or are immunocompromised but sacrifices the security of others, like essential workers or those at risk of depression or loneliness due to a lack of care and social contact. This critique of the biopolitics of differential vulnerabilities should push us to articulate an affirmative biopolitics that sustains life in general and constructs the political institutions to secure that sustenance, as Esposito suggests. Second, the ecological crisis puts into question the anthropocentrism of the biopolitical paradigm in general. Biopolitical theory, both in Italy and beyond, has predominantly discussed the government of *human* populations without considering non-human entities. This not only ignores the animality underlying human life itself, as Agamben suggests, but also disregards the *zōè*-politics and *geo*-politics that inform our interactions with nature. If we want to meet the challenges of climate catastrophe and environmental degradation, we ought to expand the scope of biopolitics to include a posthuman dimension, as Braidotti, Luisetti and Coccia argue. Third, we have studied the rise of a new general intellect composed of social media platforms, AI, and algorithmic management software. Especially post-workerists argue that new technologies are subjecting our mental processes to the logic of capital accumulation. Big Tech is turning human social interactions into data assets that generate financial rents and allow tech companies to surreptitiously influence human conduct in their favor. Yet post-workerism reminds us also of the Foucauldian adage that wherever there is power, there is also resistance. Technology is a stake in class struggle, and collectives possess the persistent capacity to exceed the commands of mental subsumption and reappropriate the general intellect. Fourth, the cyberfascist war machine on social media should make us reconsider the democratic promises of new communication technologies and internet-based political activism so popular around the time of the Twitter revolutions. Social media platforms display an elective affinity with fascism that the left has been unable to replicate for its own political strategies. The rise of cyberfascism, documented by Lazzarato, Eco, Toscano, and others, reveals how the breakdown of social community under neoliberalism has generated a mass society vulnerable to swindling promises of racist nostalgia. Lastly, the notion of social identity itself has become a major site of political struggle. The far right pushes for a populist discourse of ethnic and traditional identity that essentializes white and Western supremacy. It presents the perverted double of a narrative in Italian thought about the vibrant potential of the common folk, as expressed in the works of Pasolini or Agamben. While the latter still focused on the *plebs'* capacity to differ from traditional norms, far-right politicians like Giorgia Meloni nowadays claim to speak in the name of this same *plebs* in order to reassert traditional values. To combat this revival of nationalist nostalgia, authors like Mezzadra and Negri argue for a decolonization of Western and Italian thought in order to reveal alternative trajectories toward modernization that oppose the combination of global capitalism and liberal democracy that has delivered our *faux* end of history in the first place.

In other words, if politics concerns the collective articulation of the good life in a common *polis,* then the contemporary *polis* is in bad shape. Collectives are torn apart by identitarian politics, the good life is turning into wishful thinking haunted by climate catastrophe, the common *polis* is falling apart under a global civil war. We are living through an experience of a radical crisis. On the etymology of the Ancient Greek term "*krisis,*" Agamben argues:

"Crisis" in ancient medicine meant a judgement, when the doctor noted at the decisive moment whether the sick person would survive or die. The present understanding of crisis, on the other hand, refers to an enduring state. So this uncertainty is extended into the future, indefinitely. It is exactly the same with the theological sense; the Last Judgement was inseparable from the end of time. Today, however, judgement is divorced from the idea of resolution and repeatedly postponed. So the prospect of a decision is ever less, and an endless process of decision never concludes.[1]

"Crisis" used to be a temporary yet decisive episode in which the fate of an individual's health or the world's salvation would be decided. Yet today we are stumbling from one crisis into the next without any sense of resolution. Gramsci already formulated a similar insight when he identified the organic crisis of Italian society in the 1930s: "The old is dying and the new cannot be born: in this interregnum, morbid phenomena of the most varied kind come to pass."[2] When the *polis* suffers from multiple organ failure, signs of sickness appear across social spheres. From the interaction with nature to social media or identity politics, the current era of global capital and liberal democracy is dying, and yet we are at a loss for alternatives. Two possible outcomes reveal themselves in this interregnum: either we remain stuck in a crisis without resolution, the end of a world that keeps on ending, or we discover new potential futures hidden in the current political conjuncture. The first option aligns with the dystopian scenario delineated by the Gramscian political phenomenologist Ernesto De Martino as an "apocalypse without *eschaton*,"[3] while the second route leads to a politics of invisible cities in line with Calvino's novel, a politics that pursues promising potentialities in the actual present.

## The Unending End of the World

De Martino died on May 9, 1965, leaving a treasure trove of notes on the cultural history of apocalyptic thought that would in 1977 be published as *La fine del mondo*.[4] Virtually unknown outside of Italy, De Martino was a major cultural anthropologist in the 1950s and 60s, particularly well regarded for his studies of folklore and popular culture in the Italian South. He was both a member of the Italian Communist Party and sympathizer of the Italian phenomenological movement in Milan, centered around Enzo Paci, Antonio Banfi, and the still-running academic journal *Aut Aut*. He combined these influences in his research notes by synthesizing a Gramscian analysis of popular apocalyptic imaginaries with Heideggerian existential phenomenology. *The End of the World* opens on the psychopathological case study of a young Swiss farmer suffering from schizophrenia and his "*Weltuntergangserlebnis*," i.e., his experience of the end of the world.

> The world … has entered into a radical crisis beginning the previous
> spring, when it happened that the patient had uprooted some shrubs,
> and with this guilty act of his started off a process of breakdown. But
> blame for the ominous alteration was even more attributable to the
> fact that in autumn, his father had uprooted an oak tree in order to sell
> it: from the hole in the ground left after the uprooting, water flowed
> that spilled on the ground.[5]

The schizophrenic farmer imagines the complete unsettling of the land
after a series of events that leaves the world unhinged. The familiar shape
of the landscape dissolves in a quagmire of delusions, and his world
experience sinks into a radical crisis without any prospect of being
resolved. This perceived loss of control over his surroundings is mirrored
in his experienced loss of self.[6] Feeling overpowered by a hostile and
chaotic world, the patient loses any sense of identity and falls apart into
psychotic delusions. The farmer feels haunted by hallucinations of the
world coming to an end, and yet it never truly does. The water takes up
more of the land and his self-control slips through his fingers, and yet
neither he nor the world are ever fully destroyed. The world just keeps
on ending.

De Martino identifies more healthy experiences of the apocalypse in
cultural movements like Marxism. According to De Martino, Marxism
puts forward a secular version of the Christian apocalyptic narrative
that successfully converts people to a shared emancipatory project.
While Christianity warned for the end of days to convince believers
to change their lives for the better, Marxism predicts the impending
doom of capitalism to mobilize the working class for its liberation. This
prophecy of world crisis is not an outcry of despair but a revolutionary
call. In Christianity and Marxism, the apocalypse holds out the promise
of an *eschaton*, a resolution that puts an end to the end of the world. It
contains the seed of something new and subsequently motivates people
to act in the here and now to make this emancipatory future possible.[7]
The experience of radical crisis is not paralyzing but productive in this
style of thought. Just like Christ's words moved his followers to live a life
free from sin right now to prepare for redemption in Heaven, and Marx
and Engels wrote *The Communist Manifesto* to persuade all workers of
the world to unite against capitalism and forge a new communist future.

Such narratives articulate what De Martino calls an "ethos of
transcendence," i.e., a collective project that negates the dying old

world in favor of a new world in the process of being born.[8] This is not "transcendence" in the sense of awaiting some form of divine intervention as if only a God could save us. De Martino's ethos of transcendence rather aligns with Gramsci's call for the political construction of a national-popular will that can break with capitalist hegemony. According to Gramsci, capitalism has successfully held its ground in Western Europe because it has convinced people of the ideology that there is no alternative. Counter-hegemonic opposition, on the other hand, requires "the concrete formation and operation of a collective will" that posits a new society against the capitalist status quo.[9] Such a strategy for transcending the status quo can succeed only if the political conjuncture lays bare society's deep contradictions in a radical crisis and the victims of this crisis can effectively posit a new society to replace the old order. The ethos of transcendence not only confronts the apocalyptic crisis of the present but also identifies potentialities hidden within the actual world that transcend this crisis.

This ethos of transcendence is lacking in the pathological manifestations of the crisis experience, like the Swiss farmer's schizophrenic delusions. He fails to identify potentialities that offer an alternative to the uprooting of the world. Nothing within his predicament promises to transcend the morbid phenomena of his dying world. According to De Martino, however, Western modernity is also entering a pathological state of an apocalypse without *eschaton*. In the 1960s, De Martino witnessed the rise of economic crises and the beginnings of the social unrest around the factories that would later birth the workerist movement in Italy, the threat of atomic bombs leading the world's superpowers into mutually assured destruction, anti-imperialist uprisings in the colonies of the Global South, and a wave of modernist novels struggling to find any meaning in a cold and absurd universe. According to De Martino, apocalyptic threats were looming over the globe, yet no collective will was available to posit a radical new alternative.

> The current cultural climate in the West is familiar with the theme of the end outside of any religious horizon of salvation, that is, as a desperate catastrophe of the worldly, the domestic, the settled, of the signifying and the practicable: a catastrophe that narrates with meticulous, and at times obsessive, accuracy the undoing of what has been formed, the alienation of what is domestic, the unsettling of what has been settled, the loss of sense of signifiers, the impracticability

of the practicable ... The moment of abandoning oneself without compensation to the experience of the end undeniably constitutes an elective orientation of our epoch.[10]

De Martino never finished his research project. He kept piling on notes about the most diverse topics like the novels of Alberto Moravia, Heideggerian phenomenology, or Benedetto Croce's philosophy of history in a desperate search for an *eschaton* at the end of the tunnel. He kept looking for a perspectival shift that would end the end of the world, but he died trying.

# Italian Thought and the Politics of Potentiality

In this book, we suggest that the history of Italian thought offers us glimpses of a different opportunity. Esposito names in *Living Thought: The Origins and Actuality of Italian Philosophy*, as one of the recurrent motifs in Italian thought, the "historicization of the non-historical." Italian thought uniquely emphasizes the historical role of potentialities that have not been enacted in actual history. It puts into focus the historical efficacy of a primordial potential that destitutes the current order and institutes new orders instead. While most philosophies privilege the actual, Italian thought highlights that the actual is just one potentiality among many that just happens to have been the one that has been historically enacted. These alternative potentialities have not thereby disappeared, but still linger as a haunting presence with the current state of actuality. Writing about Giambattista Vico's philosophy of history, Esposito writes that "history must always contain or curb the obscure vital power that underlies it in order to proceed along the path that divine providence and human reason trace."[11] When most modern philosophies of history identify a uniform logic of history—the unfolding of divine providence or the Hegelian cunning of reason, for example—Italian philosophers stressed that there is no unilinear course of history locked into the present. The origins of time, the moment at which anything was still possible, is still with us today. Every actual state of the world contains an excess of unrealized potentialities that are just as existent or real as the current world order. Underneath the status quo lies a magma of potentialities demanding realization. "This originary element … never completely fades away, but rather, moves in a covert fashion, so to speak, into history itself."[12]

Italian political theory has been especially attentive to the force of potentiality to destitute the status quo of the *polis* in its actual shape and institute a new political order instead. According to Esposito, Italian thought is persistently intent on the revolutionary potentialities hidden in political conjunctures. Esposito describes the writings of Machiavelli as strategic reflections on how to birth the new from the old and dying. As evidence, he cites Machiavelli's celebration of political tactics that enact a "return to principles" (*ritorno ai principi*) in *The Discourses*.[13] While political calls for a return to principles usually mean a nostalgic push for conservative and traditional values, in Machiavelli it designates the complete opposite. At the origins of any political regime lies the chaos of revolutionary upheaval. In those moments, anything is possible, and what futures end up being realized depends on the construction of a national-popular will that forces itself on reality. A healthy political order possesses the power to tap into this excess of potentialities to revitalize itself, a capacity Esposito later dubbed "instituent praxis" (see Chapter 1). As Esposito writes about Machiavelli, "the return to the beginning, like a ricochet movement, coincides with the drive toward the new. Freed from any regressive mythology, the origin is the moment when— skipping over the present current—the past projects life into the free and open space of its future."[14] The dominant political conjuncture can always regress into an originary moment of omnipotentiality. Of course, not all potential futures are worth pursuing. But at least this eye for unrealized potential allows us to identify those particular futures that hold out a promise of ending our current radical crisis. Politics is the art of taming the world's omnipotentiality in the name of a hegemonic project.

The Italian politics of potentiality is beautifully captured in Calvino's *Invisible Cities*. When Marco Polo narrates about the wondrous cities of the Khan's empire, he is carefully tracing the potential cities that have gone lost in the rubble of actuality.

It is the desperate moment when we discover that this empire, which had seemed to us the sum of all wonders, is an endless, formless ruin, that corruption's gangrene has spread too far to be healed by our scepter, that the triumph over enemy sovereigns has made us the heirs of their long undoing. Only in Marco Polo's accounts was Kublai Khan able to discern, through the walls and towers destined to crumble, the tracery of a pattern so subtle it could escape the termites' gnawing.[15]

Within this critical conjuncture, a tracery of a pattern emerges that enables an exodus from catastrophe. At the end of the novel, Marco Polo specifies why he belabors the recounting of these imaginary cities so fondly. He argues that

> it is all useless, if the last landing place can only be the infernal city, and it is there that, in ever-narrowing circles, the current is drawing us. … The inferno of the living is not something that will be; if there is one, it is what is already here, the inferno where we live every day, that we form by being together. There are two ways to escape suffering it. The first is easy for many: accept the inferno and become such a part of it that you can no longer see it. The second is risky and demands constant vigilance and apprehension: seek and learn to recognize who and what, in the midst of the inferno, are not inferno, then make them endure, give them space.[16]

We either accept the inferno to which modern history has brought us, or we look for the potentialities hidden within the political order that are not infernal and give them space. Marco Polo recounts all the invisible cities that could have been but were cast aside along the unilinear course of history, not as mere escapist entertainment for the Khan but to give voice to the potentialities that cry out for existence against the status quo. If we are looking for a way out of the Khan's crumbling empire, we must first attend to the omnipotentiality haunting the present from which new hegemonic projects can be born. Just before the final passage just quoted, Marco Polo presents Berenice as the final city of his story.[17] It is the pinnacle of injustice, a city of absolute dystopia, its citizens enslaved to meat-grinding machines. Yet within the unjust Berenice is an invisible network of individuals who make new use of the clunky tools of the master. These citizens recognize each other through small signs and gestures of solidarity and plant the seed of a just Berenice that keeps on growing until it takes over the city. Within this evil city, new social relations form that slowly wash away the inferno of the living. However, buried deep within the just Berenice lies a germ of corruption that, yet again, will spread and take over the city. Berenice represents a perpetual struggle between a corrupt empire and a network of social relations that escape this empire's clutching grasp. However, Calvino does not double down on the tragedy of an endless cycle of booms and busts.

> From my words you will have reached the conclusion that the real Berenice is a temporal succession of different cities. alternately just and unjust. But what I wanted to tell you is something else: all the future Berenices are already present in this instant, wrapped one within the other, confined, crammed, inextricable.[18]

Calvino is not interested in the actual tragic course of history but in the potentialities wrapped within the present. The city today contains within itself all potential future cities inextricably crammed into one tight spot. Some of these potentialities lead to horrendous injustice, others to emancipatory futures. What is required of political thought is discerning the distinction. In this context, it is worth remarking that the Ancient Greek word "*krisis*," which Agamben links to the medical paradigm of a critical episode that will determine whether a patient will live, originally derives from the Greek verb "*krinein*," which means "to discern" or "to judge." Crisis constitutes the moment in which emancipatory possibilities are separated from catastrophic possibilities, and in which political judgment is required to determine which course to take.

When Italian thought celebrates the historicization of the non-historical, in Esposito's phrasing, or the alternative potentialities hidden in every concrete political conjuncture, it is not merely reveling in the contingency of the present. It is not just a matter of saying that everything could have been different or that there are infinite potentialities unrealized in the actual present. Not all potentialities are worth pursuing. Esposito calls upon us to develop the capacity of discernment to see and identify those potentialities within the present that promise the deliverance of a just city. It is an exhortation to uncover the invisible cities that offer an emancipatory alternative to the current *polis*, the tracery of a pattern so subtle it could escape the termites' gnawing. In Machiavelli, for example, Esposito discovers this capacity of discernment in the philosophers' notion of *virtù*.[19] This is not "virtue" in the traditional sense of the capacity to obey God's will or some natural law but the strategic ingenuity to take advantage of the vagaries of political conflict to further the cause of democratic politics. If at the heart of politics lies a persistent possibility of a "return to principles," a regression into revolutionary upheaval where anything is possible, political virtue is the capacity to discern and identify those potentialities that escape the inferno of the living.

## The *Entwicklungsfähigkeit* of Italian Thought

Excavating emancipatory potentialities buried in the present and worthy of constituting a counter-hegemonic will is no easy feat. Italian thought in the 2000s and early 2010s successfully articulated a reading lens for the political present to reveal the potential for an emancipatory exodus, but one could wonder whether the moment of its realization has since then passed. Esposito's work on affirmative biopolitics seemingly voiced a promising alternative to the immunitary paradigm that lets refugees and migrants die at the borders of Europe, Lazzarato's critique of financial capitalism gave voice to a generation ravaged by the global financial crisis, Agamben's destituent politics pushed back against the rising tide of emergency government powers, Federici's genealogy of early modern witch hunts gave legitimacy to a global politics of commons, and Negri's theory of the multitude offered a strategic roadmap for social movements' struggle against Empire across the globe. All these initiatives were rooted in a deep reflection on the politics of potentiality and its regenerative force against the sclerosis of the political present. Negri, for example, identified the multitude as a constituent political subject capable of putting modernity on a new, "altermodern" track. Like Esposito, Negri refers to Machiavelli's *virtù*.[20] The multitude is not just a crowd of individuals rebelling against the status quo but an intelligent mass that discerns within the present potential alternatives to this status quo. The Machiavellian Prince of today is not an individual aristocrat like Lorenzo de Medici, to whom Machiavelli dedicated *Il principe,* nor a political party, as Gramsci's theory of the modern Prince posits, but the multitude itself. The communication and networking of minds via new social movements, digital technologies, and new forms of work foster the collective capacity to discern and determine our own future. One can criticize Negri's optimism with the benefit of hindsight, but he did show a potential hidden in the political conjuncture of the 2000s worth pursuing against the hegemony of the end of history, capitalist globalization, and liberal democracy. The multitude named the excess potentialities that resisted this status quo. As Negri and Hardt argued, "a constituent power that connects mass intellectuality and self-valorization in all the arenas of the flexible and nomadic productive social cooperation is the order of the day."[21]

Negri's call sounded very attractive when the alter-globalization movement was protesting WTO and G8 meetings, Occupy Wall Street was resisting the power of finance, and the Arab Spring was ravaging dictatorial regimes in the Middle East. But in the age of Trump, climate catastrophe, and global pandemics, this picture seems off. In our present times, the political conjuncture has shifted, and we must recalibrate our conceptual apparatus to see clearly again the emancipatory potentialities, the invisible cities buried in today's *polis*. We cannot simply repeat Negri's words and hope for the best. In his volume on philosophical method, Agamben emphasizes the need to respect the "*Entwicklungsfähigkeit*" of concepts. As he writes, "the genuine philosophical element in every work … is its capacity to be developed, which Ludwig Feuerbach defined as *Entwicklungsfähigkeit*."[22] Philosophical concepts do not have a fixed, pre-established meaning but contain a capacity to generate new meanings. When applied in new contexts or linked to new discourses, concepts show new sides of themselves and present novel understandings of the world. As changing political conjunctures call for novel conceptual constellations to make sense of them, novel conceptual developments also promise to put political reality in a new light. This has been the interpretative effort of this book. We have attempted to construct new conceptual tools from the recent history of Italian thought to render the political order legible again and discern potential counter-hegemonic lines of flight.

Five tracks of *Entwicklungsfähigkeit* have emerged in our present study. The tradition of Italian thought still offers a conceptual apparatus to reveal the political dangers and emancipatory potentialities of today's political conjuncture. We have stressed the avenue of affirmative biopolitics and instituent praxis to tackle the negative biopolitics of current politics. While biopolitical government too often amounts to a differential exposure of populations to the sovereign decision over life and death, we must build institutions that sustain and strengthen life without enforcing caesurae within the population to delineate a *homo sacer*. We have also noted the importance of moving beyond the anthropocentric focus of biopolitical theory if we want to address the impending environmental catastrophe. Posthuman politics considers the agency of non-human entities to sustain and strengthen life in a more durable fashion than the current phase of cannibal capitalism allows.[23] Italian thought also shows the political ambivalence of digital technologies as a general intellect. While they currently enact a mental subsumption of our social lifeworld, they also offer means of emancipation insofar as the people whose lives are increasingly being datafied can reappropriate the general intellect to make it serve the project of collective autonomy. We subsequently noted how cyberfascism is exploiting the elective affinities between social media infrastructures and right-wing predilections for plebiscitarian authoritarianism. While a major threat to popular emancipation, this observation also contains a lesson for the left not to recklessly mimic the right's tactics and combat the mass atomization of society enacted under neoliberalism that is making cyberfascism attractive in the first place. Lastly, we noted how an essentialist discourse of social identity is rapidly taking over political debates. While this bears some eerie affinities to populist narratives among Italian philosophers themselves, it also falls flat against Italian thought's project of altermodernity carried forth by, among others, Negri and Mezzadra. Identitarian essentialism inevitably loses against the multitude's persistent capacity to rearticulate itself and cultivate excessive potentialities that do not fit conservative pre-established casts.

# NOTES

## Introduction

**1**     See Enrica Lisciani-Petrini and Giusi Strummiello (eds.), *Effetto Italian Thought* (Marcerata: Quodlibet, 2017).

**2**     See, for example, Roberto Esposito, *Living Thought: The Origins and Actuality of Italian Philosophy*, translated by Zakiya Hanafi (Stanford: Stanford University Press, 2012) and Antonio Negri, "Post-Operaism? No, Operaism," in *Italian Critical Thought*, eds. Dario Gentili, Elettra Stimilli, and Glenda Garelli (London and New York: Rowman and Littlefield International, 2018).

**3**     Giacomo Marramao argues that Italian Thought "is divided into two components: a first component continues in an original way the work of French Theory, as in the case of Roberto Esposito, while a second component, which belongs to Tronti, Cacciari, or myself, privileging the relationship with the Germanic area, has always focused on the concept of the 'political.'" In Federica Buongiorno and Antonio Lucci (eds.), "La differenza italiana: Filosofi(e) nell'Italia di oggi," *Lo Sguardo: Rivista di filosofia* 15, no. 2 (2014): 12–13, our translation.

**4**     See Esposito's *Living Thought* and Buongiorno and Lucci's introduction to *La differenza italiana*, 5.

**5**     Buongiorno and Lucci, *La differenza italiana*, 6.

**6**     See Steve Wright, *Storming Heaven: Class Composition and Struggle in Italian Autonomist Marxism* (London: Pluto Press, 2002); *Semiotext(e): Autonomia, Post-Political Politics* (Los Angeles, Semiotext(e), [1980] 2007); see Nanni Balestrini and Primo Moroni (eds), *The Golden Horde: Revolutionary Italy, 1960–1977*, translated by Richard Braude (London and Calcutta: Seagull Books, 2020); Franco Berardi Bifo, *Dell'innocenza. 1977: l'anno della premonizione* (Verona: Ombre Corte Edizioni, 1997); see also Toni Negri's autobiography *Storia di una communista* (3 volumes) (Firenze: Ponte Alle Grazie, 2015–2021).

**7**     See *Semiotext(e): Autonomia, Post-Political Politics*; Michael Hardt and Paolo Virno (eds.), *Radical Thought in Italy: A Potential Politics* (Minneapolis: Minnesota University Press, 1996); for a critique of the alleged homogeneity of "Italian Theory," see Lorenzo Chiesa and Alberto Toscano (eds.), *The Italian Difference: Between Nihilism and Biopolitics* (Melbourne: re.press, 2009) and Silvia Contarini and Davide Luglio (eds.), *L'Italian Theory existe-t-elle?* (Sesto San Giovanni: Mimesis, 2015).

8    See also Corrado Claverini, *La tradizione filosofica italiana: quattro paradigmi interpretativi* (Macerata: Quodlibet, 2021).

9    Dario Gentili, *Italian Theory: Dall'operaismo alla biopolitica* (Bologna: Il Mulino, 2012); Elettra Stimilli (ed.), *Decostruzione o biopolitica?* (Macerata: Quodlibet, 2017); Enrica Lisciani-Petrini and Guisi Strummiello (eds.), *Effetto Italian Thought* (Macerata: Quodlibet, 2017).

10   Gentili *et al.*, *Italian Critical Thought*, 1.

11   For the growing archive of Italian thought, including authors such as Furio Jesi or Enzo Melandri, see, for example, the excellent work done by publishers like Quodlibet.

12   Gentili, *Italian Critical Thought*, 6.

13   Hardt and Virno, *Radical Thought in* Italy, 1. The idea of the "Italian laboratory" is also central to the Semiotext(e) issue on Autonomia originally published in 1980.

14   See also Jamila Squire and Seth Wheeler (eds.), *A Thousand Little Machines: A/traverso and the Movement of '77* (London: Agit Press, 2024).

15   *Semiotext(e): Autonomia, Post-Political Politics*, vi.

16   Hardt and Virno, *Radical Thought in Italy*, 2.

17   Hardt and Virno, 2.

18   Hardt and Virno, 2.

19   See also Steven Wright's *Storming Heaven*.

20   Hardt and Virno, *Radical Thought in Italy*, 3, emphasis added.

21   Hardt and Virno, 2.

22   For a history of Autonomia (or the "Movement of 77"), see Sergio Bianchi and Lanfranco Caminiti (eds.), *Gli Autonomi: Le storie, le lotte, le teorie* (Bologna: DeriveApprodi, 2020); see also Marcello Tari's *Il ghiaccio era sottile: Per una storia dell'Autonomia* (Bologna: DeriveApprodi, 2012).

23   Hardt and Virno, *Radical Thought in Italy*, 5.

24   Hardt and Virno, 4.

25   Hardt and Virno, 5

26   Hardt and Virno, 5.

27   Lorenzo Chiesa and Alberto Toscano, *The Italian Difference*, 2–3

28    For a narrative regarding the "years of lead," see for example Nanni Ballestrini's *The Unseen* (London: Verso Books, 2012).

29    Lorenzo Chiesa and Alberto Toscano, *The Italian Difference*, 2.

30    Lorenzo Chiesa and Alberto Toscano, 3 and 5.

31    Negri in Gentili et al., *Italian Critical Thought*, 14.

32    Negri in Gentili et al., 14.

33    Negri in Gentili et al., 32.

34    Negri in Gentili et al., 31.

35    Negri in Gentili et al., 31.

36    For more historical context, see *Semiotext(e): Autonomia. Post-Political Politics*.

37    Pier Aldo Rovatti, "'Deconstructing the Capital Letters. Weak Thought, Italian Theory, and Politics. A Conversation with Pier Aldo Rovatti' Interview by Andrea Muni," *Journal of Italian Philosophy* 2, no. 1 (2019): 6, emphasis added.

38    Lisciani-Petrini and Strummiello, *Effetto Italian Thought*, 175.

39    Pier Paolo Pasolini, *Scritti Corsari* (Milan: Garzanti libri, 2015). For an English translation, see https://libcom.org/article/corsair-writings-pier-paolo-pasolini.

40    Esposito, *Living Thought*, 211–13.

41    Dario Gentili in Buongiorno and Lucci (eds.), *La differenza italiana*, 17, our translation and added emphasis.

42    To consider Italian thought as sustained engagement with the contemporary does not mean that Italian thought is a kind of presentism. In fact, many Italian theorists offer well-wrought "archaeologies of the present," from Agamben's unearthing of the theological roots of political modernity and Esposito's careful genealogy of biopolitics, to Negri's politicization of Spinoza and the Renaissance.

43    Esposito, *Living Thought*, 10.

44    Esposito, 10.

45    Rovatti, "Deconstructing the Capital Letters," 2.

46    Rovatti, 2–3.

47    Rovatti, 3.

48    Esposito, 10.

49    Esposito, 14.

50   Esposito, 14–15.

51   Stimilli, *Decostruzione o biopolitica?*, 10.

52   Rovatti, 1.

53   Rovatti, 2.

54   Sandro Chignola, "Italian Theory: Elements for a Genealogy," in *Italian Critical Thought*, Dario Gentili et al., 44.

55   Stimilli, *Decostruzione o biopolitica?*, 9.

56   Esposito, "Decostruzione o biopolitica," in Stimilli (ed.). 13.

57   Esposito in Stimilli (ed.). 19.

58   Esposito in Stimilli (ed.). 23.

59   Esposito in Stimilli (ed.). 23.

60   Sandro Chignola in Gentili et al., 34.

61   Chignola in Gentili et al., 43.

62   Chignola in Gentili et al., 44.

63   Gilles Deleuze and Félix Guattari, *What is Philosophy?*, translated by Hugh Tomlinson and Graham Burchell (London: Verso Books, 1994); Massimo Cacciari, *Geofilosofia dell'Europa* (Milan: Adelphi, 1994).

64   Esposito, *Living Thought*, 12.

65   Esposito, 14.

66   Esposito, 15.

67   Esposito, 21.

68   Esposito, 21.

69   Esposito, 23.

70   Esposito, 23.

71   Esposito, 269.

72   Sandro Mezzadra, "A World to Gain: On the Borders of 'Theory,'" in Gentili et al., 78.

73   Mezzadra in Gentili et al., 78.

74   Mezzadra in Gentili et al., 79. See Rosi Braidotti, *The Posthuman* (Cambridge: Polity Press, 2013).

75   Dario Gentili, "Che cos'è Italian Theory Tavola rotonda con Roberto Esposito, Dario Gentili, Giacomo Marramao," in Buongiorno and Lucci (eds.). 14.

76 Mezzadra in Gentili et al., 79.

77 Mezzadra in Gentili et al., 73.

78 Mezzadra in Gentili et al., 75.

79 Roberto Esposito, *Common Immunity: Biopolitics in the Age of the Pandemic*, translated by Zakiya Hanafi (New York: Polity, 2023), 87–8; Roberto Esposito, *Institution*, translated by Zakiya Hanafi (New York: Polity, 2022), 78.

80 Daniele Lorenzini, "Biopolitics in the Time of Coronavirus," *Critical Inquiry* 47 (Winter 2021), 40–5.

81 Roberto Esposito, *Bios: Biopolitics and Philosophy*, translated by Timothy Campbell (Minneapolis: University of Minnesota Press, 2008).

82 Esposito, *Institution*, 9.

83 Tiziana Terranova, "Futurepublic. On Information Warfare, Bio-racism and Hegemony as Noopolitics," *Theory, Culture & Society* 24, no. 3 (2007): 125–45; Maurizio Lazzarato, *La politica dell'evento* (Cosenza: Rubbettino, 2004).


# Chapter 1

1 Giorgio Agamben, *Where Are We Now? The Epidemic as Politics*, translated by Valeria Dani (London: Rowman & Littlefield, 2021). In a text written together with Massimo Cacciari, the measures forbidding people to travel to other parts of the country, as well as the green pass that people were required to show, were compared to the travel restrictions that existed in the Soviet Union. Massimo Cacciari, Giorgio Agamben, "A proposito del decreto sul 'green pass.'" June 26, 2021. https://www.iisf.it/progetti/diario-della-crisi/item/2531-massimo-cacciari-giorgio-agamben-a-proposito-del-decreto-sul-green-pass.html For more about Agamben's views during the pandemic, see Tim Christiaens, "Biomedical Technocracy, The Networked Public Sphere and the Biopolitics of COVID-19: Notes on the Agamben Affair," *Culture, Theory and Critique* 62, no. 4 (2021): 404–21.

2 Roberto Esposito, *Common Immunity: Biopolitics in the Age of the Pandemic*, translated by Zakiya Hanafi (New York: Polity, 2023), 85.

3 Achille Mbembe, *Necropolitics*, translated by Steven Corcoran (Durham: Duke University Press, 2019); Tiziana Terranova, "Futurepublic. On Information Warfare, Bio-racism and Hegemony as Noopolitics," *Theory, Culture & Society* 24, no. 3 (2007): 125–45; Elizabeth Povinelli,

*Geontologies: A Requiem to Late Liberalism* (Durham, Duke University Press, 2016); Mariá Puig de la Bellacasa, *Matters of Care: Speculative Ethics in More than Human Worlds* (Minneapolis: University of Minnesota Press, 2017).

4    Esposito, *Common Immunity*, 87.

5    Esposito, *Institution*, 78.

6    Esposito, *Common Immunity*, 87–8.

7    For an extensive philosophical genealogy of the notion of "*bios*" or "*life*" at the heart of biopolitics even before Foucault's engagement with the term, see Davide Tarizzo, *Life: A Modern Invention*, translated by Mark William Epstein (Minneapolis: University of Minnesota Press, 2017).

8    Jean-Luc Nancy, "Communovirus," March 27, 2020. https://www.versobooks.com/blogs/news/4626-communovirus

9    Daniele Lorenzini, "Biopolitics in the Time of Coronavirus," *Critical Inquiry* 47 (Winter 2021): 40–5.

10   Michel Foucault, *"Society Must Be Defended": Lectures at the Collège de France, 1975–76*, translated by David Macey (New York: Picador, 2003), 255

11   Foucault, 254–5.

12   Lorenzini, "Biopolitics," 43.

13   Lorenzini, 43. The citation within the quote is an adapted translation from Foucault, *Society Must Be Defended*, 255.

14   Lorenzini, "Biopolitics," 43.

15   See for example the text "Bare Life" in Agamben, *Where Are We Now?*, 38–41.

16   Terranova, "Futurepublic," 135–6.

17   Terranova, 136

18   Daniele Lorenzini, "Rethinking Biopolitics: COVID-19, Differential Vulnerabilities and Biopolitical Rights," *Journal of European Studies* 54, no. 1 (2024): 1–15, 3.

19   Esposito, *Common Immunity*, 87.

20   Esposito, 113.

21   Achille Mbembe, *Critique of Black Reason*, translated by Laurent Dubois (Durham: Duke University Press, 2017), 167.

22   Tim Christiaens, *Digital Working Lives* (London: Rowman & Littlefield, 2023), 25.

23    Giorgio Agamben, *Homo Sacer: Sovereign Power and Bare Life*, translated
      by Daniel Heller-Roazen (Stanford: Stanford University Press, 1998), 6,
      emphasis in original.

24    Agamben, *Homo Sacer*, 11. During the pandemic it was tempting to
      describe measures taken as a state of exception that would become
      "the new normal." However, Esposito repeatedly clarified why the
      emergency measures cannot be called a state of exception. The measures
      were not the result of a planned sovereign decision with the aim to
      subjugate the population but the result of unforeseen, contingent, and
      temporary circumstances. Esposito, *Institution*, 7; Esposito, *Common
      Immunity*, 168–9.

25    Tim Christiaens and Stijn De Cauwer, "The Multitude Divided:
      Biopolitical Production during the Coronavirus Pandemic," in *Pandemic
      and the Crisis of Capitalism*, eds. Yahya Madra, Vincent Lyon-Callo,
      Chizu Sato, Boone Shear, Maliha Safri, Marcus Green, Serap Kayatekin,
      Ceren Özselçuk, Jared Randall (Brighton: ReMarx Books, 2020): 118–27.

26    Esposito, *Institution*, 80.

27    Roberto Esposito, "Community, Immunity, Biopolitics," translated by
      Zakiya Hanafi, *Angelaki: Journal of the Theoretical Humanities*, 18, no. 3
      (2013): 83–90, 84.

28    Esposito, "Community, Immunity, Biopolitics," 84.

29    Esposito, 85.

30    This aspect of his work has been extensively discussed by various
      scholars: Tilottama Rajan and Antonio Calcagno (eds.), *Roberto Esposito:
      New Directions in Biophilosophy* (Edinburgh: Edinburgh University Press,
      2023); Greg Bird and Jon Short (eds.), *Community, Immunity and the
      Proper: Roberto Esposito* (New York: Routledge, 2017); Inna Viriasova
      and Antonio Calcagno (eds.), *Roberto Esposito: Biopolitics and Philosophy*
      (New York: SUNY University Press, 2017).

31    Esposito, *Institution*, 78.

32    Esposito, 90.

33    Esposito, 91.

34    Esposito, 2.

35    Esposito, 10.

36    Esposito, 9.

37    Roberto Esposito, *Persons and Things*, translated by Zakiya Hanafi
      (Malden, MA: Polity, 2015), 147.

38    Esposito, *Institution*, 13.

39    Esposito, 81–4.

40    Esposito, *Common Immunity*, 118.

41    Esposito, *Institution*, 13.

42    For more about Negri's constituent power and Agamben's destituent potential, see Stijn De Cauwer, "Potentiality and Uprisings: Georges Didi-Huberman in Dialogue with Giorgio Agamben and Antonio Negri," *Italian Studies* 76, no. 2 (2021), 186–99.

43    Antonio Negri, *Insurgencies: Constituent Power and the Modern State*, translated by Maurizia Boscagli (Minneapolis: University of Minnesota Press, 1999).

44    Antonio Negri, "'The European Union is a Cage'. Interview and translation by Stijn De Cauwer and Gert-Jan Meyntjens," in *Critical Theory at a Crossroads: Conversations on Resistance in Times of Crisis*, ed. Stijn De Cauwer (New York: Columbia University Press, 2018): 87–98, 88–9. Various prominent scholars from different fields have also pleaded for such a politics of two levels. Fredric Jameson has updated the idea of developing a "dual power," and anthropologist Philippe Descola has pleaded for the formation of more horizontally organized communities, while at the national level a governing structure with a limited mandate takes care of the issues that cannot be managed by local communities, from national defense and transnational geopolitical tension to dealing with large environmental challenges, such as managing our nuclear waste. This national level, however, would respect the organizing principles of the local communities. Fredric Jameson, *An American Utopia: Dual Power and the Universal Army*, ed. Slavoj Zizek (London: Verso Books, 2016); Philippe Descola & Alessandro Pignocchi, *Ethnographies des mondes à venir* (Paris: Éditions du Seuil, 2022), 128–31.

45    Giorgio Agamben, *The Use of Bodies*, translated by Adam Kotsko (Stanford: Stanford University Press, 2016), 226.

46    Agamben, *Where Are We Now?*, 72–4.

47    Agamben, 74.

48    Agamben, 73.

49    Roberto Esposito, "The Biopolitics of Immunity in Times of COVID-19: An Interview with Roberto Esposito," Interview by Tim Christiaens and Stijn De Cauwer, *Antipode online*, 16th June 2020. https://antipodeonline.org/2020/06/16/interview-with-roberto-esposito/.

50    Esposito, *Persons and Things*; Roberto Esposito, *Third Person*, translated by Zakiya Hanafi (New York, Polity, 2012).

51    Safiya Umoja Noble, *Algorithms of Oppression: How Search Engines Reinforce Racism* (New York: New York University Press, 2018);

Ramon Amaro, *The Black Technical Object: On Machine Learning and the Aspiration of Black Being* (London: Sternberg Press, 2023).

52    Matteo Pasquinelli, *The Eye of the Master: A Social History of Artificial Intelligence* (London: Verso Books, 2023); Tiziana Terranova, "Free Labor: Producing Culture for the Digital Economy," *Social Text* 18, no. 2 (summer 2000): 33–58.

53    The term "Noopolitik" was first coined by John Arquilla and David Ronfeldt in a publication by the RAND corporation (John Arquilla and David Ronfeldt, "The Emergence of Noopolitik: Toward An American Information Strategy," *RAND*, published in 1999. https://www.rand.org/pubs/monograph_reports/MR1033.html). In that publication, they argued for the potential of online networks to control information flows and public opinion for the purposes of warfare. At the time of writing, proxy warfare and online manipulation are standard practices in the ongoing wars and occupations. Authors such as Lazzarato and Terranova critically reclaim the term for their own purposes.

54    Lazzarato, *La politica dell'evento*, 44. Yves Citton clarifies the difference between a crowd and a public in the following way: "Whereas the notion of a crowd refers to a group of individuals gathered together in the same place whose affective interferences and contagions relies on the fact that they can see and hear each other in real time, a public refers to a collection of apparently autonomous and independent individuals who neither see nor hear each other, but who, notwithstanding this spatial separation, tend to think and act in the same way." See Yves Citton, *Mythocracy: How Stories Shape Our Worlds*, translated by David Broder (London: Verso Books, 2025), 23.

55    Terranova, "Futurepublic," 139.

56    Terranova, 139.

57    Michel Foucault, *Security, Territory, Population: Lectures at the Collège de France, 1977–78*, translated by Graham Burchell (New York: Picador, 2007), 105.

58    Terranova, "Futurepublic," 140

59    Terranova, 140.

60    Terranova, 140.

61    Terranova, 140–1.

62    Esposito, *Bios*, 108.

63    Esposito, *Common Immunity*, 187.

64    Esposito, 185.

65    Esposito, "The Biopolitics of Immunity in Times of COVID-19."

66    Esposito, "The Biopolitics of Immunity in Times of COVID-19";
      Esposito, "Community, Immunity, Biopolitics," 89.

67    Esposito, *Common Immunity*, 188–90.

68    See, among others, Carla Lonzi, *Sputiamo su Hegel* (Rome: Rivolta
      femminile, 1970); Mariarosa Dalla Costa, *Women and the Subversion
      of Community: A Mariarosa Dalla Costa Reader* (Oakland: PM Press,
      2019); Leopoldina Fortunati, *The Arcana of Reproduction: Housework,
      Prostitution, Labour, and Capital* (London: Verso Books, 2025).

69    Silvia Federici, *Caliban and the Witch: Women, the Body and Primitive
      Accumulation* (Brooklyn: Autonomedia, 2004).

70    Adriana Cavarero, *Donne che allattano cuccioli di lupo. Icone
      dell'ipermaterno* (Roma: Castelvecchi, 2023). Adriana Cavarero, "Il corpo
      come luogo di transito," *Doppiozero* 30th September 2014. https://www.
      doppiozero.com/il-corpo-come-luogo-di-transito.

71    For commentaries of Cavarero's relational ontology of care, see Tim
      Christiaens. "Towards Affirmative Economic Theologies: Responses to
      the Problem of Evil in Contemporary Italian Thought," *Political Theology*
      21, no. 7 (2020): 634–49; Tim Christiaens. "Agamben's 'Bare Life' and
      Grossman's Ethics of Senseless Kindness," *Journal of European Studies* 52,
      no. 1 (2022): 36–53; Paula Landerreche Cardillo & Rachel Silverbloom
      (eds.), *Political Bodies: Writings on Cavarero's Political Thought* (New
      York: SUNY Press, 2024).

72    Adriana Cavarero, *Inclinations: A Critique of Rectitude*, translated by
      Amanda Minervini and Adam Sitze (Stanford: Stanford University Press,
      2016), 13.

73    Cavarero, 13.

74    Federici, *Revolution*; Silvia Federici, *Re-enchanting the World: Feminism
      and the Politics of the Commons* (New York: PM Press, 2019).

75    Federici, *Revolution*, 139–40.

76    Federici, 142.

77    Federici, 143.

78    Federici (143) is referring to practices such as showing pictures of women
      who are unable to pay off their debt in public places, which happened for
      example in Niger and which drove some to suicide.

79    Federici, 141.

80    Federici, 145.

81    Federici, 145.

82    Federici, 145.

83    Esposito, *Common Immunity*, 187.

84    Esposito, 190.

85    Foucault, *Security, Territory, Population*, 21.

86    Foucault, 21.

87    Judith Butler, "Leaving Out, Caught in the Fall," in *Toward a Feminist Ethics of Nonviolence. Adriana Cavarero, with Judith Butler, Bonnie Honig, and Other Voices*, eds. Timothy J. Huzar and Clare Woodford (New York: Fordham University Press, 2021): 46–62, 59.

88    Butler, 59.

89    Esposito, *Bios*, 191.

90    Esposito, 194.

91    Esposito, 193.

92    Esposito, 194.

93    Gilles Deleuze, *The Logic of Sense*, translated by Mark Lester with Charles Stivale and edited by Constantin V. Boundas (London: The Athlone Press, 1990), 107.

94    Baptiste Morizot, *Ways of Being Alive*, translated by Andrew Brown (New York: Polity, 2022), 5.

95    Morizot, 167–231.

96    Baptiste Morizot, *L'inexploré* (Marseille: Éditions Wildproject, 2023), 267–71.

97    Morizot, *Ways of Being Alive*; Nastassja Martin, *In the Eye of the Wild*, translated by Sophie R. Lewis (New York: New York Review Books, 2021); Sylvain Tesson, *The Art of Patience: Seeking the Snow Leopard in Tibet*, translated by Frank Wynne (New York: Penguin, 2021).

98    Iwona Janicka, "Reinventing the Diplomat: Isabelle Stengers, Bruno Latour and Baptiste Morizot," *Theory, Culture & Society*, 40, no. 3 (2023): 23–40, 35. It should be emphasized that Morizot is only thinking of non-human animal life. He explicitly disagrees with Bruno Latour about his proposal to develop a politics of all non-human life. Morizot, *L'inexploré*, 300–1.

# Chapter 2

1    Esposito, *Living Thought*, 8, emphasis added.

2    Esposito, 8.

3       Esposito, *Bios,* 9.

4       Esposito, *Living Thought,* 269.

5       Esposito, 10.

6       Esposito, 51.

7       Esposito, 49.

8       Felice Cimatti and Carlo Salzani, *Animality in Contemporary Italian Philosophy* (Cham: Palgrave MacMillan, 2020): 7.

9       Cimatti and Salzani, 7.

10      Cimatti and Salzani, 8.

11      Cimatti and Salzani, 11.

12      Esposito, *Living Thought,* 45.

13      See Giacomo Marramao's *Dopo Il Leviatano* (Torino: Bollati Boringhieri, 2000).

14      See Esposito, *Bios; Communitas: The Origin and Destiny of Community,* translated by Timothy Campell (Stanford: Stanford University Press, 2010); Esposito, *Terms of the Political: Community, Immunity, Biopolitics,* translated by Rhiannon Noel Welch (New York: Fordham University Press, 2013).

15      Federico Luisetti, "Dopo il Leviatano: Gaia, Chthulu e i mostri dell'Antropocene," in *Effetto Italian Thought,* eds. Enrica Lisciani-Petrini and Giusi Strumiello (Macerata: Quodlibet, 2017): 151–2.

16      Luisetti, 152.

17      See Donna Haraway, *Staying with the Trouble* (Durham: Duke University Press, 2016); and James Lovelock and Lynn Margulis, *Writing Gaia* (Cambridge: Cambridge University Press, 2022).

18      For an extensive overview of theories of animality in Italian philosophy, see Cimatti and Salzani, *Animality in Contemporary Italian Philosophy.*

19      Giorgio Agamben, *The Open: Man and Animal,* translated by Kevin Attell (Stanford: Stanford University Press, 2004): 77.

20      Agamben, *The Open,* 76.

21      Agamben, 76–7, emphasis added.

22      Agamben, 77.

23      Agamben, 49--7. For brief overviews of Agamben's reception of Heidegger on the notion of life, see Timothy Campbell, *Improper Life: Technology and Biopolitics from Heidegger to Agamben* (Minneapolis: University of Minnesota Press, 2011): 32–60; Sergei Prozorov,

*Agamben and Politics: A Critical Introduction* (Edinburgh: Edinburgh University Press, 2014): 150–76; Claire Colebrooke and Jason Maxwell, *Agamben* (Cambridge: Polity Press, 2016): 167–78; Adam Kotsko, *Agamben's Philosophical Trajectory* (Edinburgh: Edinburgh University Press, 2020): 109–10.

24    Colby Dickinson and Adam Kotsko, *Agamben's Coming Philosophy: Finding a New Use of Theology* (London: Rowman and Littlefield, 2015): 59.

25    Agamben, *The Open*, 21.

26    Agamben, 26.

27    Agamben, 36

28    Agamben, 80.

29    Agamben, 37–8.

30    For a reading of Aristotle's endorsement of slavery as an example of the workings of "the anthropological machine," see Tim Christiaens, "Aristotle's Anthropological Machine and Slavery," in *Epoché: A Journal for the History of Philosophy* 23, no. 1 (2018): 239–62.

31    Giorgio Agamben, *Use of Bodies*, 264.

32    Agamben, 263.

33    However, Agamben is careful not to draw any equivalences between different forms and scales of suffering: for him, "bare life" is, first and foremost, a vital category and concept for understanding (modern) politics and thought.

34    For a similar analysis, see Agamben's *Gaia e Ctonia*: https://www. quodlibet.it/giorgio-agamben-gaia-e-ctonia; English translation: https://lenabloch.medium.com/gaia-and-ctonia-by-giorgio-agamben-32e11d542ce8.

35    Agamben, *Use of Bodies*, 265.

36    Agamben, *The Open*, 81.

37    Agamben, 83.

38    Agamben, 83.

39    See also Tarizzo, *Life: A Modern Invention*, 185–220.

40    Carlo Salzani "Beyond Human and Animal: Giorgio Agamben and Life as Potential," in *Animality in Contemporary Italian Philosophy*, eds. Felice Cimatti and Carlo Salzani (Edinburgh: Edinburgh University Press, 2020): 108.

41    Salzani, 110.

**42**    Giorgio Losi and Niccolò Bertuzzi, "What is Italian Anti-Speciesism? An Overview of Recent Tendencies in Animal Advocacy," in *Animality in Contemporary Italian Philosophy*, eds. Felice Cimatti and Carlo Salzani (Edinburgh: Edinburgh University Press, 2020): 82.

**43**    Braidotti, *The Posthuman,* 49.

**44**    Braidotti, 120.

**45**    Braidotti, 120.

**46**    Braidotti, 121, emphasis added.

**47**    See https://letztegeneration.org and https://rebellion.global

**48**    Braidotti, 50.

**49**    Braidotti, 50.

**50**    Braidotti, 60.

**51**    Braidotti, 60.

**52**    Braidotti, 60.

**53**    Braidotti, 189–90.

**54**    Braidotti, 140.

**55**    Braidotti, 60.

**56**    Braidotti, 190.

**57**    Rosi Braidotti, "'A Critical Europe Can Do It!'" Interview by Joost de Bloois in *Critical Theory at A Crossroads: Conversations on Resistance in Times of Crisis*, ed. Stijn De Cauwer (New York: Columbia University Press, 2017): 40.

**58**    For Braidotti, this is also an epistemological issue. Agamben's critique of biopolitics, and the anthropological machine that operates at its heart, remains a fairly cerebral exercise. The painstaking archaeological and philological excavation of the conceptual genealogies of biopolitics, its subsequent deconstruction and rendering "inoperative" of biopolitical mechanisms of exclusion, all remain operations of the critical, scholarly mind. Even in Esposito, the more practical proposition of affirmative biopolitics remains something of an afterthought following his minute analyses of philosophical or legal texts. Braidotti is radically opposed to such residual idealism. The primary affirmation of living matter also questions the superiority of the thinking (speaking and writing) human subject that supposedly finds itself separated from *zōè*.

**59**    Braidotti, *The Posthuman,* 111.

**60**    Braidotti, 195.

**61**    Braidotti, 111.

62    Braidotti, 111.

63    Braidotti, 115.

64    Emanuele Coccia, "Don't Call me Gaia," in *e-flux Architecture* "Hydroreflexivity" (October 2023): 3, https://www.e-flux.com/architecture/hydroreflexivity/571453/don-t-call-me-gaia/.

65    Coccia, 3.

66    Federico Luisetti, *Non-Human Subjects: An Ecology of Earth-Beings* (Cambridge: Cambridge University Press, 2023), 2.

67    Coccia, "Don't Call Me Gaia," 1.

68    See Joost de Bloois, "The Death of Vitruvian Man: Anomaly, Anomie, Autonomy," in *The Anomie of the Earth: Philosophy, Politics and Autonomy in Europe and the Americas*, eds. Federico Luisetti, John Pickles and Wilson Kaiser (Durham: Duke University Press, 2015): 23–43.

69    Emanuele Coccia, "Don't Call Me Gaia," 1.

70    Emanuele Coccia, 4.

71    Federico Luisetti, "Geopower: On the States of Nature of Late Capitalism," *European Journal of Social Theory* 22, no. 3 (2019): 357, emphasis added.

72    Luisetti, "Geopower," 348.

73    Luisetti, 348.

74    Luisetti, 348, emphasis added.

75    Luisetti, 348–9.

76    Luisetti, 348–9. We will here not delve into the debates over Foucault's alleged conversion to neoliberalism. On this topic, see Daniel Zamora, ed., *Critiquer Foucault* (Bruxelles: Aden, 2014); Michael Behrent, "Accidents Happen: François Ewald, the 'Antirevolutionary' Foucault, and the Intellectual Politics of the French Welfare State," *The Journal of Modern History* 82, no. 3 (2010): 585–624. Exemplary critical responses are Gavin Walker, "Introduction: The Late Foucault and the Allegories of Theory," *South Atlantic Quarterly* 121, no. 4 (2022): 645–53; Tim Christiaens, 'On the Limitations of Michel Foucault's Genealogy of Neoliberalism', *Journal of French and Francophone Philosophy—Revue de la philosophie française et de langue française* 31, no. 1/2 (2023): 24–45.

77    Luisetti, 349.

78    Luisetti, 349.

79    Luisetti, *Non-Human Subjects*, 7.

80    Luisetti, 7.

81   See also Dario Gentili, "Potentiality and Adaptability: Neoliberalism and Italian Thought," *Italian Studies* 76, no. 2 (2021): 148–60.

82   Luisetti, *Non-Human Subjects*, 7.

83   Stefania Barca, *Forces of Reproduction* (Cambridge: Cambridge University Press, 2020), 15.

84   Barca, 5; See also Stefania Barca, *Workers of the Earth: Labour, Ecology and Reproduction in the Age of Climate Change* (London: Pluto Press, 2024), 77–89.

85   Luisetti, *Non-Human Subjects*, 8.

86   Luisetti, 9.

87   Luisetti, 9.

88   Luisetti, 9.

89   See Povinelli, *Geontologies*; Kathryn Yusoff, *A Billion Black Anthropocenes or None* (Minneapolis: University of Minnesota Press, 2018).

90   Luisetti, *Non-Human Subjects*, 10.

91   Luisetti, 10.

92   Luisetti, 10–11.

93   Luisetti, 32.

94   Luisetti, 33.

95   Luisetti, 11.

96   For an earlier appeal to decolonize European thought, from the perspective of the Italian South, see Ernesto de Martino, *The End of the World: Cultural Apocalypse and Transcendence*, translated by Dorothy Louise Zinn (Chicago: Chicago University Press, 2023).

97   Luisetti, *Non-Human Subjects*, 11–12.

98   See Eduardo Kohn, *How Forests Think? An Anthropology Beyond the Human* (Berkeley: University of California Press, 2013); and Donna Haraway, *The Companion Species Manifesto: Dogs, People and Significant Others* (Chicago: Prickly Paradigm Press, 2003).

99   Federico Luisetti, *Non-Human Subjects*, 61.

100   Luisetti, 13 and 19.

101   Luisetti, 19.

102   See recent examples of "rights" and legal personhood granted to the Whanganui (New Zealand) and Rhône (France/Switzerland) rivers, as well as to the Mar Menor lagoon near Murcia, Spain.

103  Luisetti, 22–3.

104  Luisetti, 33–4.

105  Luisetti, 61.

106  Emanuele Coccia, "Don't Call Me Gaia," 6.

107  Coccia, 6.

108  Coccia, 6.

109  Emanuele Coccia, *The Life of Plants: A Metaphysics of Mixture*, translated by Dylan J. Montanari (Cambridge: Polity Press, 2018), 91.

110  Coccia, "Don't Call Me Gaia," 4.

111  Coccia, 4.

112  Coccia, 5.

113  Emanuele Coccia, *Metamorphosis*, translated by Robin Mackay (Cambridge: Polity Press, 2021), 130.

114  Coccia, 130.

115  Coccia, 130.

116  Coccia, 132.

117  Coccia, 133.

118  Coccia, 137.

119  Coccia, 140.

120  Coccia, 141.

121  Coccia, 142.

122  Coccia, 140–1, emphasis added.

123  Coccia, 147.

124  Coccia, 156.

125  Coccia, 150–1.

126  Coccia, 150–1.

127  Coccia, 153.

128  Coccia, 159.

129  Coccia, *Life of Plants*, 81.

130  Coccia, 81.

131  Coccia, 81.

132  Coccia, 82.

133     See Isabelle Stengers, *Cosmopolitics*, translated by Roberto Bononno (Minneapolis: University of Minnesota Press, 2010).

134     Coccia, *Life of Plants*, 87.

135     Coccia, 91. The English "radical" comes from the Latin "*radix*" meaning "root."

136     Coccia, 93.

137     Coccia, 94.

138     Coccia, 94.


# Chapter 3

1       Veena Dubal, "The House Always Wins: The Algorithmic Gamblification of Work," LPE Project, January 23, 2023, https://lpeproject.org/blog/the-house-always-wins-the-algorithmic-gamblification-of-work/.

2       Matteo Pasquinelli, *The Eye of the Master,* 4.

3       See, among others, Callum Cant, *Riding for Deliveroo: Resistance in the New Economy* (Cambridge: Polity Press, 2020); James Muldoon and Paul Raekstad, "Algorithmic Domination in the Gig Economy," *European Journal of Political Theory* 22, no. 4 (2023): 587–607; James Hickson, "Freedom, Domination and the Gig Economy," *New Political Economy* 29, no. 2 (2024): 321–36; Tim Christiaens, "Platform Cooperativism and Freedom as Non-Domination in the Gig Economy," *European Journal of Political Theory* 24, no. 2 (2024): 176–99.

4       Karl Marx, *Capital: Vol. 1*, translated by Samuel Moore and Edward Aveling (London: Lawrence & Wishart, 1996): 349.

5       Pasquinelli, *The Eye of the Master*, 18. See also Mario Tronti, "Italy," in *Karl Marx' Grundrisse: Foundations of the Critique of Political Economy 150 Years Later*, ed. Marcello Musto (London: Routledge, 2008): 229–35. The same issue also contained Raniero Panzieri's seminal text on the role of technology in capitalism. For an English translation, see Raniero Panzieri, "The Capitalist Use of Machinery: Marx versus the Objectivists," translated by Quintin Hoare, in *Outlines for a Critique of Technology*, ed. Phil Slater (London: Ink Links, 1980): 44–68.

6       Karl Marx, *Grundrisse: Foundations of the Critique of Political Economy*, translated by Martin Nicolaus (London: Penguin Books, 2005): 706.

7       Remo Bodei, *Dominio e Sottomissione: Schiavi, Animali, Macchine, Intelligenza Artificiale* (Bologna: Il Mulino, 2023): 279.

8    Paolo Virno, "Notes on the General Intellect," in *Marxism Beyond Marxism*, translated by Arianna Bove, ed. Saree Makdisi, Cesare Casarino, and Rebecca Karl (London: Routledge, 1996): 265.

9    Antonio Negri, *Marx Oltre Marx* (Rome: Manifestolibri, 1998): 194; Kathi Weeks, *The Problem with Work: Feminism, Marxism, Antiwork Politics, and Postwork Imaginaries* (Durham: Duke University Press, 2011): 103.

10   Michael Hardt and Antonio Negri, *Assembly* (Oxford: Oxford University Press, 2017): 273.

11   Franco Berardi Bifo, *Futurability: The Age of Impotence and the Horizon of Possibility* (London: Verso Books, 2017): 106.

12   Pasquinelli, *The Eye of the Master*, 236.

13   Nicolas Scheiber, "How Uber Pushes Drivers' Buttons," *New York Times*, April 3, 2017, https://www.nytimes.com/interactive/2017/04/02/technology/uber-drivers-psychological-tricks.html; Krishnan Vasudevan and Ngai Keung Chan, "Gamification and Work Games: Examining Consent and Resistance Among Uber Drivers," *New Media & Society* 24, no. 4 (2022): 866–86.

14   Tim Christiaens, "Convivial Autonomy and Platform Capitalism," in *Autonomy: Interdisciplinary Perspectives*, eds. Oliver Davis and Chris Watkin (London: Routledge, 2022): 69–82, 71.

15   Michael Hardt, *The Subversive Seventies* (Oxford: Oxford University Press, 2023): 113.

16   For histories of Italian workerism and its political impact, see Robert Lumley, *States of Emergency: Cultures of Revolt in Italy from 1968 to 1978* (London: Verso Books, 1990); Wright, *Storming Heaven*; Giuseppe Trotta, Fabio Milana, and Mario Tronti, *L'operaismo Degli Anni Sessanta: Da "Quaderni Rossi" a "Classe Operaia"* (Roma: Derive Approdi, 2008); Tim Christiaens, "Uit Verzet Geboren: De Filosofische Erfenis van Het Operaismo," *Ethische Perspectieven* 28, no. 2 (2018): 87–111; Gigi Roggero, *Italian Operaismo: Genealogy, History, Method*, translated by Clara Pope (Cambridge: MIT Press, 2023).

17   See, among others, Maurizio Lazzarato, "Immaterial Labor," in *Radical Thought in Italy*, 133–47; Michael Hardt and Antonio Negri, *Empire* (Cambridge: Harvard University Press, 2000): 280–303; Yann Moulier Boutang, *Cognitive Capitalism*, translated by Ed Emery (Cambridge: Polity Press, 2011); Carlo Vercellone, "The Becoming Rent of Profit? The New Articulation of Wage, Rent and Profit," *Knowledge Cultures* 1, no. 2 (2013): 194–207.

18   Nick Srnicek, *Platform Capitalism* (Cambridge: Polity Press, 2017).

**19**   Shoshana Zuboff, *The Age of Surveillance Capitalism: The Fight for the Future at the New Frontier of Power* (London: Profile Books, 2019): 47–8.

**20**   Franco Berardi Bifo, *The Soul at Work: From Alienation to Autonomy* (Los Angeles, CA: Semiotext(e), 2009): 75.

**21**   Franco Berardi Bifo, *And: Phenomenology of the End: Sensibility and Connective Mutation* (Los Angeles, CA: Semiotext(e), 2015): 205.

**22**   Franco Berardi Bifo, *After the Future*, translated by Gary Genosko and Nicholas Thoburn (Oakland: AK Press, 2011), 90.

**23**   Alex Rosenblat, *Uberland: How Algorithms Are Rewriting the Rules of Work* (Oakland: University of California Press, 2018), 179; Jamie Woodcock and Mark Graham, *The Gig Economy: A Critical Introduction* (Cambridge: Polity Press, 2020), 66; Paris Marx, *Road to Nowhere: What Silicon Valley Gets Wrong about the Future of Transportation* (London: Verso Books, 2022), 116.

**24**   Tiziana Terranova, "Free Labor: Producing Culture for the Digital Economy," *Social Text* 18, no. 2 (2000): 33–58. See also Tiziana Terranova, *Network Culture: Politics for the Information Age* (London: Pluto Press, 2004); Tiziana Terranova, *After the Internet* (Los Angeles, CA: Semiotext(e), 2022).

**25**   Adam Arvidsson and Elanor Colleoni, "Value in Informational Capitalism and on the Internet," *The Information Society* 28, no. 3 (2012): 135–50; Christiaens, *Digital Working Lives,* 39–58.

**26**   Brett Christophers, *Rentier Capitalism: Who Owns the Economy, and Who Pays for it?* (London: Verso Books, 2020): 95.

**27**   Carlo Vercellone, "The Crisis of the Law of Value and the Becoming-Rent of Profit," in *Crisis in the Global Economy*, ed. Andrea Fumagalli and Sandro Mezzadra (Los Angeles: Semiotext(e), 2010): 85–118.

**28**   Javier Moreno Zacarés, "Euphoria of the Rentier?," *New Left Review* 129, no. 3 (2021): 48.

**29**   Berardi Bifo, *Futurability*, 106.

**30**   Armin Beverungen, Steffen Böhm, and Chris Land, "Free Labour, Social Media, Management: Challenging Marxist Organization Studies," *Organization Studies* 36, no. 4 (2015): 483.

**31**   Luciano Floridi, *The 4th Revolution: How the Infosphere is Reshaping Human Reality* (Oxford: Oxford University Press, 2016): 43.

**32**   Maartje Roelofsen and Claudio Minca, "The Superhost: Biopolitics, Home and Community in the Airbnb Dream-World of Global Hospitality," *Geoforum* 91 (May 2018): 170–81; Sarah Gainsforth, *Airbnb città merce: storie di resistenza alla gentrificazione digitale* (Roma: DeriveApprodi, 2019).

33    Zuboff, *The Age of Surveillance Capitalism*, 338–9.

34    Zuboff, 8.

35    Antoinette Rouvroy and Thomas Berns, "Gouvernementalité Algorithmique et Perspectives d'émancipation," *Réseaux* 177, no. 1 (2013): 163–96.

36    Christiaens, "Convivial Autonomy and Platform Capitalism," 72.

37    Rob Kitchin and Alistair Fraser, *Slow Computing: Why We Need Balanced Digital Lives* (Bristol: Bristol University Press, 2020): 100–2.

38    Zuboff, *The Age of Surveillance Capitalism*, 378.

39    Berardi Bifo, *And*, 314.

40    Donald MacKenzie, "Cookies, Pixels and Fingerprints," *London Review of Books* 43, no. 7 (2021): 31–4.

41    Karl Marx, *Capital: Vol. 1*, 406, emphasis added.

42    Hardt and Negri, *Empire*, 218.

43    Pasquinelli, *The Eye of the Master*, 253.

44    Cant, *Riding for Deliveroo*; Jamie Woodcock and Callum Cant, "Platform Worker Organising at Deliveroo in the UK: From Wildcat Strikes to Building Power," *Journal of Labor and Society* 25 (2022): 220–36.

45    Niloufar Salehi et al., "We Are Dynamo: Overcoming Stalling and Friction in Collective Action for Crowd Workers," in *Proceedings of the 33rd Annual ACM Conference on Human Factors in Computing Systems* (CHI '15: CHI Conference on Human Factors in Computing Systems, Seoul Republic of Korea: ACM, 2015): 3; Antonio Casilli, *En Attendant Les Robots: Enquête Sur Le Travail Du Clic* (Paris: Éditions du Seuil, 2019), 157.

46    Romano Alquati, "Struggle at FIAT," translated by Evan Calder Williams, *Viewpoint Magazine*, September 26, 2013, https://viewpointmag. com/2013/09/26/struggle-at-fiat-1964/.

47    See Trebor Scholz, *Uberworked and Underpaid: How Workers are Disrupting the Digital Economy* (Cambridge: Polity Press, 2017): 31–2; Karen Gregory, "'My Life is More Valuable than This': Understanding Risk among On-Demand Food Couriers in Edinburgh," *Work, Employment and Society* 35, no. 2 (2020): 316–31; Tim Christiaens, "Digital Biopolitics and the Problem of Fatigue in Platform Capitalism," in *Big Data: A New Medium?*, ed. Natasha Lushetich (London: Routledge, 2020): 80–93; Alessandro Delfanti, *The Warehouse: Workers and Robots at Amazon* (London: Pluto Press, 2021): 30–54.

48    Berardi Bifo, *The Soul at Work*, 167.

49    Franco Berardi Bifo, *The Uprising: On Poetry and Finance* (Los Angeles, CA: Semiotext(e), 2012), 68.

50    Gavin Mueller, *Breaking Things at Work: The Luddites Are Right about Why You Hate Your Job* (London: Verso Books, 2021), 129.

51    Veena Dubal, "Wage Slave or Entrepreneur?: Contesting the Dualism of Legal Worker Identities," *California Law Review* 105, no. 1 (2017): 103; Rosenblat, *Uberland*, 36; Edouard Pignot, "Who is Pulling the Strings in the Platform Economy? Accounting for the Dark and Unexpected Sides of Algorithmic Control," *Organization* 30, no. 1 (2023): 148.

52    Maurizio Lazzarato, *Signs and Machines: Capitalism and the Production of Subjectivity*, translated by Joshua David Jordan (Los Angeles, CA: Semiotext(e), 2014): 89.

53    Maurizio Lazzarato, *Governing by Debt*, translated by Joshua David Jordan (Los Angeles, CA: Semiotext(e), 2015): 188.

54    Lazzarato, *Signs and Machines*, 184–7.

55    Lazzarato, 188.

56    Lazzarato, 180.

57    Vili Lehdonvirta, "Flexibility in the Gig Economy: Managing Time on Three Online Piecework Platforms," *New Technology, Work and Employment* 33, no. 1 (2018): 21.

58    Roberto Ciccarelli, *Forza Lavoro: Il Lato Oscuro Della Rivoluzione Digitale* (Roma: DeriveApprodi, 2018); Marco Marrone, "Rights against the Machines! Food Delivery, Piattaforme Digitali e Sindacalismo Informale: Il Caso Riders Union Bologna," *Labour & Law Issues* 5, no. 1 (2019): 1–28; Federico Chicchi and Marco Marrone, 'A New Subjectivity in Digital Platform Capitalism? Marginal Notes on Power and Conflict in the Time of Algorithms', *Work Organisation, Labour, and Globalization* 17, no. 2 (2023): 197–204; Gianmarco Peterlongo, *Nella Trama Dell'algoritmo* (Torino: Rosenberg & Sellier, 2023).

59    Lorenzo Cini, "Resisting Algorithmic Control: Understanding the Rise and Variety of Platform Worker Mobilisations," *New Technology, Work and Employment* 38, no. 1 (2023): 125–44; Donatella Della Porta, Riccardo Emilio Chesta, and Lorenzo Cini, *Labour Conflicts in the Digital Age: A Comparative Perspective* (Bristol: Bristol University Press, 2023).

60    Rafael Grohmann, "Not Just Platform, nor Cooperatives: Worker-Owned Technologies from Below," *Communication, Culture & Critique* 16, no. 4 (2023): 274–82.

61    Evangelos Papadimitropoulos, 'Platform Capitalism, Platform Cooperativism, and the Commons', *Rethinking Marxism* 33, no. 2 (2021): 246–62; Ana Sofia Acosta Alvarado, Laura Aufrère, and Cynthia Srnec,

"CoopCycle, Un Projet de Plateforme Socialisée et de Régulation de La Livraison à Vélo," HAL Archives Ouvertes, October 4, 2021, https://hal.archives-ouvertes.fr/hal-03364001/document; Christiaens, 'Platform Cooperativism'.

62    *Enabling Workers to Govern Their Work*, Democratize Work, 2024, https://www.youtube.com/watch?v=U8jf90X1KYc.

63    Paolo Virno, *A Grammar of the Multitude: For an Analysis of Contemporary Forms of Life*, translated by Isabella Bertoletti, James Cascaito, and Andrea Casson (Los Angeles, CA: Semiotext(e), 2003): 41.

64    Antonio Negri, *From the Factory to the Metropolis*, translated by Ed Emery (Cambridge: Polity Press, 2018): 162.

65    Negri, 171.

66    Pasquinelli, *The Eye of the Master*, 84–5.

67    Hardt and Negri, *Assembly*, 115.

68    Hardt and Negri, 287.

69    See Shaked Spier, "The Ethics and Politics of Platform Cooperatives" (New York: Institute for Digital Cooperative Economy, 2022), https://resources.platform.coop/resources/the-ethics-and-politics-of-platform-cooperatives/; Grohmann, "Not Just Platform, Nor Cooperatives."


# Chapter 4

1    Adrienne Massanari, "#Gamergate and The Fappening: How Reddit's Algorithm, Governance, and Culture Support Toxic Technocultures," *New Media & Society* 19, no. 3 (2017): 329–46; Emily Rosamond, "From Reputation Capital to Reputation Warfare: Online Ratings, Trolling, and the Logic of Volatility," *Theory, Culture & Society* 37, no. 2 (2020): 105–29; William Davies, "The Politics of Recognition in the Age of Social Media," *New Left Review* 128, no. 2 (2021): 83–99.

2    Roger Griffin, *The Nature of Fascism* (London: Routledge, 1993): 38.

3    Angela Nagle, *Kill All Normies: The Online Culture Wars from Tumblr and 4chan to the Alt-Right and Trump* (Winchester: Zero Books, 2017): 7.

4    Maurizio Lazzarato, *Capital Hates Everyone: Fascism or Revolution*, translated by Robert Hurley (Los Angeles: Semiotext(e), 2021): 119.

5    Lazzarato, 119.

6    Mark Ledwich and Anna Zaitsev, "Algorithmic Extremism: Examining YouTube's Rabbit Hole of Radicalization," *Working Paper*, 2019: 2; Alice Marwick, Benjamin Clancy, and Katherine Furl, "Far-Right Online

Radicalization: A Review of the Literature," *The Bulletin of Technology and Public Life* (Chapel Hill: Center for Information, Technology, and Public Life, 2022): 7.

7    Marwick, Clancy, and Furl, "Far-Right Online Radicalization: A Review of the Literature," 32; Kevin Munger and Joseph Phillips, "Right-Wing YouTube: A Supply and Demand Perspective," *The International Journal of Press/Politics* 27, no. 1 (2022): 198.

8    Lazzarato, *Capital Hates Everyone*, 9.

9    Aaron Winter, "Online Hate: From the Far-Right to the 'Alt-Right' and from the Margins to the Mainstream," in *Online Othering*, ed. Karen Lumsden and Emily Harmer (Cham: Springer International Publishing, 2019): 51.

10   For a similar claim defending an elective affinity between social media and populism, see Paolo Gerbaudo, "Social Media and Populism: An Elective Affinity?," *Media, Culture & Society* 40, no. 5 (2018): 745–53; Caroline Stockman and Vincenzo Scalia, "Democracy on the Five Star Movement's Rousseau Platform," *European Politics and Society* 21, no. 5 (2020): 603–17; Alan Finlayson, "YouTube and Political Ideologies: Technology, Populism and Rhetorical Form," *Political Studies* 70, no. 1 (2022): 62–80.

11   Michael Hardt, *The Subversive Seventies*, 206.

12   Ryan Kor-Sins, "The Alt-Right Digital Migration: A Heterogeneous Engineering Approach to Social Media Platform Branding," *New Media & Society* 25, no. 9 (2023): 2321–8.

13   Hardt and Negri, *Empire*; Yochai Benkler, *The Wealth of Networks: How Social Production Transforms Markets and Freedom* (New Haven: Yale University Press, 2006); Manuel Castells, *Networks of Outrage and Hope: Social Movements in the Internet Age* (Cambridge: Polity Press, 2015); Zeynep Tufekci, *Twitter and Tear Gas: The Power and Fragility of Networked Protest* (New York: Yale University Press, 2018).

14   Hardt and Negri, *Assembly*, 48.

15   Mario Tronti, *Workers and Capital*, translated by David Broder (London: Verso Books, 2019): 61.

16   Antonio Negri, *Marx Oltre Marx*, 247.

17   Negri, 51–2. See also Stefano Micali, "The Capitalistic Cult of Performance," *Philosophy Today* 54, no. 4 (2010): 379–91; Dario Gentili, *Crisi Come Arte Di Governo* (Macerata: Quodlibet, 2018); Dario Gentili, "Potentiality and Adaptability"; Tim Christiaens, "Esposito's Critique of Personhood and the Neoliberalization of Potentiality," *Italian Studies* 76, no. 2 (2021): 161–73.

18  For Foucault's theory of neoliberalism, see Lois McNay, "Self as Enterprise: Dilemmas of Control and Resistance in Foucault's The Birth of Biopolitics," *Theory, Culture & Society* 26, no. 6 (2009): 55–77; Terry Flew, "Michel Foucault's The Birth of Biopolitics and Contemporary Neo-Liberalism Debates," *Thesis Eleven* 108, no. 1 (2012): 44–65; Pierre Dardot and Christian Laval, *The New Way of the World: On Neoliberal Society* (London: Verso Books, 2013); Daniele Lorenzini, "Governmentality, Subjectivity, and the Neoliberal Form of Life," *Journal for Cultural Research* 22, no. 2 (2018): 154–66; Tim Christiaens, "Financial Neoliberalism and Exclusion with and beyond Foucault," *Theory, Culture & Society* 36, no. 4 (2018): 95–116.

19  Michel Foucault, *The Birth of Biopolitics: Lectures at the Collège de France, 1978–79*, translated by Graham Burchell (Basingstoke: Palgrave Macmillan, 2010): 259.

20  On Foucault's surprisingly positive description of neoliberalism, see Michael Behrent, "Liberalism without Humanism: Michel Foucault and the Free-Market Creed, 1976–1979," *Modern Intellectual History* 6, no. 3 (2009): 539–68; Zamora, *Critiquer Foucault*; Serge Audier, *Penser Le "Néolibéralisme": Le Moment Néolibéral, Foucault et La Crise Du Socialisme* (Latresne: Le Bord de l'eau, 2015); Mitchell Dean and Daniel Zamora, *The Last Man Takes LSD: Foucault and the End of Revolution* (London: Verso Books, 2021); Christiaens, "Foucault's Genealogy of Neoliberalism."

21  Hardt and Negri, *Assembly*, 218.

22  Maurizio Lazzarato, *Governing by Debt*, 218–9.

23  Franco Berardi Bifo, *Futurability: The Age of Impotence and the Horizon of Possibility* (London: Verso Books, 2017): 113.

24  Franco Berardi Bifo, *Heroes: Mass Murder and Suicide* (London: Verso Books, 2015): 159–60.

25  Nadia Urbinati, *Me the People: How Populism Transforms Democracy* (Cambridge: Harvard University Press, 2019), 172.

26  Urbinati, 7–8. See also Nadia Urbinati, *Democracy Disfigured: Opinion, Truth and the People* (Cambridge: Harvard University Press, 2014): 16–80.

27  Urbinati, 151.

28  Urbinati, 24–5.

29  Urbinati, 164.

30  Urbinati, 20–1.

31  Berardi Bifo, *Heroes*, 123.

32    Berardi Bifo, 129.

33    This politics of resentment is a common explanation for the affective
      pull of reactionary ideologies beyond Italian thought as well. See, among
      others, Oliver Nachtwey, *Germany's Hidden Crisis: Social Decline in the
      Heart of Europe* (London: Verso Books, 2018); Arlie Russell Hochschild,
      *Strangers in Their Own Land: Anger and Mourning on the American
      Right* (New York: The New Press, 2018); Jason Read, *The Double Shift:
      Spinoza and Marx on the Politics and Ideology of Work* (London: Verso
      Books, 2024).

34    Alberto Toscano, *Late Fascism: Race, Capitalism and the Politics of Crisis*
      (London: Verso Books, 2023): 7.

35    Toscano, 9.

36    Hardt and Negri, *Assembly*, 52.

37    Umberto Eco, *Il Fascismo Eterno* (Milano: La nave di Teseo, 2018), 43.

38    Eco, 39.

39    Toscano, *Late Fascism*, 118.

40    Luke Munn, "Alt-Right Pipeline: Individual Journeys to Extremism
      Online," *First Monday* 24, no. 6 (2019); Alan Finlayson, "Neoliberalism,
      the Alt-Right and the Intellectual Dark Web," *Theory, Culture & Society*
      38, no. 6 (2021): 167–90.

41    Finlayson, "YouTube and Political Ideologies," 67.

42    Nagle, *Kill All Normies*, 106–7.

43    Gerbaudo, "Social Media and Populism," 750.

44    Mitchell Dean, "Political Acclamation, Social Media and the Public
      Mood," *European Journal of Social Theory* 20, no. 3 (2017): 429; Mitchell
      Dean, "Three Forms of Democratic Political Acclamation," *Telos* 179
      (2017): 27.

45    Toscano, *Late Fascism*, 16.

46    The most advanced articulation of the liberal public sphere is Jürgen
      Habermas, *The Structural Transformation of the Public Sphere*
      (Cambridge: Polity, 2011).

47    Immanuel Kant, "An Answer to the Question: What Is Enlightenment?,"
      in *What Is Enlightenment?: Eighteenth-Century Answers and Twentieth-
      Century Questions*, ed. James Schmidt (Stanford: University of California
      Press, 1996): 59.

48    Eco, *Il Fascismo Eterno*, 44–5.

49    Toscano, *Late Fascism*, 55.

50   Eco, *Il Fascismo Eterno*, 23.

51   Giorgio Agamben, *Opus Dei: An Archaeology of Duty*, translated by
     Adam Kotsko (Stanford: Stanford University Press, 2013), 1; Nicholas
     Heron, *Liturgical Power: Between Economic and Political Theology* (New
     York: Fordham University Press, 2018): 8.

52   Émile Benveniste, *Dictionary of Indo-European Concepts and Society*
     (Chicago: Hau Books, 2016): 378.

53   Eco, *Il Fascismo Eterno*, 45–6.

54   Eco, 46. For Urbinati's similar views on direct representation,
     see Urbinati, *Democracy Disfigured*, 171–227; Urbinati, *Me the
     People*, 158–89.

55   For helpful introductions to Agamben's notion of liturgy and its role
     in politics, see Mitchell Dean, *The Signature of Power: Sovereignty,
     Governmentality and Biopolitics* (London: SAGE, 2013); Colby Dickinson
     and Adam Kotsko, *Agamben's Coming Philosophy: Finding a New Use for
     Theology* (New York: Rowman & Littlefield International, 2015); Heron,
     *Liturgical Power*; Tim Christiaens, "Agamben's Theories of the State of
     Exception: From Political to Economic Theology," *Cultural Critique* 110,
     no. 1 (2021): 49–74.

56   Giorgio Agamben, *The Kingdom and the Glory*, translated by Lorenzo
     Chiesa (Stanford: Stanford University Press, 2011): 192–3. Agamben's
     main source of inspiration for the theory of plebiscitary democracy
     is Carl Schmitt, who defends it against the defects of the liberal
     parliamentary democracy of the Weimar Republic. Agamben takes a
     more critical stance, showing how Schmitt's notion of the public sphere
     actually accelerates the decline of political democracy into fascism
     rather than immunizing democracy from any deficits of political
     legitimacy. See Carl Schmitt, *The Crisis of Parliamentary Democracy*,
     translated by Ellen Kennedy (Cambridge: MIT Press, 1988); Carl Schmitt,
     *Legality and Legitimacy*, translated by Jeffrey Seitzer (New York: Duke
     University Press, 2004); Duncan Kelly, "Carl Schmitt's Political Theory
     of Representation," *Journal of the History of Ideas* 65, no. 1 (2004):
     113–34; Andreas Kalyvas, *Democracy and the Politics of the Extraordinary*
     (Cambridge: Cambridge University Press, 2009); William Scheuerman,
     "Donald Trump Meets Carl Schmitt," *Philosophy & Social Criticism*
     45, no. 9–10 (2019): 1170–85; Tim Christiaens, "The Populist Promise
     in Carl Schmitt's Political Theology," in *100 Years after Carl Schmitt*,
     ed. Lotte List, Stefan Schwarzkopf, and Mitchell Dean (New York:
     Bloomsbury Academic, 2023): 30–44.

57   Agamben, *The Kingdom and the Glory*, 177.

58   Agamben, 253–4.

59    Agamben, 256.

60    For an overview, see Dean, *The Signature of Power*.

61    Dean, "Three Forms," 28.

62    See Jodi Dean, "Communicative Capitalism: Circulation and the Foreclosure of Politics," *Cultural Politics* 1, no. 1 (2005): 51–74; Zizi Papacharissi, *Affective Publics: Sentiment, Technology, and Politics* (Oxford: Oxford University Press, 2015).

63    Nidesh Lawtoo, *(New) Fascism: Contagion, Community, Myth* (East Lansing: Michigan State University Press, 2019): 185.

64    Mark Fielitz and Holger Marcks, "Digital Fascism: Challenges for the Open Society in Times of Social Media," Berkeley Center for Right-Wing Studies (Los Angeles: Institute for the Study of Societal Issues, 2019): 8; Finlayson, "YouTube and Political Ideologies," 68.

65    Alessandro Baricco, *The Game*, translated by Manon Smits (Amsterdam: Bezige Bij, 2019): 281–308.

66    Baricco, 291.

67    Baricco, 306–7.

68    Maurizio Lazzarato, "How to Think a War Machine: Interview with Maurizio Lazzarato," Interview by Tim Christiaens and Stijn De Cauwer, in *Critical Theory at a Crossroads*, 139; Lazzarato, *Capital Hates Everyone*, 117.

69    Lazzarato, *Capital Hates Everyone*, 133.

70    Donatella Di Cesare, *Virus Sovrano? L'asfissia Capitalistica* (Torino: Bollati Boringhieri, 2020): 55, our translation.

71    Donatella Di Cesare, *Conspiracy and Power* (Cambridge: Polity Press, 2023), 54.

72    Di Cesare, 13, 56.

73    Di Cesare, 107–8.

74    Hardt and Negri, *Empire*, 204.

75    Paolo Gerbaudo, *The Digital Party: Political Organisation and Online Democracy* (London: Pluto Press, 2019): 81.

76    Gerbaudo, 10–11.

77    Gerbaudo, 127.

78    Gerbaudo, 38.

79    Gerbaudo, 145.

80    Gerbaudo, 161.

81    Gerbaudo, 98.

82    Gerbaudo, 140.

83    Gerbaudo, 104.

84    Toscano, *Late Fascism*, 13.

85    Meagan Day, "Americans are Starting to Love Unions Again," Jacobin, February 9, 2019, https://jacobin.com/2019/09/unions-us-labor-movement-americans-gallup-poll-bernie-sanders.


# Chapter 5

1     For a video recording of Meloni's speech, see for example: https://video.corriere.it/politica/meloni-sono-donna-madre-cristiana-non-me-toglierete/acfae0ee-f291-11e9-a8b5-b5f95b99eb6a

2     Meloni expands these ideas in her autobiography: *Io sono Giorgia: Le mie radici, le mie idee* (Rizzoli, Milano: 2021).

3     Pier Paolo Pasolini, "A Study of the Anthropological Revolution in Italy," English translation: https://files.libcom.org/files/Corsair%20Writings%20–%20Pier%20Paolo%20Pasolini.pdf. For the original Italian text, see Pier Paolo Pasolini, *Scritti corsari* (Milano: Garzanti Libri, 2015).

4     English translation: https://files.libcom.org/files/Corsair%20Writings%20–%20Pier%20Paolo%20Pasolini.pdf and https://www.diagonalthoughts.com/?p=2107 For the original text, see *Scritti Corsari*.

5     See Pasolini's "Repudiation of the Trilogy of Life," in *Heretical Empiricism* (Washington: New Academia Publishing, 2005).

6     See Pasolini, *Scritti Corsari*. English translation: https://files.libcom.org/files/Corsair%20Writings%20–%20Pier%20Paolo%20Pasolini.pdf

7     See Giorgio Agamben, "Form of Life," in *Means without Ends*, translated by Vincenzo Binetti and Cesare Casarino (Minneapolis: University of Minnesota Press, 2000): 3–12.

8     Pier Paolo Pasolini, "Repudiation of the Trilogy of Life," in *Heretical Empiricism*, xix.

9     Pier Paolo Pasolini, "A Study of the Anthropological Revolution in Italy," in *Scritti Corsari*. English translation: https://files.libcom.org/files/Corsair%20Writings%20–%20Pier%20Paolo%20Pasolini.pdf

10    "The Real Fascism and Therefore the Real Antifascism," in *Scritti Corsari*. English translation: https://files.libcom.org/files/Corsair%20Writings%20–%20Pier%20Paolo%20Pasolini.pdf

11   Giorgio Agamben, *When the House Burns Down*, translated by Kevin Attell (London and Kolkata: Seagull Books, 2023): 3.

12   Agamben, *When the House Burns Down*, 3.

13   Agamben, 3.

14   Agamben, 4.

15   Agamben, 3 and 6.

16   See Guy Debord, *The Society of the Spectacle*, translated by Donald Nicholson-Smith (New York: Zone Books, 1995).

17   Agamben, *When the House Burns Down*, 5.

18   Agamben, 5.

19   Agamben, 5.

20   Giorgio Agamben, "Leviathan's Riddle," in *Leviathans Rätsel* translated by Paul Silas Peterson (Tübingen: Mohr Siebeck, 2014): 20.

21   Agamben, "Leviathan's Riddle," 20.

22   Agamben, 30–2.

23   Agamben, 34–6.

24   Giorgio Agamben, *Stasis: Civil War as a Political Paradigm* (Stanford: Stanford University Press, 2015). For an extensive critique of Agamben's peculiar "populism," see Joost de Bloois, "*Tutti i popoli sono bande*: Giorgio Agamben's Populism," in *'Us versus Them': Exploring Transatlantic Practices of Fascism(s) and Populism(s) from the Margins*, eds. R. Dhondt, Jansen, and M. B. Urban (London: Routledge, 2025).

25   In this "anarchist" sense, Agamben's conceptualization of "the people" is in line with his theory of the "coming community": a community that remains undefined, open-ended; a community of potentiality, not identity. On the other hand, this potentiality, especially in Agamben's work of the past decade or so, is, paradoxically, explicitly located by Agamben in cultural, geographical, and linguistic particularisms. See Giorgio Agamben, *The Coming Community*, translated by Michael Hardt (Minneapolis: Minnesota University Press, 1993).

26   English translation: https://voxeurop.eu/en/the-latin-empire-should-strike-back/

27   Agamben, "The Latin Empire Should Strike Back," emphasis added.

28   Giorgio Agamben, "Beyond Human Rights," *Open* 15 (2008): 90.

29   Agamben, "Beyond Human Rights," 90, emphasis added.

30   Agamben even writes that we should conceive of "political philosophy anew starting from the one and only figure of the refugee" (90).

31 Agamben, 92.

32 Agamben, 93.

33 Agamben, 94.

34 Agamben, 94.

35 Agamben, 95.

36 Agamben, 95.

37 Agamben, *When the House Burns Down*, 16.

38 Agamben, 11. For a critique of Agamben's "gnostic" rejection of the modern world as inherently "evil," see Simon Critchley's *The Faith of the Faithless: Experiments in Political Theology* (London: Verso Books, 2014).

39 Agamben, 2.

40 Agamben, 14.

41 Gianni Vattimo, "Dialectics, Difference, Weak Thought," in *Weak Thought*, eds. Gianni Vattimo and Pier Aldo Rovatti, translated by Peter Caravetta (Albany: State University of New York Press, 2013): 43.

42 Vattimo, "Dialectics, Difference, Weak Thought," 45.

43 Vattimo, 47.

44 Vattimo, 47.

45 Vattimo, 48–50.

46 Vattimo, 51.

47 Vattimo, 51.

48 See Gianni Vattimo, *Belief*, translated by Luca d'Isanto and David Webb (Stanford: Stanford University Press, 1999).

49 Vattimo, "Dialectics, Difference, Weak Thought," 51.

50 Vattimo, "Dialectics, Difference, Weak Thought," 51.

51 See Sandro Mezzadra and Brett Neilson, *The Rest and the West: Capital and Power in a Multipolar World* (London: Verso Books, 2024).

52 Sandro Mezzadra and Brett Neilson, *Border as Method, Or, The Multiplication of Labor* (Durham: Duke University Press, 2013): ix–x.

53 Mezzadra and Neilson, *Border as Method*, xi.

54 Mezzadra and Neilson, ix.

55 Mezzadra and Neilson, ix.

56 Mezzadra and Neilson, ix.

57    See Giorgio Agamben, "What is a Camp?" in *Means without Ends* (Minneapolis: University of Minnesota Press, 2000): 37–48.

58    Mezzadra and Neilson, *Border as Method*, 149.

59    Mezzadra and Neilson, 149.

60    Mezzadra and Neilson, 155.

61    Mezzadra and Neilson, 155.

62    Mezzadra and Neilson, 149.

63    Mezzadra and Neilson, 149.

64    Mezzadra and Neilson, 149.

65    Mezzadra and Neilson, 99.

66    Mezzadra and Neilson, 99.

67    Mezzadra and Neilson, 99.

68    Mezzadra and Neilson, 100.

69    Sandro Mezzadra, *La condizione postcoloniale. Storia e politica nel mondo globale* (Verona: Ombre Corte, 2008).

70    Mezzadra and Neilson, *Border as Method*, 100.

71    Mezzadra and Neilson, 124.

72    Mezzadra and Neilson, 125.

73    Mezzadra and Neilson, 125–6.

74    Mezzadra and Neilson, 126.

75    Mezzadra and Neilson, 125.

76    Mezzadra and Neilson, 125.

77    Sandro Mezzadra, *La condizone postcoloniale*, 14. See also Dipesh Chakrabarty, *Provincializing Europe: Postcolonial Thought and Historical Difference* (Princeton: Princeton University Press, 2007).

78    Mezzadra, *La condizione postcoloniale*, 31.

79    Mezzadra, 36.

80    Mezzadra, 37.

81    Mezzadra, 146.

82    Antonio Negri and Michael Hardt, *Commonwealth* (Cambridge, Massachusetts: Belknap and Harvard University Press, 2009): 346.

83    Negri and Hardt, *Commonwealth*, 346.

84    Negri and Hardt, 347.

85    Negri and Hardt, 350.

86    Negri and Hardt, 351.

87    See Karl Marx, *The Poverty of Philosophy*, anonymous translation (New York: International Publishers, 1992); Vladimir Lenin, "Left-Wing Communism: An Infantile Disorder," translated by Julius Katzer https://www.marxists.org/archive/lenin/works/1920/lwc/; Theodor Adorno, *Minima Moralia: Refelctions on a Damaged Life*, translated by E.F.N. Jephcott (London: Verso 2005); Walter Benjamin, "Theses on the Philosophy of History," in *Illuminations: Essays and Reflections*, translated by Harry Zohn (New York: Schocken Books 1968): 253–64.

88    Negri and Hardt, *Commonwealth*, 97.

89    See also Silvia Federici, *Caliban and the Witch*.

90    Negri and Hardt, *Commonwealth*, 98.

91    Negri and Hardt, 102.

92    Negri and Hardt, 102.

93    Negri and Hardt, 108.

94    Negri and Hardt, 110.

95    Negri and Hardt, 111.

96    Negri and Hardt, 111.

97    Negri and Hardt, 111.

98    See Jodie Dean and Paul Passavant (eds.), *Empire's New Clothes: Reading Hardt and Negri* (London: Routledge, 2004) and see Bruce Braun and Sarah Nelson (eds.), *Autonomia in the Anthropocene: New Challenges to Radical Politics* (*South Atlantic Quarterly* 116: 2, April 2017).

99    Negri and Hardt, *Commonwealth*, 85.

100   Negri and Hardt, 87.

101   Negri and Hardt, 88.

102   As it had its heyday in Bologna in the spring of 1977.

103   See Francis Fukuyama, *The End of History and the Last Man* (New York: Free Press, 1992).

104   Berardi Bifo, *Dell'innocenza. 1977: l'anno della premonizione* (Verona: Ombre Corte, 1997): 49; see also Jamilla Squire and Seth Wheeler (eds.) *A Thousand Little Machines*.

105   Berardi Bifo, *Dell'innocenza*, 11.

106   See Mario Troni's "The Strategy of Refusal," in *Workers and Capital,* and https://libcom.org/article/strategy-refusal-mario-tronti

107 Franco Berardi Bifo, *Precarious Rhapsody: Semiocapitalism and the Pathologies of Post-Alpha Generation* (New York: Autonomedia, 2009): 15.

108 Berardi Bifo, *Precarious Rhapsody*, 15.

109 Berardi Bifo, 30.

110 Bruce Braun and Sarah Nelson, "Autonomia in the Anthropocene: New Challenges to Radical Politics," *South Atlantic Quarterly* 116, no. 2 (2017): 223–36.

111 Berardi, *Precarious Rhapsody*, 31.

112 Marcello Tari, *Autonomie! Italie, les années 1970* (Paris: La fabrique éditions, 2011): 50, 53.

113 Tari, *Autonomie!*, 28.

114 Bruce Braun and Sarah Nelson, "Autonomia in the Anthropocene: New Challenges to Radical Politics," in *South Atlantic Quarterly* 116, no. 2 (2017): 230.

115 Braun and Nelson, 229.

# Conclusion

1 Giorgio Agamben, "The Endless Crisis as an Instrument of Power: In Conversation with Giorgio Agamben," Verso Blog, June 4, 2013, https://www.versobooks.com/blogs/news/1318-the-endless-crisis-as-an-instrument-of-power-in-conversation-with-giorgio-agamben.

2 Antonio Gramsci, *Prison Notebooks: Volume II*, translated by Joseph Buttigieg (New York: Columbia University Press, 2011): 33.

3 Ernesto de Martino, *The End of the World: Cultural Apocalypse and Transcendence*, translated by Dorothy Louise Zinn (Chicago: University of Chicago Press, 2023): 192.

4 See also Dorothy Louise Zinn, "An Introduction to Ernesto de Martino's Relevance for the Study of Folklore," *Journal of American Folklore* 128, no. 507 (2015): 3–17; Carlo Ginzburg, "On Ernesto de Martino's 'The End of the World' and its Genesis," *Chicago Review* 60–1, no. 4/1 (2017): 77–91; Nicolas Guilhot, "The Man Who Lived at the End of History," *New Statesman*, February 15, 2024, https://www.newstatesman.com/ideas/2024/02/ernesto-de-martino-history-apocalypse.

5 De Martino, *End of the World*, 17.

6 De Martino, 62.

7   De Martino, 95. See also Elettra Stimilli, "Apocalyptic Time," *Political Theology* 21, no. 5 (2020): 391–2.

8   De Martino, 280.

9   Antonio Gramsci, *Selections from the Prison Notebooks of Antonio Gramsci*, translated by Quintin Hoare and Geoffrey Nowell-Smith (London: Lawrence & Wishart, 1971): 130.

10  De Martino, *End of the World*, 191.

11  Esposito, *Living Thought*, 27.

12  Esposito, 27.

13  Niccolo Machiavelli, *Discourses on Livy* (Oxford: Oxford University Press, 2009), 246.

14  Esposito, *Living Thought*, 51.

15  Italo Calvino, *Invisible Cities* (Boston: Houghton Mifflin Harcourt, 2013): 5–6.

16  Calvino, 165.

17  Calvino, 161–3.

18  Calvino, 163. Translation slightly altered.

19  Esposito, *Living Thought*, 48.

20  Negri, *Insurgencies*, 304.

21  Hardt and Negri, *Empire*, 410.

22  Giorgio Agamben, *The Signature of All Things: On Method*, translated by Kevin Attell (New York: Zone Books, 2009): 7–8.

23  See Nancy Fraser, *Cannibal Capitalism* (London: Verso Books, 2022).

# BIBLIOGRAPHY


Acosta Alvarado, Ana Sofia, Laura Aufrère, and Cynthia Srnec. "CoopCycle, Un Projet de Plateforme Socialisée et de Régulation de La Livraison à Vélo." HAL Archives Ouvertes, 4 October 2021. https://hal.archives-ouvertes.fr/hal-03364001/document.

Adorno, Theodor. *Minima Moralia: Reflections on a Damaged Life*. Translated by E.F.N. Jephcott. London: Verso, 2005.

Agamben, Giorgio. *Gaia e Ctonia*: https://www.quodlibet.it/giorgio-agamben-gaia-e-ctonia

Agamben, Giorgio. *Homo Sacer: Sovereign Power and Bare Life*. Translated by Daniel Heller-Roazen. Stanford: Stanford University Press, 1998.

Agamben, Giorgio. *Leviathans Rätsel*. Translated by Paul Silas Peterson. Tübingen: Mohr Siebeck, 2014.

Agamben, Giorgio. *Means Without Ends*. Translated by Vincenzo Binetti and Cesare Casarino. Minneapolis: University of Minnesota Press, 2000.

Agamben, Giorgio. *Opus Dei: An Archaeology of Duty*. Translated by Adam Kotsko. Stanford: Stanford University Press, 2013.

Agamben, Giorgio. *Stasis: Civil War as a Political Paradigm*. Translated by Nicholas Heron. Stanford: Stanford University Press, 2015

Agamben, Giorgio. *The Coming Community*. Translated by Michael Hardt. Minneapolis: Minnesota University Press, 1993.

Agamben, Giorgio. "The Endless Crisis as an Instrument of Power: In Conversation with Giorgio Agamben." Verso Blog, 4 June 2013. https://www.versobooks.com/blogs/news/1318-the-endless-crisis-as-an-instrument-of-power-in-conversation-with-giorgio-agamben.

Agamben, Giorgio. *The Kingdom and the Glory*. Translated by Lorenzo Chiesa. Stanford: Stanford University Press, 2011.

Agamben, Giorgio. "The Latin Empire Should Strike Back." https://voxeurop.eu/en/the-latin-empire-should-strike-back/

Agamben, Giorgio. *The Signature of All Things: On Method*. Translated by Kevin Attell. New York: Zone Books, 2009.

Agamben, Giorgio. *The Use of Bodies*. Translated by Adam Kotsko. Stanford: Stanford University Press, 2016.

Agamben, Giorgio. *Where Are We Now? The Epidemic as Politics*. Translated by Valeria Dani, London: Rowman & Littlefield, 2021.

Agamben, Giorgio. *When the House Burns Down*. Translated by Kevin Attell. London and Kolkata: Seagull Books, 2023.

Alquati, Romano. "Struggle at FIAT." Translated by Evan Calder Williams. *Viewpoint Magazine*, 26 September 2013. https://viewpointmag. com/2013/09/26/struggle-at-fiat-1964/.

Amaro, Ramon. *The Black Technical Object: On Machine Learning and the Aspiration of Black Being*. London: Sternberg Press, 2023.

Arquilla, John, and Ronfeldt, David. "The Emergence of Noopolitik: Toward an American Information Strategy." RAND7 1999. https://www.rand.org/pubs/ monograph_reports/MR1033.html.

Arvidsson, Adam, and Elanor Colleoni. "Value in Informational Capitalism and on the Internet." *The Information Society* 28, no. 3 (2012): 135–50.

Audier, Serge. *Penser Le "Néolibéralisme": Le Moment Néolibéral, Foucault et La Crise Du Socialisme*. Latresne: Le Bord de l'eau, 2015.

Balestrini, Nanni. *The Unseen*. London: Verso Books, 2012.

Balestrini, Nanni and Primo Moroni, eds. *The Golden Horde: Revolutionary Italy, 1960–1977*. Translated by Richard Braude. London and Calcutta: Seagull Books, 2020.

Barca, Stefania. *Forces of Reproduction*. Cambridge: Cambridge University Press, 2020.

Barca, Stefania. *Workers of the Earth: Labour, Ecology and Reproduction in the Age of Climate Change*. London: Pluto Press, 2024.

Baricco, Alessandro. *The Game*. Translated by Manon Smits. Amsterdam: Bezige Bij, 2019.

Behrent, Michael. "Liberalism without Humanism: Michel Foucault and the Free-Market Creed, 1976–1979." *Modern Intellectual History* 6, no. 3 (2009): 539–68.

Benjamin, Walter. "Theses on the Philosophy of History" in *Illuminations: Essays and Reflections*. Translated by Harry Zohn. New York: Schocken Books, 1968.

Benkler, Yochai. *The Wealth of Networks: How Social Production Transforms Markets and Freedom*. New Haven: Yale University Press, 2006.

Benveniste, Émile. *Dictionary of Indo-European Concepts and Society*. Chicago: Hau Books, 2016.

Berardi Bifo, Franco. *After the Future*. Translated by Gary Genosko and Nicholas Thoburn. Oakland: AK Press, 2011.

Berardi Bifo, Franco. *And: Phenomenology of the End: Sensibility and Connective Mutation*. Los Angeles: Semiotext(e), 2015.

Berardi Bifo, Franco. *Dell'innocenza. 1977: l'anno della premonizione*. Verona: Ombre Corte, 1997.

Berardi Bifo, Franco. *Futurability: The Age of Impotence and the Horizon of Possibility*. London: Verso Books, 2017.

Berardi Bifo, Franco. *Heroes: Mass Murder and Suicide*. London: Verso Books, 2015.

Berardi Bifo, Franco. *Precarious Rhapsody: Semiocapitalism and the Pathologies of Post-Alpha Generation*. New York: Autonomedia, 2009.

Berardi Bifo, Franco. *The Soul at Work: From Alienation to Autonomy*. Los Angeles: Semiotext(e), 2009.

Berardi Bifo, Franco. *The Uprising: On Poetry and Finance*. Los Angeles: Semiotext(e), 2012.

Beverungen, Armin, Steffen Böhm, and Chris Land. "Free Labour, Social Media, Management: Challenging Marxist Organization Studies." *Organization Studies* 36, no. 4 (2015): 473–89.

Bianchi, Sergio and Lanfranco Caminiti (eds.). *Gli Autonomi: Le storie, le lotte, le teorie*. Bologna: DeriveApprodi, 2020.

Bird, Greg, and Short, John (eds.). *Community, Immunity and the Proper: Roberto Esposito*. New York: Routledge, 2017.

Bodei, Remo. *Dominio e Sottomissione: Schiavi, Animali, Macchine, Intelligenza Artificiale*. Bologna: Il Mulino, 2023.

Braidotti, Rosi. "'A Critical Europe Can Do It!' Interview by Joost de Bloois." In Stijn De Cauwer (ed.), *Critical Theory at A Crossroads: Conversations on Resistance in Times of Crisis*. New York: Columbia University Press, 2018.

Braidotti, Rosi. *The Posthuman*. Cambridge: Polity Press, 2013.

Braun, Bruce and Sarah Nelson (eds.). "Autonomia in the Anthropocene." *South Atlantic Quarterly* 116, no. 2 (2017).

Buongiorno, Federica and Antonio Lucci, "La differenza italiana: Filosofi(e) nell'Italia di oggi." *Lo Sguardo: Revista di filosofia* 15, no. 2 (2014): 5–10.

Butler, Judith. "Leaving Out, Caught in the Fall." In *Toward a Feminist Ethics of Nonviolence. Adriana Cavarero, with Judith Butler, Bonnie Honig, and Other Voices* edited by Timothy J. Huzar, and Clare Woodford, 46–62. New York: Fordham University Press, 2021.

Cacciari, Massimo. *Geofilosofia dell'Europa*. Milano: Adelphi, 1994.

Cacciari, Massimo, and Giorgo Agamben. "A proposito del decreto sul 'green pass.'" 26 June 2021. https://www.iisf.it/progetti/diario-della-crisi/item/2531-massimo-cacciari-giorgio-agamben-a-proposito-del-decreto-sul-green-pass.html

Calvino, Italo. *Invisible Cities*. Boston: Houghton Mifflin Harcourt, 2013.

Campbell, Timothy. *Improper Life: Technology and Biopolitics from Heidegger to Agamben*. Minneapolis: University of Minnesota Press, 2011.

Cant, Callum. *Riding for Deliveroo: Resistance in the New Economy*. Cambridge: Polity Press, 2020.

Casilli, Antonio. *En Attendant Les Robots: Enquête Sur Le Travail Du Clic*. Paris: Éditions du Seuil, 2019.

Castells, Manuel. *Networks of Outrage and Hope: Social Movements in the Internet Age*. Cambridge: Polity Press, 2015.

Cavarero, Adriana. *Donne che allattano cuccioli di lupo. Icone dell'ipermaterno*. Roma: Castelvecchi, 2023.

Cavarero, Adriana. "Il corpo come luogo di transito." *Doppiozero* 30th September 2014. https://www.doppiozero.com/il-corpo-come-luogo-di-transito

Cavarero, Adriana. *Inclinations: A Critique of Rectitude.* Translated by Adam Sitze and Amanda Minervini, Stanford: Stanford University Press, 2016.

Chakrabarty, Dipesh. *Provincializing Europe: Postcolonial Thought and Historical Difference.* Princeton: Princeton University Press, 2007.

Chicchi, Federico, and Marco Marrone. "A New Subjectivity in Digital Platform Capitalism? Marginal Notes on Power and Conflict in the Time of Algorithms." *Work Organisation, Labour, and Globalization* 17, no. 2 (2023): 197–204.

Chiesa, Lorenzo and Alberto Toscano, (eds.). *The Italian Difference: Between Nihilism and Biopolitics.* Melbourne: re.press, 2009.

Christiaens, Tim. "Agamben's 'bare life' and Grossman's ethics of senseless kindness." *Journal of European Studies* 52, no. 1 (2022): 36–53.

Christiaens, Tim. "Agamben's Theories of the State of Exception: From Political to Economic Theology." *Cultural Critique* 110, no. 1 (2021): 49–74.

Christiaens, Tim. "Aristotle's Anthropological Machine and Slavery." *Epoché: A Journal for the History of Philosophy* 23, no. 1 (2018): 239–62.

Christiaens, Tim. "Biomedical Technocracy, the Networked Public Sphere and the Biopolitics of COVID-19: Notes on the Agamben Affair." *Culture, Theory and Critique*, 62, no. 4 (2021): 404–21.

Christiaens, Tim. "Convivial Autonomy and Platform Capitalism." In *Autonomy: Interdisciplinary Perspectives.* Edited by Oliver Davis and Chris Watkin, 69–82. London: Routledge, 2022.

Christiaens, Tim. "Digital Biopolitics and the Problem of Fatigue in Platform Capitalism." In *Big Data: A New Medium?* Edited by Natasha Lushetich, 80–93. London: Routledge, 2020.

Christiaens, Tim. *Digital Working Lives: Worker Autonomy and the Digital Gig Economy.* London: Rowman & Littlefield, 2022.

Christiaens, Tim. "Esposito's Critique of Personhood and the Neoliberalization of Potentiality." *Italian Studies* 76, no. 2 (2021): 161–73.

Christiaens, Tim. "Financial Neoliberalism and Exclusion with and beyond Foucault." *Theory, Culture & Society* 36, no. 4 (2018): 95–116.

Christiaens, Tim. "On the Limitations of Michel Foucault's Genealogy of Neoliberalism." *Journal of French and Francophone Philosophy* 31, no. 1/2 (2024): 24–45.

Christiaens, Tim. "Platform Cooperativism and Freedom as Non-Domination in the Gig Economy." *European Journal of Political Theory*, 24, no. 2 (2024): 176–99.

Christiaens, Tim. "The Populist Promise in Carl Schmitt's Political Theology." In *100 Years after Carl Schmitt.* Edited by Lotte List, Stefan Schwarzkopf, and Mitchell Dean, 30–44. New York: Bloomsbury Academic, 2023.

Christiaens, Tim. "Towards Affirmative Economic Theologies: Responses to the Problem of Evil in Contemporary Italian Thought." *Political Theology* 21, no. 7 (2020): 634–49.

Christiaens, Tim. "Uit Verzet Geboren: De Filosofische Erfenis van Het Operaismo." *Ethische Perspectieven* 28, no. 2 (2018): 87–111.

Christiaens, Tim, and De Cauwer, Stijn. "The Multitude Divided: Biopolitical Production during the Coronavirus Pandemic." In *Pandemic and the Crisis of Capitalism*. Edited by Vincent Lyon-Callo, Yahira Madra, Ceren Özselçuk, Jared Randall, Malihu Safri, Chizu Sato, Boone W. Shear, 118–27. Brighton: ReMarx Books, 2020.

Christophers, Brett. *Rentier Capitalism: Who Owns the Economy, and Who Pays for It?* London: Verso Books, 2020.

Ciccarelli, Roberto. *Forza Lavoro: Il Lato Oscuro Della Rivoluzione Digitale*. Roma: DeriveApprodi, 2018.

Cimatti, Felice and Carlo Salzani, (eds.). *Animality in Contemporary Italian Philosophy*. Cham: Palgrave MacMillan, 2020.

Cimatti, Felice and Carlo Salzani, eds. *The Biopolitical Animal*. Edinburgh: Edinburgh University Press, 2024.

Cini, Lorenzo. "Resisting Algorithmic Control: Understanding the Rise and Variety of Platform Worker Mobilisations." *New Technology, Work and Employment* 38, no. 1 (2023): 125–44.

Citton, Yves. *Mythocracy: How Stories Shape Our Worlds*. Translated by David Broder. London: Verso Books, 2025.

Claverini, Corrado. *La tradizione filosofica italiana: quattro paradigmi interpretativi*. Marcerata: Quodlibet, 2021.

Coccia, Emanuele. "Don't Call me Gaia" in *e-flux Architecture* "Hydroreflexivity." October 2023, 3. https://www.e-flux.com/architecture/hydroreflexivity/571453/don-t-call-me-gaia/

Coccia, Emanuele. *Metamorphosis*. Translated by Robin Mackay. Cambridge: Polity Press, 2021.

Coccia, Emanuele. *The Life of Plants: A Metaphysics of Mixture*. Cambridge: Polity Press, 2018.

Colebrooke, Claire and Jason Maxwell. *Agamben*. Cambridge: Polity Press, 2016.

Contarini, Silvia and Davide Luglio, eds. *L'Italian Theory existe-t-elle?* Sesto San Giovanni: Il Mulino, 2015.

Critchley, Simon. *The Faith of the Faithless: Experiments in Political Theology*. London: Verso Books, 2014.

Dardot, Pierre, and Christian Laval. *The New Way of the World: On Neoliberal Society*. Translated by Gregory Elliott. London: Verso Books, 2013.

Davies, William. "The Politics of Recognition in the Age of Social Media." *New Left Review* 128, no. 2 (2021): 83–99.

Day, Meagan. "Americans Are Starting to Love Unions Again." *Jacobin*, 9 February 2019. https://jacobin.com/2019/09/unions-us-labor-movement-americans-gallup-poll-bernie-sanders.

Dean, Jodi. "Communicative Capitalism: Circulation and the Foreclosure of Politics." *Cultural Politics* 1, no. 1 (2005): 51–74.

Dean, Jodi and Paul Passavant (eds.). *Empire's New Clothes: Reading Hardt and Negri*. London: Routledge, 2004.

Dean, Mitchell. "Political Acclamation, Social Media and the Public Mood." *European Journal of Social Theory* 20, no. 3 (2017): 417–34.

Dean, Mitchell. *The Signature of Power: Sovereignty, Governmentality and Biopolitics*. London: SAGE, 2013.

Dean, Mitchell. "Three Forms of Democratic Political Acclamation." *Telos* 179 (2017): 9–32.

Dean, Mitchell, and Daniel Zamora. *The Last Man Takes LSD: Foucault and the End of Revolution*. London: Verso Books, 2021.

De Bloois, Joost. "*Tutti i popoli sono bande*": Giorgio Agamben's Philosophical Populism' in Dhondt, R., Jansen, M., and Urban, M. B. (eds.), "*Us versus Them*": *Exploring Transatlantic Practices of Fascism(s) and Populism(s) from the Margins*. London: Routledge, 2025.

De Bloois, Joost "The Death of Vitruvian Man: Anomaly, Anomie, Autonomy" in Federico Luisetti, John Pickles and Wilson Kaiser (eds.). *The Anomie of the Earth: Philosophy, Politics and Autonomy in Europe and the Americas*. Durham: Duke University Press, 2015: 25–53.

De Cauwer, Stijn. "Potentiality and Uprisings: Georges Didi-Huberman in Dialogue with Giorgio Agamben and Antonio Negri." *Italian Studies* 76, no. 2 (2021): 186–99.

De Martino, Ernesto. *The End of the World: Cultural Apocalypse and Transcendence*. Translated by Dorothy Louise Zinn. Chicago: University of Chicago Press, 2023.

Debord, Guy. *The Society of the Spectacle*. Translated by Donald Nicholson-Smith. New York: Zone Books, 1995.

Deleuze, Gilles. *The Logic of Sense*. Translated by Mark Lester and Charles Stivale, edited by Constantin V. Boundas. London: The Athlone Press, 1990.

Deleuze, Gilles and Félix Guattari. *What is Philosophy?* translated by Hugh Tomlinson. London: Verso Books, 1994.

Delfanti, Alessandro. *The Warehouse: Workers and Robots at Amazon*. London: Pluto Press, 2021.

Della Porta, Donatella, Riccardo Emilio Chesta, and Lorenzo Cini. *Labour Conflicts in the Digital Age: A Comparative Perspective*. Bristol: Bristol University Press, 2023.

Descola, Philippe, and Pignocchi, Alessandro. *Ethnographies des mondes à venir*. Paris: Éditions du Seuil, 2022.

Di Cesare, Donatella. *Conspiracy and Power*. Cambridge: Polity Press, 2023.

Di Cesare, Donatella. *Virus Sovrano? L'asfissia Capitalistica*. Torino: Bollati Boringhieri, 2020.

Dickinson, Colby, and Adam Kotsko. *Agamben's Coming Philosophy: Finding a New Use for Theology*. New York: Rowman & Littlefield International, 2015.

Dubal, Veena. "The House Always Wins: The Algorithmic Gamblification of Work." LPE Project, 23 January 2023. https://lpeproject.org/blog/the-house-always-wins-the-algorithmic-gamblification-of-work/.

Dubal, Veena. "Wage Slave or Entrepreneur?: Contesting the Dualism of Legal Worker Identities." *California Law Review* 105, no. 1 (2017): 65–123.

Eco, Umberto. *Il Fascismo Eterno*. Milano: La nave di Teseo, 2018.

*Enabling Workers to Govern Their Work*. Democratize Work, 2024. https://www. youtube.com/watch?v=U8jf90X1KYc.

Esposito, Roberto. *Bios: Biopolitics and Philosophy*. Translated by Timothy Campbell, Minneapolis: University of Minnesota Press, 2008.

Esposito, Roberto. *Common Immunity: Biopolitics in the Age of the Pandemic*. Translated by Zakiya Hanafi, New York: Polity, 2023.

Esposito, Roberto. *Communitas: The Origin and Destiny of Community*. Translated by Timothy Campell. Stanford: Stanford University Press, 2010.

Esposito, Roberto. "Community, Immunity, Biopolitics." Translated by Zakiya Hanafi, *Angelaki: Journal of the Theoretical Humanities* 18, no. 3 (2013): 83–90.

Esposito, Roberto. *Immunitas: The Protection and Negation of Life*. Translated by Zakiya Hanafi. Cambridge: Polity Press, 2011.

Esposito, Roberto. *Institution*. Translated by Zakiya Hanafi, New York: Polity, 2022.

Esposito, Roberto. *Living Thought: The Origins and Actuality of Italian Philosophy*. Translated by Zakiya Hanafi. Stanford: Stanford University Press, 2012.

Esposito, Roberto. *Persons and Things*. Translated by Zakiya Hanafi, Malden: Polity, 2015.

Esposito, Roberto. *Terms of the Political: Community, Immunity, Biopolitics*. Translated by Rhiannon Noel Welch. New York: Fordham University Press, 2013.

Esposito, Roberto. "The Biopolitics of Immunity in Times of COVID-19: An Interview with Roberto Esposito." Interview by Tim Christiaens, and Stijn De Cauwer, *Antipode online*, 16th June 2020. https://antipodeonline. org/2020/06/16/interview-with-roberto-esposito/

Esposito, Roberto. *Third Person*. Translated by Zakiya Hanafi. New York: Polity, 2012.

Federici, Silva. *Caliban and the Witch: Women, the Body and Primitive Accumulation*. New York: Autonomedia, 2014.

Esposito, Roberto. *Re-enchanting the World: Feminism and the Politics of the Commons*. New York: PM Press, 2019.

Esposito, Roberto. *Revolution at Point Zero: Housework, Reproduction, and Feminist Struggle*. New York: PM Press, 2012.

Fielitz, Mark, and Holger Marcks. "Digital Fascism: Challenges for the Open Society in Times of Social Media." Berkeley Center for Right-Wing Studies. Los Angeles: Institute for the Study of Societal Issues, 2019.

Finlayson, Alan. "Neoliberalism, the Alt-Right and the Intellectual Dark Web." *Theory, Culture & Society* 38, no. 6 (2021): 167–90.

Finlayson, Alan. "YouTube and Political Ideologies: Technology, Populism and Rhetorical Form." *Political Studies* 70, no. 1 (2022): 62–80.

Flew, Terry. "Michel Foucault's The Birth of Biopolitics and Contemporary Neo-Liberalism Debates." *Thesis Eleven* 108, no. 1 (2012): 44–65.

Floridi, Luciano. *The 4th Revolution: How the Infosphere Is Reshaping Human Reality*. Oxford: Oxford University Press, 2016.

Fortunati, Leopoldina. *The Arcana of Reproduction: Housework, Prostitution, Labour and Capital*. London: Verso Books, 2025.

Foucault, Michel. *Security, Territory, Population: Lectures at the Collège de France, 1977–78*. Translated by Graham Burchell. New York: Picador, 2007.

Foucault, Michel. *"Society Must Be Defended" Lectures at the Collège de France, 1975–76*. Translated by David Macey. New York: Picador, 2003.

Foucault, Michel. *The Birth of Biopolitics: Lectures at the Collège de France, 1978–79*. Translated by Graham Burchell. Basingstoke: Palgrave Macmillan, 2010.

Fraser, Nancy. *Cannibal Capitalism*. London: Verso Books, 2022.

Fukuyama, Francis. *The End of History and the Last Man*. New York: Free Press, 1992

Gainsforth, Sarah. *Airbnb città merce: storie di resistenza alla gentrificazione digitale*. Roma: DeriveApprodi, 2019.

Gentili, Dario. *Crisi Come Arte Di Governo*. Macerata: Quodlibet, 2018.

Gentili, Dario. *Italian Theory: Dall'operaismo alla biopolitica*. Bologna: Il Mulino, 2012.

Gentili, Dario. "Potentiality and Adaptability: Neoliberalism and Italian Thought." *Italian Studies* 76, no. 2 (2021): 148–60.

Gentili, Dario, Elettra Stimilli and Glenda Garelli (eds.). *Italian Critical Thought*. London and New York: Rowman & Littlefield International, 2018.

Gerbaudo, Paolo. "Social Media and Populism: An Elective Affinity?" *Media, Culture & Society* 40, no. 5 (2018): 745–53.

Gerbaudo, Paolo. *The Digital Party: Political Organisation and Online Democracy*. London: Pluto Press, 2019.

Ginzburg, Carlo. "On Ernesto de Martino's 'The End of the World' and its Genesis." *Chicago Review* 60–61, no. 4/1 (2017): 77–91.

Gramsci, Antonio. *Prison Notebooks: Volume II*. Translated by Joseph Buttigieg. New York: Columbia University Press, 2011.

Gramsci, Antonio. *Selections from the Prison Notebooks of Antonio Gramsci*. Translated by Quintin Hoare and Geoffrey Nowell-Smith. London: Lawrence & Wishart, 1971.

Gregory, Karen. "'My Life is More Valuable than This': Understanding Risk among On-Demand Food Couriers in Edinburgh." *Work, Employment and Society* 35, no. 2 (2020): 316–31.

Griffin, Roger. *The Nature of Fascism*. London: Routledge, 1993.

Grohmann, Rafael. "Not Just Platform, nor Cooperatives: Worker-Owned Technologies from Below." *Communication, Culture & Critique* 16, no. 4 (2023): 274–82.

Guilhot, Nicolas. "The Man Who Lived at the End of History." *New Statesman*, 15 February 2024. https://www.newstatesman.com/ideas/2024/02/ernesto-de-martino-history-apocalypse.

Habermas, Jürgen. *The Structural Transformation of the Public Sphere*. Cambridge: Polity, 2011.

Haraway, Donna. *The Companion Species Manifesto: Dogs, People and Significant Others*. Chicago: Prickly Paradigm Press, 2003.

Haraway, Donna. *Staying with the Trouble*. Durham: Duke University Press, 2016.

Hardt, Michael. *The Subversive Seventies*. Oxford: Oxford University Press, 2023.

Hardt, Michael, and Antonio Negri. *Assembly*. Oxford: Oxford University Press, 2017.

Hardt, Michael, and Antonio Negri. *Empire*. Cambridge: Harvard University Press, 2000.

Heron, Nicholas. *Liturgical Power: Between Economic and Political Theology*. New York: Fordham University Press, 2018.

Hickson, James. "Freedom, Domination and the Gig Economy." *New Political Economy* 29, no. 2 (2024): 321–33.

Hochschild, Arlie Russell. *Strangers in Their Own Land: Anger and Mourning on the American Right*. New York: The New Press, 2018.

Jameson, Fredric. *An American Utopia: Dual Power and the Universal Army*. Edited by Slavoj Zizek, London: Verso Books, 2016.

Janicka, Iwona. "Reinventing the Diplomat: Isabelle Stengers, Bruno Latour and Baptiste Morizot." *Theory, Culture & Society* 40, no. 3 (2023): 23–40.

Kalyvas, Andreas. *Democracy and the Politics of the Extraordinary*. Cambridge: Cambridge University Press, 2009.

Kant, Immanuel. "An Answer to the Question: What Is Enlightenment?" In *What Is Enlightenment?: Eighteenth-Century Answers and Twentieth-Century Questions* edited by James Schmidt, 58–64. Stanford: University of California Press, 1996.

Kelly, Duncan. "Carl Schmitt's Political Theory of Representation." *Journal of the History of Ideas* 65, no. 1 (2004): 113–34.

Kitchin, Rob, and Alistair Fraser. *Slow Computing: Why We Need Balanced Digital Lives*. Bristol: Bristol University Press, 2020.

Kohn, Eduardo. *How Forests Think? An Anthropology Beyond the Human*. Berkeley: University of California Press, 2013.

Kotsko, Adam. *Agamben's Philosophical Trajectory*. Edinburgh: Edinburgh University Press, 2020.

Kor-Sins, Ryan. "The Alt-Right Digital Migration: A Heterogeneous Engineering Approach to Social Media Platform Branding." *New Media & Society* 25, no. 9 (2023): 2321–38.

Landerreche Cardillo, Paula, and Silverbloom, Rachel (eds.). *Political Bodies: Writings on Cavarero's Political Thought*. New York: SUNY Press, 2024.

Lawtoo, Nidesh. *(New) Fascism: Contagion, Community, Myth*. East Lansing: Michigan State University Press, 2019.

Lazzarato, Maurizio. *Capital Hates Everyone: Fascism or Revolution*. Translated by Robert Hurley. Los Angeles: Semiotext(e), 2021.

Lazzarato, Maurizio. *Governing by Debt*. Translated by Joshua David Jordan. Los Angeles: Semiotext(e), 2015.

Lazzarato, Maurizio. "Immaterial Labor." In *Radical Thought in Italy: A Potential Politics*. Edited by Michael Hardt and Paolo Virno, 133–47. Minneapolis: University of Minnesota Press, 1996.

Lazzarato, Maurizio. *La politica dell'evento*. Cosenza: Rubbettino, 2004.

Lazzarato, Maurizio. *Signs and Machines: Capitalism and the Production of Subjectivity*. Translated by Joshua David Jordan. Los Angeles: Semiotext(e), 2014.

Lazzarato, Maurizio. "How to Think a War Machine: Interview with Maurizio Lazzarato." Interview and translation by Tim Christiaens and Stijn De Cauwer. In *Critical Theory at a Crossroads* edited by Stijn De Cauwer, 134–45. New York: Columbia University Press, 2017.

Ledwich, Mark, and Anna Zaitsev. "Algorithmic Extremism: Examining YouTube's Rabbit Hole of Radicalization." *Working Paper*, 2019.

Lehdonvirta, Vili. "Flexibility in the Gig Economy: Managing Time on Three Online Piecework Platforms." *New Technology, Work and Employment* 33, no. 1 (2018): 13–29.

Lenin, Vladimir I. "Left-Wing Communism: An Infantile Disorder." Translated by Julius Katzer https://www.marxists.org/archive/lenin/works/1920/lwc/

Lisciani-Petrini, Enrica and Giusi Strumiello (eds.). *Effetto Italian Thought*. Macerata: Quodlibet, 2017.

Lorenzini, Daniele. "Biopolitics in the Time of Coronavirus." *Critical Inquiry* 47 (winter 2021): 40–5.

Lorenzini, Daniele. "Governmentality, Subjectivity, and the Neoliberal Form of Life." *Journal for Cultural Research* 22, no. 2 (2018): 154–66.

Lorenzini, Daniele. "Rethinking Biopolitics: COVID-19, differential vulnerabilities and biopolitical rights." *Journal of European Studies* 54, No. 1(2024): 1–15.

Lovelock, James and Lynn Margulis. *Writing Gaia*. Cambridge: Cambridge University Press, 2022.

Luisetti, Federico. "Geopower: On the States of Nature of Late Capitalism." *European Journal of Social Theory*, 2019: 22/3, 342–63.

Luisetti, Federico. *Non-Human Subjects: An Ecology of Earth-Beings*. Cambridge: Cambridge University Press, 2023.

Lumley, Robert. *States of Emergency: Cultures of Revolt in Italy from 1968 to 1978*. London: Verso Books, 1990.

Machiavelli, Niccolo. *Discourses on Livy*. Translated by Julia Conway Bondanella and Peter Bondanella. Oxford: Oxford University Press, 2009.

MacKenzie, Donald. "Cookies, Pixels and Fingerprints." *London Review of Books* 43, no. 7 (2021): 31–4.

Marramao, Giacomo. *Dopo Il Leviatano*. Torino: Bollati Boringhieri, 2000.

Marrone, Marco. "Rights against the Machines! Food Delivery, Piattaforme Digitali e Sindacalismo Informale: Il Caso Riders Union Bologna." *Labour & Law Issues* 5, no. 1 (2019): 1–28.

Martin, Nastassja. *In the Eye of the Wild*. Translated by Sophie R. Lewis. New York: New York Review Books, 2021.

Marwick, Alice, Benjamin Clancy, and Katherine Furl. "Far-Right Online Radicalization: A Review of the Literature." *The Bulletin of Technology and Public Life*. Chapel Hill: Center for Information, Technology, and Public Life, 2022.

Marx, Karl. *Capital: Vol.* 1. Translated by Samuel Moore and Edward Aveling. London: Lawrence & Wishart, 1996.

Marx, Karl. *Grundrisse: Foundations of the Critique of Political Economy*. Translated by Martin Nicolaus. London: Penguin Books, 2005.

Marx, Karl. *The Poverty of Philosophy*. Anonymous translation. New York: International Publishers, 1992.

Marx, Paris. *Road to Nowhere: What Silicon Valley Gets Wrong about the Future of Transportation*. London: Verso Books, 2022.

Massanari, Adrienne. "#Gamergate and The Fappening: How Reddit's Algorithm, Governance, and Culture Support Toxic Technocultures." *New Media & Society* 19, no. 3 (2017): 329–46.

Mbembe, Achille. *Critique of Black Reason*. Translated by Laurent Dubois, Durham: Duke University Press, 2017.

Mbembe, Achille. *Necropolitics*. Translated by Steven Corcoran, Durham: Duke University Press, 2019.

McNay, Lois. "Self as Enterprise: Dilemmas of Control and Resistance in Foucault's The Birth of Biopolitics." *Theory, Culture & Society* 26, no. 6 (2009): 55–77.

Mezzadra, Sandro and Brett Neilson, *Border as Method, Or, The Multiplication of Labor*. Durham: Duke University Press, 2013.

Mezzadra, Sandro and Brett Neilson. *The Rest and the West: Capital and Power in a Multipolar World*. London: Verso Books, 2024.

Mezzadra, Sandro. *La condizione postcoloniale. Storia e politica nel mondo globale*. Verona: Ombre Corte, 2008.

Micali, Stefano. "The Capitalistic Cult of Performance." *Philosophy Today* 54, no. 4 (2010): 379–91.

Moreno Zacarés, Javier. "Euphoria of the Rentier?" *New Left Review* 129, no. 3 (2021): 47–67.

Morizot, Baptiste. *Ways of Being Alive*. Translated by Andrew Brown, New York: Polity, 2022.

Morizot, Baptiste. *L'inexploré*. Marseille: Éditions Wildproject, 2023.

Moulier Boutang, Yann. *Cognitive Capitalism* translated by Ed Emery. Cambridge: Polity Press, 2011.

Mueller, Gavin. *Breaking Things at Work: The Luddites Are Right about Why You Hate Your Job*. London: Verso Books, 2021.

Muldoon, James, and Paul Raekstad. "Algorithmic Domination in the Gig Economy." *European Journal of Political Theory* 22, no. 4 (2023): 587–607.

Munger, Kevin, and Joseph Phillips. "Right-Wing YouTube: A Supply and Demand Perspective." *The International Journal of Press/Politics* 27, no. 1 (2022): 186–219.

Munn, Luke. "Alt-Right Pipeline: Individual Journeys to Extremism Online." *First Monday* 24, no. 6 (2019).

Nachtwey, Oliver. *Germany's Hidden Crisis: Social Decline in the Heart of Europe*. London: Verso Books, 2018.

Nagle, Angela. *Kill All Normies: The Online Culture Wars from Tumblr and 4chan to the Alt-Right and Trump*. Winchester: Zero Books, 2017.

Nancy, Jean.-Luc. "Communovirus." *Verso Blog* 27 March 2020. https://www.versobooks.com/blogs/news/4626-communovirus.

Negri, Antonio. *From the Factory to the Metropolis*. Translated by Ed Emery. Cambridge: Polity Press, 2018.

Negri, Antonio. *Insurgencies: Constituent Power and the Modern State*. Minneapolis: University of Minnesota Press, 2009.

Negri, Antonio. *Marx Oltre Marx*. Rome: Manifestolibri, 1998.

Negri, Antonio. *Storia di una communista* (3 volumes). Firenze: Ponte Alle Grazie, 2015–2021.

Negri, Antonio. "The European Union is a Cage." Interview and translation by Stijn De Cauwer and Gert-Jan Meyntjens. In *Critical Theory at a Crossroads: Conversations on Resistance in Times of Crisis*. Edited by Stijn De Cauwer, 87–98, New York: Columbia University Press, 2018.

Negri, Antonio and Michael Hardt, *Commonwealth*. Cambridge, Massachusetts: Belknap and Harvard University Press, 2009.

Noble, Safiya Umoja. *Algorithms of Oppression: How Search Engines Reinforce Racism*. New York: New York University Press, 2018.

Panzieri, Raniero. "The Capitalist Use of Machinery: Marx versus the Objectivists." Translated by Quintin Hoare, in *Outlines for a Critique of Technology*. Edited by Phil Slater, 44–68. London: Ink Links, 1980.

Papacharissi, Zizi. *Affective Publics: Sentiment, Technology, and Politics*. Oxford: Oxford University Press, 2015.

Papadimitropoulos, Evangelos. "Platform Capitalism, Platform Cooperativism, and the Commons." *Rethinking Marxism* 33, no. 2 (2021): 246–62.

Pasolini, Pier Paolo. *Heretical Empiricism*. Washington: New Academia Publishing, 2005.

Pasolini, Pier Paolo. *Scritti corsari*. Milan: Garzanti Libri, 2015.

Pasquinelli, Matteo. *The Eye of the Master: A Social History of Artificial Intelligence*. London: Verso Books, 2023.

Peterlongo, Gianmarco. *Nella Trama Dell'algoritmo*. Torino: Rosenberg & Sellier, 2023.

Pignot, Edouard. "Who is Pulling the Strings in the Platform Economy? Accounting for the Dark and Unexpected Sides of Algorithmic Control." *Organization* 30, no. 1 (2023): 140–67.

Prozorov, Sergei. *Agamben and Politics: A Critical Introduction*. Edinburgh: Edinburgh University Press, 2014.

Povinelli, Elizabeth, *Geontologies: A Requiem to Late Liberalism*. Durham, Duke University Press, 2016.

Puig de la Bellacasa, Maria. *Matters of Care: Speculative Ethics in More than Human Worlds*. Minneapolis: University of Minnesota Press, 2017.

Rajan, Tilottama, and Antonio Calcagno, eds. *Roberto Esposito: New Directions in Biophilosophy*. Edinburgh: Edinburgh University Press, 2023.

Read, Jason. *The Double Shift: Spinoza and Marx on the Politics and Ideology of Work*. London: Verso Books, 2024.

Roelofsen, Maartje, and Claudio Minca. "The Superhost: Biopolitics, Home and Community in the Airbnb Dream-World of Global Hospitality." *Geoforum* 91 (May 2018): 170–81.

Roggero, Gigi. *Italian Operaismo: Genealogy, History, Method*. Translated by Clara Pope. Cambridge: MIT Press, 2023.

Rosamond, Emily. "From Reputation Capital to Reputation Warfare: Online Ratings, Trolling, and the Logic of Volatility." *Theory, Culture & Society* 37, no. 2 (2020): 105–29.

Rosenblat, Alex. *Uberland: How Algorithms are Rewriting the Rules of Work*. Oakland: University of California Press, 2018.

Rouvroy, Antoinette, and Thomas Berns. "Gouvernementalité Algorithmique et Perspectives d'émancipation." *Réseaux* 177, no. 1 (2013): 163–96.

Rovatti, Pier Aldo. "Deconstructing the Capital Letters. Weak Thought, Italian Theory, and Politics. A Conversation with Pier Aldo Rovatti." Interview by Andrea Muni in *Journal of Italian Philosophy*, 2 (2019): 1–7.

Salehi, Niloufar, Lilly C. Irani, Michael S. Bernstein, Ali Alkhatib, Eva Ogbe, Kristy Milland, and Clickhappier. "We Are Dynamo: Overcoming Stalling and Friction in Collective Action for Crowd Workers." In *Proceedings of the 33rd Annual ACM Conference on Human Factors in Computing Systems*, 1621–30. Seoul Republic of Korea: ACM, 2015.

*Semiotext(e): Autonomia, Post-Political Politics*. Edited by Sylvère Lotringer and Christian Marazzi. Los Angeles, Semiotext(e), 2007.

Scheiber, Nicolas. "How Uber Pushes Drivers' Buttons." *New York Times*, 3 April 2017. https://www.nytimes.com/interactive/2017/04/02/technology/uber-drivers-psychological-tricks.html.

Scheuerman, William. "Donald Trump Meets Carl Schmitt." *Philosophy & Social Criticism* 45, no. 9/10 (2019): 1170–85.

Schmitt, Carl. *Legality and Legitimacy*. Translated by Jeffrey Seitzer. New York: Duke University Press, 2004.

Schmitt, Carl. *The Crisis of Parliamentary Democracy*. Translated by Ellen Kennedy Ellen. Cambridge: MIT Press, 1988.

Scholz, Trebor. *Uberworked and Underpaid: How Workers are Disrupting the Digital Economy*. Cambridge: Polity Press, 2017.

Squire, Jamilla and Seth Wheeler, eds.) *A Thousand Little Machines: A/Traverso and the Movement of '77*. London: Agit Press, 2024.

Spier, Shaked. "The Ethics and Politics of Platform Cooperatives." New York: Institute for Digital Cooperative Economy, 2022. https://resources.platform.coop/resources/the-ethics-and-politics-of-platform-cooperatives/.

Srnicek, Nick. *Platform Capitalism*. Cambridge: Polity Press, 2017.

Stengers, Isabelle. *Cosmopolitics*. Translated by Roberto Bononno. Minneapolis: University of Minnesota Press, 2010.

Stimilli, Elettra. "Apocalyptic Time." *Political Theology* 21, no. 5 (2020): 391–2.

Stimilli, Elettra (ed.). *Decostruzione o biopolitica?* Macerata: Quodlibet, 2017.

Stockman, Caroline, and Vincenzo Scalia. "Democracy on the Five Star Movement's Rousseau Platform." *European Politics and Society* 21, no. 5 (2020): 603–17.

Tari, Marcello. *Autonomie! Italie, les années 1970.* Paris: La fabrique éditions, 2011.

Tari, Marcello. *Il ghiacco era sottile: Per una storia dell'Autonomia.* Bologna: DeriveApprodi, 2012.

Tarizzo, Davide. *Life: A Modern Invention.* Translated by Mark William Epstein. Minneapolis: University of Minnesota Press, 2017.

Terranova, Tiziana. *After the Internet.* Los Angeles: Semiotext(e), 2022.

Terranova, Tiziana. "Free Labor: Producing Culture for the Digital Economy." *Social Text* 18, no. 2 (2000): 33–58.

Terranova, Tiziana. "Futurepublic. On Information Warfare, Bio-racism and Hegemony as Noopolitics." *Theory, Culture & Society* 24, no.3 (2007): 125–45.

Terranova, Tiziana. *Network Culture: Politics for the Information Age.* London: Pluto Press, 2004.

Tesson, Sylvain. *The Art of Patience: Seeking the Snow Leopard in Tibet.* Translated by Frank Wynne, New York: Penguin, 2021.

Toscano, Alberto. *Late Fascism: Race, Capitalism and the Politics of Crisis.* London: Verso Books, 2023.

Tronti, Mario. "Italy." In *Karl Marx' Grundrisse: Foundations of the Critique of Political Economy 150 Years Later.* Edited by Marcello Musto, 229–35. London: Routledge, 2008.

Tronti, Mario. *Workers and Capital.* Translated by David Broder. London: Verso Books, 2019.

Trotta, Giuseppe, Fabio Milana, and Mario Tronti. *L'operaismo Degli Anni Sessanta: Da "Quaderni Rossi" a "Classe Operaia."* Roma: DeriveApprodi, 2008.

Tufekci, Zeynep. *Twitter and Tear Gas: The Power and Fragility of Networked Protest.* New York: Yale University Press, 2018.

Urbinati, Nadia. *Democracy Disfigured: Opinion, Truth and the People.* Cambridge: Harvard University Press, 2014.

Urbinati, Nadia.*Me the People: How Populism Transforms Democracy.* Cambridge: Harvard University Press, 2019.

Vattimo, Gianni. *Belief.* Translated by Luca d'Isanto and David Webb. Stanford: Stanford University Press, 1999.

Vattimo, Gianni and Pier Aldo Rovatti (eds.). *Weak Thought.* Translated by Peter Caravetta. Albany: State University of New York Press, 2012.

Vasudevan, Krishnan, and Ngai Keung Chan. "Gamification and Work Games: Examining Consent and Resistance among Uber Drivers." *New Media & Society* 24, no. 4 (2022): 866–86.

Vercellone, Carlo. "The Becoming Rent of Profit? The New Articulation of Wage, Rent and Profit." *Knowledge Cultures* 1, no. 2 (2013): 194–207.

Vercellone, Carlo. "The Crisis of the Law of Value and the Becoming-Rent of Profit." In *Crisis in the Global Economy* edited by Andrea Fumagalli and Sandro Mezzadra, 85–118. Los Angeles: Semiotext(e), 2010.

Viriasova, Inna, and Calcagno, Antonio, eds. *Roberto Esposito: Biopolitics and Philosophy*. New York: SUNY University Press, 2017.

Virno, Paolo. *A Grammar of the Multitude: For an Analysis of Contemporary Forms of Life*. Translated by Isabella Bertoletti, James Cascaito, and Andrea Casson. Los Angeles: Semiotext(e), 2003.

Virno, Paolo. "Notes on the General Intellect." Translated by Arianna Bove. In *Marxism Beyond Marxism*. Edited by Saree Makdisi, Cesare Casarino, and Rebecca Karl, 265–72. London: Routledge, 1996.

Virno, Paolo and Michael Hardt (eds.). *Radical Thought in Italy: A Potential Politics*. Minneapolis: Minnesota University Press, 1996.

Weeks, Kathi. *The Problem with Work: Feminism, Marxism, Antiwork Politics, and Postwork Imaginaries*. Durham: Duke University Press, 2011.

Winter, Aaron. "Online Hate: From the Far-Right to the 'Alt-Right' and from the Margins to the Mainstream." In *Online Othering*. Edited by Karen Lumsden and Emily Harmer, 39–63. Cham: Springer International Publishing, 2019.

Woodcock, Jamie, and Callum Cant. "Platform Worker Organising at Deliveroo in the UK: From Wildcat Strikes to Building Power." *Journal of Labor and Society* 25 (2022): 220–36.

Woodcock, Jamie, and Mark Graham. *The Gig Economy: A Critical Introduction*. Cambridge: Polity Press, 2020.

Wright, Steve. *Storming Heaven: Class Composition and Struggle in Italian Autonomist Marxism*. London: Pluto Press, 2002.

Yusoff, Kathryn. *A Billion Black Anthropocenes or None*. Minneapolis: University of Minnesota Press, 2018.

Zamora, Daniel (ed.). *Critiquer Foucault*. Bruxelles: Aden, 2014.

Zinn, Dorothy Louise. "An Introduction to Ernesto de Martino's Relevance for the Study of Folklore." *Journal of American Folklore*, 128, no. 507 (2015): 3–17.

Zuboff, Shoshana. *The Age of Surveillance Capitalism: The Fight for the Future at the New Frontier of Power*. London: Profile Books, 2019.

# ABOUT THE AUTHORS

**Tim Christiaens** is assistant professor of economic ethics at Tilburg University. He is the author of *Digital Working Lives* (2022) on the gig economy and worker autonomy, and has published on topics like Italian thought, philosophy of technology, neoliberalism, and biopolitical theory in journals such as the *European Journal of Social Theory*, *Italian Studies*, *Big Data & Society*, and *Foucault Studies*.

**Joost de Bloois** is senior lecturer of cultural and literary analysis at the University of Amsterdam. His publications include *Politics of Withdrawal* (with Pepita Hesselberth), a special issue of *Rethinking Marxism* on Italian post-workerism (with Monica Jansen and Frans-Willem Korsten), essays on Giorgio Agamben, Roberto Esposito, and Erri de Luca, as well as a monograph on the work of Alain Badiou and several co-authored handbooks in cultural studies.

**Stijn De Cauwer** is assistant professor at the Leiden University Centre for the Arts in Society. His publications include *Critical Theory at a Crossroads: Conversations on Resistance in Times of Crisis* (2018), *Critical Image Operations: The Work of Georges Didi-Huberman* (2019) and writings on topics such as visual studies, cultural theory, German literature (including a monograph on the work of Robert Musil), Italian philosophy, and biopolitics.